THE DRAGON'S TRAIL

The Biography of Raphael's Masterpiece

JOANNA PITMAN

A TOUCHSTONE BOOK
Published by Simon & Schuster
NEW YORK   LONDON   TORONTO   SYDNEY

 Touchstone
Rockefeller Center
1230 Avenue of the Americas
New York, NY 10020

First Touchstone edition 2007

Originally published in Great Britain in 2006 by Ebury Press as
The Raphael Trail.

TOUCHSTONE and colophon are registered trademarks
of Simon & Schuster, Inc.

For information regarding special discounts for bulk purchases,
please contact Simon & Schuster Special Sales
at 1–800–456–6798 or business@simonandschuster.com.

Designed by Elliott Beard

Manufactured in the United States of America

10 9 8 7 6 5 4 3 2 1

Library of Congress Cataloging-in-Publication Data

Pitman, Joanna.
  [Raphael trail]
  The dragon's trail : the biography of Raphael's masterpiece / Joanna
Pitman. — 1st Touchstone ed.
    p. cm.
  "Originally published in Great Britain in 2006 by Ebury Press as The
Raphael trail"—T.p. verso.
  Includes index.
  1. Raphael, 1483–1520. St. George and the dragon (National Gallery
of Art (U.S.)) 2. Art—Provenance. I. Title.
ND623.R2A765 2007
759.5—dc22   2006051130

ISBN–13: 978–0–7432–6513–3
ISBN–10:   0–7432–6513–0

In memory of Giles
and for our daughters,
Alice, Emma and Lucy

CONTENTS

ACKNOWLEDGMENTS

IN WRITING THIS BOOK I have encountered immense generosity among experts in the fields of art and history. I am indebted to many more than I can name, but I would like particularly to thank Carol Plazotta, Edward Chaney, June Osborne, Jerry Brotton, Geraldine Norman, Catherine Phillips, Mikhail Piotrovsky, Elena Solomakha, David Cannadine—to whom I owe the whole of Mellon's story, David Brown, Nicholas Penny, Gretchen Hirschauer, Sarah Fisher, Anne Halpern, Edye Weissler, and Bernice Davison. Cordelia Hattori's thesis on Pierre Crozat proved invaluable, as did Geraldine Norman's book *The Hermitage.*

This book would not have been possible without the help and encouragement of my agent, George Lucas, and my editor, Trish Todd. On a more personal note, I would like to thank Professor David Cunningham and his team at the Royal Marsden Hospital as well as our families and friends for their support during Giles's battle with cancer. Giles was immensely generous, as always, with his inspiration during the writing of this book. But it was his courage and continuing warm humor during his last months that were a source of exceptional strength to all of us. This book is dedicated to his memory, with very much love, and to Alice, Emma, and Lucy, our greatest achievement together.

THE DRAGON'S TRAIL

1·

ONE EXHILARATING SPRING DAY in 1506, a brilliant young Italian painter named Raffaello Santi was summoned to the grand ducal palace in his home town of Urbino. There, in the presence of Duke Guidobaldo and his simpering courtiers, the painter was to receive a commission that was to change his life. Raffaello was still very young, just twenty-three years old, living only for artistic advancement and ravenous for recognition and fame. Behind him stretched years of hard-bitten apprenticeship: ever since he had been old enough to handle a paintbrush, Raffaello had devoted himself to his art, gradually focusing his precocious talents on the possibilities of sublime creation. But now, unfurling in front of him like a great golden banner, lay honor, glory, and immortal fame.

A recent self-portrait showed a pale, meek-looking youth, his pearly, opalescent skin licked with dark, damp curls, his full feminine lips troubled only by the slightest shadow of fuzz. But the portrait's vacuous beauty was a fiction. It betrayed none of the extraordinary energy and determination of Raffaello's paintings, no hint of the skillful manipulator of powerful patrons and the mercenary careerist that without doubt he had become even at this stage. Raffaello, now known to us as Raphael, reeked of ambition, certainly. He knew he would go far, perhaps to the top of his profession. But even he, in his most vainglorious moments, could never have imagined that he was poised on the brink of an artistic maturity that was to turn him into a mortal god of the Italian Renaissance. His name would be universally famous for the next five hundred years.

Raphael reached the palace and was admitted through the decoratively carved stone entrance. A contingent of armored guards conducted him, clanking along in their steel, through the beautiful pillared courtyard, up the stone staircase, and on through a sequence of vaulted halls, chambers, and apartments. Ushered past noblemen and ambassadors waiting in attitudes of stiff formality, Raphael was propelled toward the seat of power itself. Finally he stood in front of Guidobaldo da Montefeltro, duke of Urbino and ruler of one of the most powerful courts in Italy.

The duke had a high regard for Raphael, and his choice of the brilliant young painter had been a careful one. For on that spring morning, to the melodious sound of quills totting up ducats on parchment, the duke commissioned Raphael to paint a picture of St. George and the dragon. It was essential, Guidobaldo explained, that this should be his finest work yet. This jewel of a painting, he went on, this portrait of the great and romantic, chivalric hero was to be sent to England as a gift for King Henry VII.

Five hundred years later, fascinated by the extraordinary life of the painting that Raphael created for the Duke of Urbino, I stood in the same piazza, looking up at the monumental façade of the ducal palace. I had been intrigued by this picture, by its travels, by the people who had wanted it, ever since stumbling on the outlines of its story a couple of years earlier. Across the sweep of half a millennium and spread out over the breadth of half the world, a string of rulers and rich men had gone out of their way to possess this gem. Several had clambered their way to power by devious means. Most had filled their purses and bank accounts dishonestly. All were rapacious consumers of art, obsessed with the glamour and power it conferred. But who were these people, and why had they wanted Raphael's painting so badly?

I first saw the painting many years ago, hanging, where it is now, in the Raphael room at the National Gallery of Art in Washington. As I gazed at it, I had no inkling of what momentous events it had witnessed, the dangers it had survived, the passions it had engendered, and the mysteries it contained. In the intervening years, it continued to dance before my eyes. This exquisite work of art had unleashed its magic on me too. Of course I was in no position to have it for myself, but instead, now that I knew something of its story, I was possessed with the urge to pursue this mystery, to follow the trail and discover what lay beyond the aesthetic attractions of this masterpiece.

Although Urbino is no longer the place of patronage and power it was in the sixteenth century, its architectural glories are still there, reassuringly little changed, and the shrill and gaudy melee of continuing life swirls in little eddies all over its piazzas and up and down its precariously steep surrounding streets. If you were to go there today, you could still inhale something of the place where this painting was born, perhaps catch a glimpse of a ghostly footprint.

It was autumn when I was there, a time of ungraciously bitter winds, which stung my cheeks as I spun round trying to imagine the scene of Raphael's summons. Dozens of university students hurried across the piazza, trailing long knitted scarves and bags of books. They stopped here and there to confer in little huddles before disappearing into cafés for coffee and canoodling. Tourists ambled across the uneven flagstones, their heads buried in their guidebooks, trailed, perhaps unwittingly, at a distance by pickpockets. And all around were shops and stalls flogging cheap goods, their determinedly jocular proprietors the descendants of the colorful hustlers of old. As I walked around, I tried to flesh out imagined pictures of that earlier reality, with all its maddening and unpossessable detail.

The massively precocious Raphael must have been barely able to contain his jubilation at the news of his commission. Here was one of the most influential and enlightened courts in Italy summoning him to paint a greatly symbolic picture for the king of England. It was to be beautiful. It was to convey an important message and carry with it a strange power. And although Raphael did not know it at the time, its many-sided allure was to take it on a journey to fabulous worlds as yet undreamed of.

For one so young the request was almost unimaginable. How could this youth, not long out of adolescence, possibly have won such a prestigious commission? The answer is that Raphael was no ordinary twenty-three-year-old. The story of his development as a painter was familiar to Guidobaldo; it is worth recounting, for it reveals much about the ruthless ambitions of Raphael, ambitions that were to be invested, at their most intensive, in this small but radiant painting that would go on to dazzle the world.

It was well known that Raphael had matured astonishingly fast as a painter. His name was already famous in the region for the many Madonna and Child devotional paintings he had completed for wealthy Florentine clients. These were small and outstandingly refined works that had succeeded in spreading Raphael's name as a rising star. But he had also made his mark with a number of larger narrative paintings. One of these was the *Marriage of the Virgin*, commissioned by the Albizzini, a leading family in nearby Città di Castello, for the church of San Francesco. For a painter just twenty years old, this work, which now hangs in the Brera Museum in Milan, was astonishingly assured. Its powers of narrative and subtleties of perspective and design, as well as its grace,

ensured that Raphael's name reached the ears of the most powerful men in the land.

Painting had always been in Raphael's blood. He was born in
1483, the only surviving child of Magia Ciarla Santi, a merchant's
daughter, and Giovanni Santi, a learned poet and minor courtier at Urbino who had taken up painting late in life, just a few
years before Raphael was born. As a child, Raphael had virtually
grown up in his father's studio, spending his days in the small air-
less workroom adjoining the family house, its whitewashed walls
hung with sketches, the floor strewn with supplies, sections of al-
tarpieces, and devotional works in progress.

If you were to go there today, you would find the structural
bones of Raphael's house little changed, but it is now a tourist
attraction, a small house-museum, cold and unbreathing in the
way house-museums so often are. It is filled with reproductions
of works by Raphael and a thin little assortment of period furniture. But at the back, in a small shady courtyard, there is the original well where the boy helped his parents draw water, and a stone
slab where pigments were ground. It had been worn down into a
hollow. I reached out and felt its smooth surface, imagining the
small boy who had stood working away there, grinding colors for
his father, unaware of the reverence that would still be attached
to his own name five hundred years later. Next door is the studio,
now an art gallery, but still laid out as a series of rooms as it would
have been in Raphael's time. I wandered round trying not to look
at the gaudy acrylic landscapes being touted for sale. The place
was full of tourists: Americans, French, Germans, and some Italians, haggling for a piece of art that had hung in Raphael's studio.
You have to half-close your eyes to imagine the eager little boy,
busying himself among his father's apprentices.

Raphael carefully observed the work going on around him as

he helped with the mixing of pigments, dabbling at sketching and painting his own pictures. He must have shown early signs of promise, for soon after Giovanni died in 1494, the eleven-year-old Raphael was sent off to work in Perugia as an apprentice in the studio of Pietro Perugino, the most popular and prolific painter in central Italy.

Perugino's achievements in the decoration of the Sistine Chapel in the 1480s had brought him many major commissions in Tuscany and Umbria, and he was famous as a painter of frescoes. During the 1490s, he was commuting frequently between Florence and Perugia and constantly receiving new commissions. To complete these works he maintained a large workshop which, given his frequent absences, was required to reproduce the master's style with complete fidelity.

Arriving with little experience to speak of and only the recommendation of his late father's colleagues, Raphael dutifully took on all sorts of menial responsibilities in Perugino's bustling studio, initially grinding pigments and preparing panels for paint and then moving on to brushing in backgrounds and completing whole sections of paintings on his own. The place was alive with activity all day long. Church representatives and the heads of wealthy families were always dropping in to view works in progress and commission their own. Traders came and went with supplies. Senior members of the studio were negotiating details and directing work. And the dozens of young apprentices went earnestly about their assigned tasks, hoping to curry favor with their master and win promotion in the studio hierarchy as they moved toward becoming fully fledged painters themselves.

As he worked, Raphael carefully studied the poses of models and in his spare time began developing his own compositions, all the while ruthlessly building and refining his skills by determined observation and experience. With month after month of trial and error, he came to grips with perspective and learned to refine his shading, in paint and charcoal, until shadows and light blended together like smoke, without lines or borders.

Artists and apprentices in the workshop were expected to follow predetermined formulas for their work, for Perugino was one of the first painters to appreciate the advantages of reusing standardized designs. Depictions of smooth-faced saints gazing heavenward surrounded by dancing angels rolled out of his studio in endless combinations and in huge numbers. The system, of course, required the complete subjugation of the pupil's individuality to the master's style. In this, Raphael was unable to conform. His extraordinary talents meant that he was always enlivening the standard pattern figures with lively flourishes of his own.

Raphael proved to be an astonishingly fast learner. Within just six years of arriving as a child in Perugino's studio, he had blossomed into a precocious young man. His painting skills matched the talents of his master and in some areas were beginning to outdo him. Branching out on his own, Raphael received his first independent commission in 1500 when his name was inked into the accounts book of the church of St. Agostino in Città di Castello, under an order for a large altarpiece for the Baroncio family chapel. The painting required was of the coronation of St. Nicholas of Tolentino, a recently canonized Augustinian friar who had been particularly popular in Umbria. The picture, which was destroyed in an earthquake in 1789, only survives in fragments, but a good idea of its style can be seen from a surviving preparatory drawing that Raphael did showing a design characteristic of the Perugino workshop. Raphael worked on this commission with another, older painter, who had been employed in his father's workshop. And it was probably owing to this shrewd collaborative arrangement that Raphael was able to attain the title of master, as he was named on the contract, at the unusually young age of seventeen.

The painting was duly completed and delivered nine months later to delighted members of the Baroncio family. It must have excited approving comment from a wider circle, for it prompted a steady stream of further commissions from admiring parishioners until by 1504 Raphael, with rising confidence and a growing local reputation, realized that the time had come for a move to Florence.

So it was that one October morning, as the sun burnt off the haze hanging over the Arno valley, Raphael stood on the road from Arrezzo looking down at the distant skyline of Florence. No visitor could fail to be impressed by this thriving city. Although unfinished, her cathedral, the Duomo, promised to be the largest in Christendom. The elegant octagonal Baptistry, with its elaborately inlaid marble façade, the huge Franciscan convent of Santa Croce, and many other magnificent palaces, villas, and churches all testified to the city's affluence. With a population of fifty thousand, this bustling, commercial city was the sixth largest in Europe, surpassed only by London, Milan, Naples, Venice, and Paris. Florence was the epicenter of artistic activity in Italy. Rivalry among artists was fiercer here than in any other city. For Raphael, no destination could have been more appealing.

Raphael made his way to the center of Florence, the smell of money and success already pricking insistently at his nostrils. The winding streets and broad piazzas were thronging with people and products, doctors visiting the sick, servants running errands, packhorses struggling under bales of wool, and the wives of rich merchants gossiping like sparrows as they promenaded in their finery. Farm trucks trundled past, laden with heads of fennel, artichokes, and wicker cages crammed with clucking chickens. Scholars, clad in as many shades of black as the jackdaw, stood engrossed in debate, oblivious to the human tide raging around them. These were perfect targets for the pickpockets who loitered, armed with quick little blades, waiting to separate leather purses from the belts from which they dangled.

Raphael saw slender houses, top-heavy with balconies, lining the narrow routes. Shops stood on street corners, their awnings hanging like lowered eyelids over their doorways. He must have wandered around in a daze, marveling at every turn, at the splendid architecture, the range of luxuries spread out for sale, and amazed at the vigor and entrepreneurial spirit of the place.

Soon he was picking up the talk of town: the competition between the fifty-one-year-old Leonardo da Vinci, famous as the consummate draftsman of his age, and his twenty-nine-year-old archrival, Michelangelo. Both of these maestros had just been commissioned to paint murals commemorating famous Florentine battle victories on opposite walls of the Grand Council Chambers, then under construction in the Palazzo della Signoria. For an artist, this was the most prestigious location in Florence. But never before had the two men been pitted against one another in a commission that was turning into a public contest. Leonardo and Michelangelo had needed no introduction. Each was aware of the other's reputation, and their esteem for their respective talents was genuine. But da Vinci did not need reminding that his output had dwindled of late. A long-commissioned painting for the altar at the Annunziata monastery was far from complete, and his overdue portrait of Isabella d'Este, the demanding and tenacious marchioness of Mantua, was not even begun.

The brash young Michelangelo, on the other hand, was fresh from a pair of successes. He had just completed his Pietà in Rome to great acclaim, and had also achieved a triumph with his statue of David in Florence. Friendly Florentines, full of pride for their creative stars, would have filled Raphael in on the background to these masterpieces. The *David* had been a true sensation, for he had carved the enormous figure from a huge block of badly hewn marble which had already been discarded by several other sculptors after their botched attempts to fashion figures from it. Michelangelo, an obsessively secretive and suspicious artist, had immediately ordered the block to be hidden from view behind a wooden enclosure. There he had chiseled and chipped at it for hour after hour, day after day, removing, as he was heard to say, "everything that was not David." When it was finally unveiled, three years later, the giant was shockingly nude and as tall as the block of marble would allow, with huge hands and an oversized head. It was a gigantic statement, a boastful trumpeting of both the city's pride and of Michelangelo's own daring.

A few weeks before Raphael's arrival in Florence, the statue had been slung up on a wooden frame and eased along greased beams by forty men, taking four days to make its precarious progress through the narrow streets to its final resting place outside the main door of the Palazzo della Signoria, now known as the Palazzo Vecchio. Then there was a furious row. The more conservative of the city's arts advisory committee objected loudly to the figure's nakedness. Michelangelo was enraged, but the elders won and arranged for a large and permanent garland of twenty-eight fig leaves to be strategically fixed to the front of the statue for modesty's sake.

Michelangelo, hailed as a master sculptor, now found himself entering da Vinci's own territory of painting, with the chance to prove himself in direct competition. Both men had reason to be rankled by the presence of the other. Michelangelo had insulted da Vinci with a rash comment about his unfinished bronze horse for the duke of Milan. Da Vinci had offended his younger rival by insisting that *David*'s nudity be less blatant. The two men nevertheless settled down to work at preliminary sketches for their paintings, and the people of Florence began to revel in the contest of intellects as if it were some kind of spectator sport.

Florence's citizens were unusually well educated. Everyone, from the grandest merchants and government officials down to the city's many bakers, cobblers, and even its humblest stable boys, went to see every new work of art, engaging in heated debates over its merits. The large Piazza della Signoria sat at the heart of sixteenth-century Florence. Here, watched by Michelangelo's *David*, people gathered all year round to sit and chat, sitting in summer under the awnings of surrounding shops, in winter wherever they could find a patch of thin sun. There they would eat and drink at the little food stalls and discuss the issues of the day. Their opinions were not always favorable. Fortunately for Raphael, the lively interest in art also translated into abundant commissions, thanks to the emergence of a thriving middle class with money to spend on art and building projects. Of course da Vinci and Michelangelo between them were scooping up all the most prestigious commissions. But the fact that even the minor commissions not only paid a stipend but also provided room and board was most welcome to a young newcomer.

Raphael immediately put out word that he was available for work. He already had in his possession a letter of introduction from Giovanna della Rovere, the Urbino-born wife of the prefect of Rome and an influential supporter of his work. She had addressed it to Piero Soderini, the *gonfalonier*, or leader, of the Republic of Florence. "The bearer of this letter," she began, "is Raphael, a painter from Urbino, who has much talent in his vocation, and wishes to spend some time in Florence to study." Soderini must have passed the letter on, for Raphael soon made contact with Taddeo Taddei, a wealthy and powerful lawyer and a generous patron of the arts.

Taddei invited Raphael to join his own household, entertained him to meals, and gave him a commission to paint a small devotional picture of the Madonna and Child. These devotional images were very popular and most households possessed at least one, choosing a cheap print or a relatively expensive painting according to their means. The works cost little to make. Raphael, shrewd as ever, with few funds to speak of, chose to concentrate on this genre because it guaranteed him a certain income while allowing him to attract the attention of other collectors by offering works of a superior quality.

Through the introductions of his friend Taddei, Raphael soon began to make his mark among the cloth merchants of Florence, painting Madonnas and Holy Families for a number of wealthy clients. For a while he was preoccupied with these commissions. He studied how others treated the same subjects, drew dozens of different variations on the theme, and worked out new solutions to compositional problems. What he had learned in Perugino's guild-controlled medieval workshop had given him an excellent grounding. But here in Florence he was astonished and exhilarated by the new metropolitan standards. He saw that he could choose freely among any number of stylistic possibilities, and he applied himself by adapting them to his own use.

He experimented with some of Leonardo's innovations, and those of Donatello and Michelangelo, all the time sketching new ideas and trying out more and more ambitious groupings and poses as he gradually found his way toward his own individual style. His work soon came to the attention of Agnolo Doni, an immensely rich but notoriously tightfisted cloth merchant, public official, and significant arts patron. Doni commissioned Raphael to paint a double portrait of himself and his plump young wife, Maddalena Strozzi. The young painter gave his social-climbing patron an aristocratic air of gravitas. Adept already at strategic flattery, he also minutely detailed their fine clothes and jewelry, positioning their hands carefully so as to best display their expensive rings.

When he was not busy preparing and painting his commissioned works, Raphael spent his spare time walking around Florence with a sketchbook, studying and drawing the finest art works to be seen in the city. He was overwhelmed by the art he was seeing, and he drew and drew as if to absorb everything. He sketched Donatello's heroic statue of St. George, which stood in a niche of Or San Michele, right in the center of Florence. He went to look at Uccello's *Battle of San Romano*, which hung in the palace of the exiled Medici. He saw works by Botticelli and studied Fra Bartolommeo's famed *Last Judgement* in the church of San Marco. Fascinated by the male nude, he sketched variations on Antonio del Pollaiuolo's famous engraving, the *Battle of the Ten Nudes*.

And of course he went to see how the two old masters had begun on their rival battle scenes. Although neither fresco was ever finished, both da Vinci's *Battle of Anghiari* and Michelangelo's *Battle of Cascina*, with their violent, muscle-bulging fighting figures, were tremendously influential in their early sketched forms. Hordes of Florentines sought admission to the Santa Maria Novella, where the large-scale drawings, known as "cartoons," were displayed. Many young artists flocked there to make copies, and Raphael was among them. Within a few years, Michelangelo's cartoon had been torn to pieces by eager students.

This was a stirring moment in Florentine artistic history. With da Vinci and Michelangelo forging the way, the canons of the great classical style, now known as the High Renaissance, were being established, and Raphael was lucky to be able to devote himself to absorbing and assimilating the finest elements of these very works. He applied his prodigious talents to his painting with extraordinary intensity. But success, for him, was measured in terms of money. Owing to the high quality of his work, he quickly got himself noticed and started to pursue rich and powerful patrons with a vigor and a native cunning that was singularly lacking in both da Vinci and Michelangelo.

Raphael was ruthless in his pursuit of excellence and did nothing to hide his ambition. He even talked his way into a personal meeting with the great Leonardo da Vinci. Perhaps he hoped for some kind of benediction from this artistic godfather, a laying of aged hands on his own perfumed young head. What Raphael got was access to da Vinci's drawings for various projects, from which he quickly picked up his master's superior pen drawing techniques. But he also managed to engineer a long-term dialogue with da Vinci, which helped Raphael to free himself from his provincial Peruginesque style and to develop his own idiom in response to the highest new standards in the arts.

His relationship with Michelangelo was less harmonious. By nature Michelangelo was a solitary, melancholy genius. He was secretive, moody, and suspicious, a burly and generally unwashed figure, slightly hunchbacked, with a quick tongue and a broken nose, earned—perhaps deservedly—in a fistfight with the sculptor Pietro Torrigiani. Raphael, on the other hand, was a man of the world, gregarious, well dressed, robustly confident, charming, and crafty too. As a result, the two were natural antagonists. Raphael thrived in the combative atmosphere of the Florentine art world and was convinced he could equal Michelangelo and even, one day, surpass him. Michelangelo naturally distrusted Raphael. He regarded him as a precocious young upstart, an artist without natural talent who had gotten where he was merely by dint of unusually persistent study. "All that Raphael knew in his art, he had from me," he wrote later, maddened by Raphael's rising star. The rivalry was to become more bitter in following years, with Michelangelo and his supporters accusing Raphael of stealing his ideas and trying to ruin him.

For the moment, Raphael blithely ignored all of this. Determined to advance at all costs, he carried on with his pattern of appropriating and exploiting ideas from the old masters, meanwhile producing undoubtedly the finest devotional pictures in Florence.

He was not exactly a copyist, but he had a power of synthesis that made him the envy of his rivals. By day he would draw, paint, and study furiously, and in the evenings he would often visit the workshop of the artist Baccio d'Agnolo, where he met other painters and idlers interested in art. Here he kept in touch with all the latest news and gossip, exchanging ideas, comparing commissions, and, as always, sniffing out more work. Honor, glory, and fame were soon to be his, but for the moment, the clink of cold cash sounded louder in Raphael's ears.

After a few hours of chatter, he would slope off into the night in search of distraction, to mask with perfume the bitter tang of his ambitious dreams. Raphael was a dedicated womanizer. In stark contrast to the ethereal purity and grace of his paintings, his private life was racy and effusively amorous. Night after night, in the streets and piazzas of Florence, the charming and handsome young Raphael had no trouble picking up women. Back in his rooms, as if releasing some sort of feverish, pent-up energy from his painting, he would assuage his sensual appetites. Around this time, an uncle in Urbino sent word to Raphael telling him that he was preparing to open negotiations to find him a suitable wife. The artist responded hotly, in some startlingly candid letters. There was absolutely no question of taking a wife, he wrote. Such an encumbrance might soften his resolve, he explained, distract him from his career, and prove to be a drain on his financial resources. Raphael could paint like an angel; at the same time he was proving to be a remarkably ruthless operator.

With two years of determined study and improvement behind him in Florence, his policy was evidently paying off. Increasingly lucrative commissions continued to pour in and Raphael's name became well known both in Florence and across all of central Italy.

At the time of his summons in 1506 by the Duke of Urbino, those in the know were referring to Raphael as an exceptional painter, the outstanding rising star of the moment.

Raphael was the perfect choice for Duke Guidobaldo da Montefeltro. At this moment the duke badly needed a painting fine enough to do justice to his precarious position as ruler of the splendid inherited court of Urbino. Unlike Raphael, Guidobaldo was a tentative, nervous man, weak, sickly, and lacking in confidence. His whole life had been overshadowed by the powerful presence of his father, Duke Federico da Montefeltro, who had died at the age of sixty the year before Raphael was born.

It is hard to overestimate the belittling effect the grand and successful Federico had on his weakling son. But ironically, it was this shaming comparison that, as we shall see, motivated Guidobaldo to commission Raphael to paint the beautiful picture of our story.

Federico was a fabulously wealthy condottiere, the leader of a powerful mercenary army who commanded huge sums to fight wars on behalf of the highest bidders. Francesco Sforza employed him for sixty thousand ducats a year in peacetime and eighty thousand for war. His annual income, above and beyond what he required to run his estate, was around fifty thousand ducats, an enormous sum when you consider that a domestic servant received about seven ducats a year, that the doge of Venice received a mere three thousand a year, and that the profits of the Medici Bank at its peak were less than twenty thousand a year. Federico was one of the richest men in Europe. Gloating at his less successful counterparts, he made sure everyone knew that he had more wealth for patronage than any other prince in Italy.

He was a large, meaty man, a great swaggering soldier hero who had lost an eye in an amorous intrigue and the upper part of his nose in a sword joust, although some said he had had it lopped off to help him see better on his blind side. He was by all accounts a prudent and cunning fighter, and politically well connected. Over the years he had built for himself what everyone in Italy aspired to have: a set of carefully nurtured links to the pope. He was also highly educated and harbored grand cultural aspirations. When Pope Sixtus IV created him Duke of Urbino in 1474 and in the same year Edward IV made him a Knight of the Garter, England's most prestigious chivalric order, Federico decided to build himself a palace. He wanted a court of a grandeur suitable to someone of his growing prestige. Spending some of his immense accumulated riches, he commissioned a program of church building and ordered ducal residences to be built in half a dozen smaller towns under his rule. He also had the castles scattered around his estate remodeled and fortified.

But the main object of his efforts and his spending was the unprepossessing Gothic family house perched on top of a rocky overhang in Urbino. Calling in the best architects and craftsmen available, he had this building dramatically enlarged into a magnificent ducal palace built around a pillared courtyard, the same one through which Raphael was escorted to see Guidobaldo, and which still stands today.

Over the course of a dozen years, Federico pushed through hugely ambitious building programs and decorative schemes.

He built up a famous library with encyclopedic scholarly ambitions, which rivaled the papal library in Rome. No expense was spared. Vespasiano, the Florentine bookseller who was responsible for the library and who supplied many of its volumes, claimed it had cost thirty thousand ducats. Many of the manuscripts were specially commissioned, written and painted on dazzling white vellum by the finest scribes and painters in Florence. Federico's two-volume Bible was bound with gold brocade with silver mounts, and many of the other books were lavish with splendidly colorful bindings.

The library was full of Greek and Latin classics, and works of the poets, historians, philosophers, astrologers, mathematicians, architects, and churchmen. It was systematically planned and worthy of a modern Caesar. Naturally, everyone who saw it agreed that it glorified the virtuous and magnificent ruler who had paid for it.

Federico also ordered a princely *studiolo* to be built. This was a private space, open only to the most favored visitors and designed to express the intellectual and moral aspirations of his life. It was an intimate room, lined with wooden paneling decorated with intricate trompe l'oeil designs. Above this hung a cycle of paintings by Justus of Ghent, twenty-eight portraits of learned men, in two dense rows: ancient philosophers, poets, and legislators above, and popes and cardinals below. Half of these are now in the Louvre.

He commissioned dozens of fine art works and bought huge, colorful tapestries enriched with gold threads. He spent lavishly on ornate detail, ordering carved door frames, decorative marble fireplaces, and gilded friezes. Splendid portraits were commissioned too, and in 1476, father and son sat to Pedro Berruguete.

You can see the painting still hanging in the ducal palace. Federico sits proud as a lion in full body armor and ceremonial robes and chains, his garter prominently displayed below his left knee, which is thrust pointedly toward the artist. His powerful hands clutch a leather-bound book, a treatise on the art of war perhaps, which he appears to be reading with a vigorous intelligence. This man, we are invited to muse, has meditated on Marcus Aurelius, learned his duties from Cicero, and discovered the universe with Lucretius. And here he is, feeding his capacious brain with more intellectual meat. Beneath his massive, steel-encased elbows, clinging like a small kitten to Federico's other knee, is his five-year-old son and heir, Guidobaldo. Dressed in miniature finery and hung with jewels, the small boy seems to stare nervously into the distance with the anticipation of failure on his tiny, pale face.

A steady flow of ambassadors from major Italian states and of poets, artists, and scholars began to stream into Urbino in the hope of securing patronage from the wealthy and cultured Federico. Scholars wrote eulogies to him; other writers dedicated their work to him and donated manuscripts to the ducal library. Piero della Francesca, Justus of Ghent, and other fine painters—including Raphael's father—produced masterpieces for his walls.

Not all aspirants to patronage received what they believed they were due: many poems and eulogies were merely acknowledged with a small gift or simply ignored. But by the end of Federico's life, there were over a hundred courtiers listed as being in his service in some form or another. Astrologers, musicians, medical doctors, inventors, painters, poets, sculptors, philosophers were all on the roll call. Entering his service provided a stipend but also carried hidden benefits. There was access to the famous ducal library but, above all, given Federico's close relationship with the Vatican as *gonfalonier* of the papal forces, a chance to catch the pope's eye, which could lead to further advancement.

Federico's patronage was not disinterested. Shrewdly, with his eye on the best value for money, he invested in tangible things: the magnificent palace buildings, the art works, the sculptures, tapestries, and other wondrous objects. He assumed it would benefit his dynasty and ensure that his name would be carried down through the centuries.

His assumptions were correct. If you were to visit the ducal palace, you would find that the place still trumpets the power of this overblown ego. Everywhere in this treasure house, on every cornice and blank patch of plaster, reproduced in the front of every library manuscript and inserted into every commissioned painting are reminders of Federico's status. Fashioned with majestic extravagance on ceilings, in the decorations around doors, and carved into stone fireplaces are Federico's initials, his coat of arms, heraldic devices, and the insignia of the various decorations and chivalric honors he received. The place screams out his triumphant potency.

Visitors to Urbino today are drawn inexorably toward the ducal palace, which sits commandingly at the top of the hill on which the city is built. This vast symbolic edifice dominates the view of the place from all angles, its orange and pink bricks glowing against the sky, the grandeur of its towers and domes and gateways proclaiming the power of its founder. When my husband, Giles, and I first arrived in Urbino, it was midday. Easing our tiny Italian rental car up the streets and back alleys and close enough to our hotel was the first challenge. Having unloaded and deposited the car outside the city walls again, we decided to spend the rest of the day exploring the city as a whole, resisting the lure of the palace, and instead roaming the little streets and steeply angled piazzas and assessing the Urbino cuisine. Later, we walked down the steep hills and across the valley, looking back at this bastion of power and marveling at how little changed the city is from its Renaissance prime.

The next day we entered the palace and found ourselves sucked into a monument to the magnificence of Federico. Wandering around the long corridors and skating across the polished floors of the enormous state rooms, I counted seventy-eight reproductions of the Order of the Garter, put there to remind visitors of Federico's singular honor. I had come with little knowledge of the Montefeltro family but soon got a sense of Federico's character, his ruthless pursuit of power, and his desire to exhibit it. Five hundred years later, the legacy of his investment is still alive: the hilltop city still attracts crowds of young and creative brains, now no longer the painters, philosophers, and poets of old but the present-day undergraduates of Urbino University.

But his presence is strangely inescapable. Touring the palace a couple of times, even I, a mere tourist and amateur art sleuth, emerged feeling somewhat crushed under the weight of Federico's ego. So it was easy to imagine how, in Raphael's time, Guidobaldo must have felt, installed as the next duke in this pulsating monument to his father. I imagine that he wore the shame of his own impotence rather heavily, like a coat of rusty armor. For Guidobaldo failed in many respects to match his father.

As a young man Guidobaldo led campaigns as a condottiere that brought pitiful returns, and his efforts to defend even his own fortress were inept. In 1502, Urbino was attacked and the ducal palace looted by the rapacious armies of Cesare Borgia, forcing Guidobaldo into exile. All the valuable tapestries were removed and the books from his father's famous library were stripped of their precious bindings and carried off. Although Guidobaldo recovered his duchy in 1503, and the books and tapestries the following year, the memory of the Borgia attack was indelible. The broken protective walls, which you can still see today around the town, now stood as a vengeful reminder of Guidobaldo's own shortcomings.

He was pigeon-chested, pasty-faced, and thin, prone to illness and unable to produce an heir. He spent his days unhappily afflicted with the solitude of state, surrounded by an obsequious throng of courtiers and noblemen. His life must have seemed a total failure until he made two profitable decisions. The first was to marry Elisabetta Gonzaga of Mantua, the sister of the next pope. This was a pairing that set Guidobaldo up with a protective insurance policy for his position as duke and gave him the significant asset of power by papal association. Secondly, he devised a scheme to acquire from the English king the Order of the Garter for himself. At least he could try to match his father in that department.

Of course we know that Guidobaldo did win the Order of the Garter, a personal triumph that prompted him to commission Raphael to produce our jewel of a painting. But the story of how Guidobaldo got his garter reveals just how cynical were the political maneuverings that governed such decisions. It also reveals an unexpected shaft of cunning in Guidobaldo.

In 1504, Guidobaldo had visited Henry VII's representative in Rome and let it be known that his father had been most honored to have been made a Knight of the Garter. The Garter was one of the oldest chivalric orders in Europe, established at Windsor by Edward III on St. George's Day, April 23rd, 1348. Its original members were the English sovereign and twenty-five knight companions who met annually in St. George's Chapel. But under Edward IV, the election of illustrious foreigners was permitted for the first time, concentrated on influential rulers with whom new alliances would strengthen English interests. A few years before Federico had received his honor, three other Italian rulers had been elected to the order: two kings of Naples and the duke of Milan. Federico, whose election was motivated by his military prowess and his papal links, had characteristically interpreted his honor as the highest Europe could offer, taking it to bestow quasi-royal status on his worthy shoulders. Guidobaldo, with his badly diminished ducal position and his emasculated pride, was desperate to claw back status with such an honor.

Subtly insinuating to Henry's man in Rome that he too coveted the honor, he offered his devotion and service in papal circles in return. It is likely that Guidobaldo was aware of Henry VII's urgent desire to win influence with the pope. A usurper of the throne, Henry Tudor was keen to establish his own dynasty through marriage alliances. He had married his daughter to the king of Scotland and, following the death of his eldest son, Arthur, he wished to marry Arthur's widow, Catherine of Aragon, to Arthur's brother, Henry, now Prince of Wales. The marriage was vital as it would guarantee powerful support for the prince's eventual succession.

A treaty for such a marriage had been concluded in June 1503, but before a marriage could take place, a papal dispensation was necessary. Obtaining this dispensation became the essence of Henry VII's policy.

Henry VII's representative in Rome discreetly suggested the advantage in naming Guidobaldo a Knight of the Order of the Garter. He was the pope's brother-in-law, highly regarded by him and a captain of the Church. He might just have some sway. The fact that, unlike his father, Guidobaldo had performed no act of bravery, nor shown any noticeable military prowess to justify the Garter, quickly became a mere detail. For Henry, expediency was all when it came to dynastic ambitions. Guidobaldo's unmerited honor was no more than a carefully considered diplomatic maneuver.

Guidobaldo's ruse worked, and in February 1504, in a grand ceremony in Rome, he received the robes and the bejeweled insignia of the order from a team of King Henry's ambassadors sent expressly to Rome. The investiture of the duke as a Garter Knight was performed in the presence of the pope and required a ceremony of staggering formality, rich with Latin recitations that had been distilled over many years. After processions and pronouncements of obscure meaning, Guidobaldo presented his left leg and the aged English peer Sir Gilbert Talbot knelt to fasten the garter below his knee.

The status imparted by this small, coveted insignia far exceeded its physical splendor. It was simply a strap of fine cloth dyed a pale shade of blue, bordered with pearls and mounted with a gold buckle and a pendant ending in a pearl. The strap bore the motto *Honi soit qui mal y pense* (Evil be to him who evil thinks), embroidered in tiny gold Gothic letters. Sir Gilbert then robed Guidobaldo in a gown of purple, placed a blue mantle over his shoulders, and draped around his neck a heavy gold chain from which dangled a pendant showing St. George killing the dragon.

Guidobaldo's proud moment was followed by a night of lavish celebration, an event which was repeated, with huge expenditure and a certain degree of private mockery from knowing courtiers, when Guidobaldo finally returned to Urbino. At last, a small spark of personal pride had begun to twitch in his chest.

His mind turned at once to how he might cement relations with the English king and thank him for the honor. As a newly ennobled knight, he was now obliged to visit the king himself or send an ambassador to London within two years to receive further badges of office. This was the moment, he decided, to send as a gift the finest painting Urbino could produce. Pondering the possible subjects that might flatter the king and maximize the strategic links between the two courts, Guidobaldo settled on the well-loved story of St. George and the dragon. St. George was the patron saint of the Order of the Garter, and a glamorous hero whose romantic cult of chivalry held a particular appeal in England.

St. George is one of our most elusive and enigmatic saints. He is supposed to have been a soldier in the Roman army, martyred early in the fourth century for refusing to renounce Christianity, somewhere on the Asiatic shores of the Bosphorus. The myth of St. George has long obscured any concrete evidence there might have been of the man. This is perhaps because his martyrdom makes such entertaining, if rather gruesome reading. According to an early text dating from the fifth century, George cheerfully underwent a series of horrific tortures including drinking poison, being cut into ten pieces, and having his bones thrown down a well. After being restored to life, he was made to drink molten lead, suspended over a fire, and then sawn in two. Resurrected again, he endured more bloodcurdling tortures before converting an entire Roman army and then finally being decapitated himself.

Given his extraordinary story, St. George quickly acquired a large and enthusiastic following and came to be known as one of the greatest military saints. With war a constant threat in early Christian times, he was much in demand, and countries and cities rushed to place themselves under his protection as their patron saint. Today he is invariably associated with his dragon, a more recent and rather compelling addition to his story, which was spread across the Christian world in a thirteen-century account of his life. The combination of a saintly knight, a damsel in distress, and a wicked dragon appealed to everyone, and the tale of St. George and the dragon became one of the great romantic stories of medieval Europe. It is of course a variant on the oldest story in the world, the struggle between good and evil, and as such has endured, even up to this day.

As a subject for a painting intended as a gift of gratitude, it could not have been better. Raphael, with his growing reputation as the next star of Italy's superlative artistic tradition, would be perfect for the job. And so it was that Duke Guidobaldo summoned Raphael on that cold spring day to an audience in the palace of Urbino.

The young painter instantly understood the significance of the task ahead of him. He had to produce a work of art that would honor his own patron, bring glory to the English Order of the Garter, win admiration from an English king, and—most important of all to him—further his own reputation in bigger, grander spheres. He knew that in taking up this commission he would be addressing the English court. But he knew also that talk of this work, if it were to succeed, would recommend him in the more knowledgeable and sophisticated circles of Rome, where the papal court, the diplomatic corps, the cardinals, and an elite of educated churchmen and discriminating patrons were gathered with the potential to elevate Raphael to the very peak of his profession.

To any other young artist, this would have seemed a hugely daunting task. But nothing was too difficult for Raphael. This was his greatest opportunity yet to establish himself as more than an exceptionally talented novice, and to rival the great Florentine masters on their home ground. The work ahead of him carried complications, even risks. But Raphael had no doubt that he could surpass all expectations.

Settling down to work, he trawled through all the images in his mind and the drawings he had done that were appropriate to the composition. His own sketchbooks were bursting already with beautifully worked impressions of famous saints, monsters, and fighting men. While in Florence, he had worked hard to develop his knowledge of anatomy and his shaping of the heroic nude, and his mastery was now evident. He had sketches of Donatello's bas-relief of St. George and the dragon and of his statue of St. George at Or San Michele in Florence. He had his own copies of Antonio del Pollaiuolo's *Battle of the Ten Nudes*. He cast his mind back to Leonardo's series of drawings of horsemen fighting dragons, and the early cartoon stages of his mural in Florence depicting the Battle of Anghiari, a scene of exceptionally powerful fighting men.

Raphael charged into his preparatory sketches with an unnerving combination of high-speed spontaneity and methodical experiment. He had always preferred to draw from life, and he borrowed a *garzone*, one of the young and eager apprentices who populated the busy studio, to pose for him. Arranging the young boy's scrawny limbs on a stool, right elbow raised and holding a lancelike pole, he thrust forward the boy's left leg in imitation of St. George's powerfully tautened horseback position. A few days later, the same *garzone* knelt on the floor, shyly impersonating the maiden, hands pressed together and head slightly bowed in prayer as he fought off sleep in the warm room, gradually lulled by the grinding of pigments and the soft industry of brushes.

Raphael's working methods were already well developed. With his industrious and professional approach, his preparations were characteristically rational and economical. He sketched out his preliminary drawings in chalk and ink, trying out different styles and characterizations of varying ferocity and dramatic power. Then he quickly and confidently reworked and reworked them on fresh sheets of paper, each time transferring a copy of the previous composition to the new page by brushing chalk or charcoal dust through pin-pricked outlines, like a pattern for petit point. No time or effort was wasted. Over the weeks, the sketches were improved and refined, all the time being invested with a far greater degree of detail and precision than those for any of Raphael's previous paintings had been. Eventually, with a fully resolved cartoon before him, he was satisfied that the essence was there for what was to become one of the most coveted pictures in the world.

Studio assistants had already prepared for him a small panel of poplar wood, washed with a grounding of white gypsum, smooth as cream. At last Raphael was ready to begin painting. The energy of his creativity poured itself into the delivery of paint onto the panel. Working fast in the rising heat of late spring, he loaded his brush with heavy, creamy paint to model the dense, knotted muscles beneath the horse's smooth white skin. He applied long, swift, multiple brushstrokes to the gleaming polished steel of the saint's armor, and placed delicate sprays of fine color to shape the horse's curling tail and the saint's billowing cape.

Here was a prodigy determined to show off his mastery of every skill in the painter's book, an artist unafraid to take risks, to match himself against the artistic giants of his age. And as he gradually closed in with his brushes toward St. George's face, he changed the saint's expression from the shouting, agonized face of his sketches to the impassive calm of a divine vengeance. Here in St. George's delicate face, Guidobaldo and King Henry VII were being prompted to find the ideal of the perfect chivalric hero, a man of grace and resolution, endowed by nature not only with talent and beauty but also with an air of nonchalance even in the face of the most daunting task.

The painting that Raphael created that spring, five hundred years ago, was like an exquisite polished diamond, its facets sparkling from within. The light, the highly finished detail, like that of a manuscript illumination, the clarity, and the sharpness all drew the eye in close and held it fast as the viewer explored the elements of the story.

Raphael's conceptual genius is there in the dynamic triangular arrangement at the center of the composition, held at its corners by the warrior saint's face, the evil head of the dragon, and the serene maiden, praying on her knees. Leonardo's influence is evident in the dragon, in its beautifully modeled muscular form, with its creeping lion's legs and claws, its scaly serpentine tail and neck, eagle wings, and rabid fanged hound of a head. And plunging his spear into the dragon's breast is noble and romantic St. George, raised powerfully up on his stirrups, his polished steel armor gleaming, his blue gray cape billowing up from his shoulders like smoke.

Behind them, the maiden kneels calmly in prayer before a smiling landscape of serene and dreamily civilized beauty. Delicately drawn trees stand like bunches of brilliant feathers, and a small picturesque citadel animates the distance, among bluish hills arranged in soft folds, hushed and slumbering in the mellow afternoon heat.

Cutting through this arrangement is the splendid bravura horse, its eyes so brimful of passion that they look almost human. With its prancing leap frozen in midair, as if seen in a flash of lightning, this huge white charger twists and turns its head to look back, straight into the eyes of the viewer. And there you see the veins throbbing beneath its skin, the nostrils flared with fear, and the hint of muscular eyebrows, ruckled with anxiety over those big round eyes. But even amidst all this action and danger, Raphael seemed to subvert the narrative with a little smile on the horse's lips, a knowing smile containing a mystery that was to be reserved for dukes, kings, empresses, and powerful men. It was a final flourish of wit from a supremely confident artist.

Within just a few months of the commission, Raphael had completed the painting. In a brilliant stroke of subtle flattery, he had made a point of the all-important garter, tied prominently below the knee on the saint's left leg, just as it was on Federico in the double portrait of Guidobaldo and his father. Raphael was introducing the idea to his patron that perhaps he, Guidobaldo, who had seen the evil dragon of Cesare Borgia out of Urbino and now, through his links to the pope, had brought peace to his people, could think of himself as the embodiment of St. George. Guidobaldo, the romantic hero, Raphael was suggesting, could now at last take his place honorably alongside his successful father.

As it turns out, Guidobaldo's name did make it into the history books, but not for his statesmanship or heroism in battle. His name is remembered as that of the earliest important patron of the painter Raphael. For soon after Raphael had completed *St. George and the Dragon*, word of his genius reached Rome. Tales of the masterpiece destined for the king of England reached the ears of the architect Donato Bramante, who was then engaged on the designs for St. Peter's. Bramante was himself from Urbino, and Raphael had engineered meetings with him on several occasions during the architect's visits to his home town. Bramante had been impressed by the young painter and now, succumbing no doubt to a degree of pressure from Raphael himself, he recommended him to the pope. Within two years, this skilled manipulator of powerful people and clever careerist was established in Rome, employed by the pope on the decoration of the papal apartments, starting with the Stanza della Segnatura.

Raphael's success in Rome was meteoric. The sheer speed of his rise to power became part of the myth of his genius, coloring attitudes to his work for hundreds of years to come. Soon after beginning work in the papal apartments, he began to eclipse the talents of the older and more experienced artists also employed there. One by one, pitted against this brilliant young newcomer, his former mentor Perugino and his collaborator Pinturicchio, Johannes Ruysch, and others were vanquished and removed from the team, their half-finished frescoes destined to be scraped from the walls to make room for Raphael's brushes.

Working furiously to spread his name, Raphael engaged engravers to make copies of his works to advertise his abilities. He persuaded leading cardinals to commission works from him and inspired Agostino Chigi, a prominent banker and probably the richest private citizen in Italy, to employ him to decorate his villa at Trastevere.

In Rome, Raphael came across Michelangelo, who was also working for the pope on the Sistine Chapel, and who by now disliked his young rival intensely. The two crossed swords frequently, but their mutual antagonism became particularly heated when Raphael painted a fresco of Isaiah that appeared to be heavily inspired by Michelangelo's prophets, then still in progress but shrouded in secrecy, on the ceiling of the Sistine Chapel. Vasari, in his biographical lives of the painters published some thirty years later, claimed that Raphael, aided by Bramante, had sneaked into the chapel behind Michelangelo's back to climb the scaffold and study the unfinished frescoes.

The farouche older recluse resented Raphael's success bitterly. Years later, after Raphael's death, Michelangelo persuaded Vasari to reassess Raphael's impact in the second edition of his *Lives*, reducing Raphael's brilliance to a secondary place, behind Michelangelo's.

But back in the 1510s, as Raphael was working away in the papal apartments, Michelangelo could do nothing about the fact that his rival had become part of a sophisticated circle at the top of Roman society, moving among the intellectuals, courtiers, and connoisseurs as a peer. After Pope Julius's death in 1513, Raphael managed to insinuate himself into papal circles so successfully that he became the favorite painter of the new pope, Leo X. He was engaged not only to continue the decoration of the papal apartments but also to serve, after Bramante's death, as architect of St. Peter's and as superintendent of antiquities.

Raphael had become a courtier who also painted. He was living like a prince in a large palazzo, designed by his friend Bramante, in central Rome. According to Vasari, he had a cardinalate in the bag and from there, the author insinuates, it was only a short step to the papal tiara. Mercenary as ever, Raphael totted up his worth in a letter to his uncle, listing property worth three thousand gold ducats and a monthly income of fifty ducats for his architectural work alone, supplemented greatly by his other commissioned incomes. He ran a huge workshop, which turned out paintings for large sums under his famous name, but worked incessantly himself on the major commissions, his last important one being the cartoons for tapestries to be hung in the Sistine Chapel. These show an extraordinary command of form and intellectual achievement for such a young painter.

Like Mozart, Raphael died prematurely, and this early end undoubtedly contributed further to the allure of his name. He died on his thirty-seventh birthday on April 6, 1520, after an illness caused, according to Vasari, by an excessive bout of lovemaking. Michelangelo's ally, the painter Sebastiano del Piombo, who had vied unsuccessfully with Raphael for commissions, immediately wrote to Michelangelo with the news, adding piously, "may God forgive him." His body lay in state for a day before being buried in the Pantheon, a privilege previously reserved only for the canons of the church. The funeral was attended by the entire papal court, and the pope himself is said to have wept publicly during the burial rites. The pomp accompanying Raphael's death and burial were unprecedented for an artist. Not even for Leonardo, who had died the previous year, had there been such a public display of grief. As one contemporary observer wrote, "Here, people are talking about nothing but the death of this exceptional man, who has completed his first life at the young age of thirty-seven. His second life—that of his fame, which is subject neither to time nor death—will endure for all eternity."

Raphael had attained a unique status during his short life and had made an indelible mark on art. Vasari, who knew many of his friends and contemporaries, described him as a mortal god. "Because of Raphael," he wrote, "art, coloring, and invention have all three been brought to a pitch of perfection that could scarcely have been hoped for; nor need anyone ever hope to surpass him."

His work was to stand for perfection in art, his star barely wavering over five hundred years. And *St. George and the Dragon*, his first true Renaissance masterpiece, which had helped to propel him to Rome and immortality, was set to go far too. A combination of Raphael's towering reputation, the painting's beauty and irresistible spirit, and the greed of collectors was to take it on some extraordinary adventures around the world.

2·

WHEN I WAS A child, museums did not have education departments. There were no scheduled story times and workshops, no young education officers hanging around the galleries, eager to help children make variations on the great works of da Vinci or Degas, out of cardboard and colored feathers. Nobody really bothered with children in museums. These were grown-up institutions for grown-up people, huge and poised and solemnly quiet like churches. Children, with their loud voices and games, were only just tolerated, certainly not encouraged. So instead, my parents used to devise complex and enticing adventures to tempt me and my brothers to go and look at art. Usually we would each choose a painting from the catalogue at home, and then when we got there, we'd race off to find our trophies, and noisily swap silly stories about them.

Occasionally some picture caught our fancy, and we sat on the floor in a trance, boring holes in the canvas with our astonished eyes. More often the paintings didn't, and we scrambled around, laughing and bumping into each other and really not noticing all the serene Madonnas and the silent, sad still lives. Our parents were blessedly unconcerned, and I remember thinking secretly that these places belonged to me. I enjoyed the absence of overbearing officials and nit-picking teachers demanding answers to questions. There was a kind of floating feel to the enormous echoing galleries, with their weird and rarefied air and their high, gilded cornices. I felt they were full of mystery and strange beings, goddesses and princesses and obscure Transylvanian kingdoms dotted with dragons. But just as I was getting carried away in some elaborate fairy tale, or staring at the gory entrails of a Goya and thinking this must be some frightful faux pas on the part of God, we would have to go home and eat fishcakes for tea.

I particularly remember a very special trip we made during a half term to the Rijksmuseum in Amsterdam. I must have been about eight at the time, and I had chosen Vermeer's *Girl with the Pearl Earring* as "my picture." I still remember the buildup of going into the museum, searching the cavernous rooms for the painting, and trying to find "mine" before my brothers found "theirs." The vast galleries teemed with imagery, landscapes, portraits, huge canvases in elaborate frames, all in exhausting quantities, enough to make a child start hallucinating. And then at last I found it, hanging right there in front of me. Here at last was Vermeer's serene girl, so beautiful and so calm. I remember standing staring at it with childish reverence, and then desperately wanting to touch it. In our attic I still have the reproduction mounted on wood that hung in my bedroom for years.

Since then, like many people, I've turned gallery going into my therapy. I've always been interested in paintings, and occasionally I've been seduced by great works of art. Sometimes certain pictures look so wonderful that I just want to stay with my eye fixed on them forever. As a teenager I dragged unwilling boyfriends to art galleries. As a young woman I went with my husband, wandering shyly, hand in hand, enjoying the delicious sexiness of these places, and getting lost in a powerful Rubens or an amazingly detailed Canaletto. Sometimes I would steal a glance at the other people, tiptoeing about, all nervous and rapt and polite, lots of them actually not looking at the paintings at all but just observing each other like cats watching mosquitoes. But now, as a mother with three young daughters of my own, I go gratefully to the sheltered treasure houses of London, to focus their hungry eyes and calm my own on one or two works of art. We always try to leave before the excitement fades.

In an earlier career as a foreign correspondent, I had adapted my reporting duties to accommodate trips to museums. For six years, traveling around the world, I had gazed at paintings and other art objects in museums in Taipei, Moscow, Lima, and dozens of other cities. Many of these national museums and galleries were fabulous, full of dizzyingly ancient and beautiful collections. A few were total fleapits, but that didn't matter. As I wandered and luxuriated in the glories and oddities of the collections, I mused momentarily, as most people do, on the subjects and the stories, and on what is known about the lives of the artists. But I seldom thought about that other hidden dimension, the provenance and history of these works of art as objects. Who else before us had gazed at these paintings? Who had commissioned them and why had they changed hands? Where had they hung, and what events had they witnessed? For years I remained oblivious to these rich tales, to the battles fought over ownership and the academic spats excited by theories surrounding their creation. What I never guessed was that behind those noble canvases and scrolls and painted panels all sorts of secrets reside, tales of power and patronage, of love and death and desire.

Raphael's little masterpiece of St. George and the dragon harbors more such mysteries and passions than any amateur sleuth could possibly hope for. When I first decided to write its story, tracing its fortunes as it moved from one rapacious collector to another, I had not appreciated the extent of its allure, nor the complexity of its ownership. I visited the cities to which its bizarre career had taken it. I foraged like a hog after truffles, burying my nose in papers and books. Whenever I found a new area of discovery, a new fact or a new detail to the story, I found I couldn't go to sleep. I would stay awake for hours at night, piecing together the bits of the puzzle, straining to get a clear picture of the life of this extraordinary painting, which was assuming a character and humanity all of its own. Slowly I uncovered a Byzantine pattern of conflicting theories and supposed truths. I found too a far-flung network of scholars and self-appointed Raphael apostles who invest their days and nights imagining and dreaming about its story.

One of the mysteries surrounds its disappearance. Just after it was painted, Raphael's *St. George* vanished without trace for more than a hundred years. All we have from this early stage of its life are five known, incontestable truths. We know that it was painted by Raphael, about 1506. Its subject is St. George and he wears a garter, an unusual detail that indicates that it was specially commissioned. Its first dated reference is 1627, when it was in the possession of the earl of Pembroke. So, between 1506 and 1627, nobody knows for sure where it was.

In the late nineteenth century, a German historian named Johann David Passavant looked at these facts and declared that the painting had traveled to England as a gift for Henry VII in 1506. Dozens of art historians agreed. According to them, it had left the city in August of that year.

I had had Passavant's theories in mind when I explored Urbino searching for details on the trail of the painting. Looking down from the beautiful carved stone loggia opening out from Federico's apartment in the ducal palace, I gazed at the roads trailing down through the wooded hills and out of Urbino, winding along the gently meandering valleys and heading off in all directions. These small roads are little changed from Raphael's day, so it is not difficult to picture a caravan of carriages and carts, setting out five hundred years ago, loaded with precious gifts destined for an English king in a distant land.

To most people, the journey from Urbino to London was an almost inconceivably long one in those days. Thought to be about two thousand miles, although no one knew precisely how many, it took the traveler through rugged and often dangerous mountain passes, across great tracts of unpredictable French territory, over the stormy English Channel to Dover and then on to England's capital.

The honor of conveying this precious symbol of Renaissance Italy's superiority on this difficult journey fell to Baldassare Castiglione, a twenty-seven-year-old courtier and intimate of Duke Guidobaldo. The official purpose of his journey was to be installed, as the duke's proxy, as a Knight of the Garter. But as we know, his other task was to deliver the duke's gifts safely into the hands of the king.

Castiglione was later to become famous as the author of *Il Cortegiano* (*The Courtier*), an influential guide to the manners and ideals of Renaissance courtly life. The book was devoured all over Europe by sovereigns and scheming courtiers alike and eventually became as widely known as Machiavelli's *The Prince*. But back in 1506, as he prepared for his long journey to London, Castiglione was still no more than a reasonably well-born, ambitious, and uncommonly wily courtier. Two years earlier, he had transferred his loyalty from the duke of Mantua to the Montefeltros in Urbino when he saw the extent of their growing power and influence in Rome. And soon after that, he had engineered an appointment as an officer of the duke of Urbino's fighting forces. In spite of his new title, Castiglione nevertheless displayed a remarkable ability to steer clear of the battlefield. Suffering from a variety of minor ailments, most of them related to the occasion when his mule had stumbled and injured his foot, Castiglione was most often to be found writing to his mother from his sickbed, set up at a safe distance from the fighting. An inveterate correspondent, he bullied her to send him the latest in Mantuan hairnets, or a new velvet-covered helmet with his fine lance, gilded and burnished and wrapped with "some beautiful silk that suits your taste." Musing from the plumped pillows of his sickbed, he seemed much more interested in what he might wear for his triumphant return to Urbino than in whatever skirmish was currently occupying his troops.

The prospect of a journey to London and an audience with Henry VII predictably awoke a new energy in Castiglione. On Easter Day, 1506, he was knighted by the duke, giving him the appropriate status to act as his emissary to the English court. And he began collecting together the various gifts destined for the English king. The consignment represented an act of homage at its most calculated, designed to confer authority on the giver as much as the receiver. The composition of the gifts had been exquisitely thought out to match the known weaknesses of the English court with the special strengths of the Urbino state: fine art, horses, falcons, and dogs. Good horses were considered a mark of aristocratic status as much in peace as in war, and Castiglione, himself a glamorously well horsed and expensively armored man, understood the prestige attached to Italy's finest, sleekest steeds.

It had been arranged that he would pick up the horses in Milan on his way north, so he busied himself supervising the packing of the other treasures. Raphael's delicate little painting would have been carefully wrapped with soft wadding, enclosed in double layers of waxed cloth, eased into a pasteboard pouch and then wedged, with more handfuls of woollen wadding and protective straw, in a sturdy wooden crate. Castiglione also packed, secretly for himself, another exquisite painting by Raphael, a small portrait of the duchess of Urbino, Elisabetta Gonzaga, which he wished to carry as a keepsake and reminder of her. As his love for the lady had to be kept secret, the portrait was craftily framed in such a way as to be normally hidden behind a sliding mirror. The space inside the frame was to carry other treasures too. A few months later, during Castiglione's mission to London, he wrote two tender little sonnets expressing his love for the unattainable Elisabetta. These were carefully concealed, tucked away inside the frame, and were only discovered sixty years later by his daughter-in-law.

Eventually, by late August, the treasury of gifts had been collected together, packed and mounted on mules and carts. The little procession set off, rumbling down the rutted roads away from the great hilltop palace of Urbino. For several days the trail of people and vehicles wound around and down precipitous slopes silvered with olive groves and musky fruit trees, between patches of beans and cabbages and aromatic herbs, demarcated by lines of ancient gnarled vines. And as they went, little clouds of dust puffed and soared up into the shimmering golden haze, punctuating their steady progress. The August of that year was a particularly sweltering month, and Castiglione made frequent stops. In the evenings he wrote to his mother, his pen scratching away to the insistent chirrup of the cicada, revealing some wholly predictable aspirations for success, glory, and honor at the English court.

In Milan, the horses delivered to Castiglione turned out to be partially blind. This was a swindling little trick played by the duke of Mantua, who was still nursing a grudge over Castiglione's decision a few years earlier to transfer his loyalty to Urbino. Castiglione was furious to have been wrong-footed so easily, but after a rapid search for some replacement horses, his party set off again, among a babel of tradesmen and other travelers, whipping the flanks of their obstinate mules all the way through the Alps and on to Lyon. Here they rested for four days, during which time Castiglione again took up his pen, lamenting to his mother the deaths since leaving Urbino of both his beloved brother and his nephew. "If fortune is as fickle as she is said to be," he wrote mournfully, "it is time we could look for some prosperity."

Castiglione's request for good fortune was granted. His passage through France and up to Calais was happily uneventful. Now he had to cross the English Channel, an adventure which in winter was dreaded by all travelers. As he waited in Calais for a ship, Castiglione heard the news of King Philip of Spain, who, a few months earlier, had set out toward Dover and had been carried in a storm to Falmouth, where his ship was almost wrecked. The king and his consort, Queen Joanna, had been forced to wade ashore in water reaching, it is said, right up to the royal waists. Castiglione was unperturbed. Fired now by the proximity of his destination, and placing his trust in the debt he reckoned fortune owed him, he organized for his party to board a sturdy vessel and set sail for Dover. The bedraggled little procession of treasure-filled carts and carriages, the mules, horses, and their travel-weary Italian masters eventually stumbled off the boat and onto English soil on October 20. There, standing slightly unsteadily beneath the towering white cliffs and whipped by a savage wind, they met a reception of which even Castiglione had not dreamed.

The arrival in England of an Italian knight, standing proxy for the duke of Urbino and having traveled two thousand miles to be installed as a Knight of the Order of the Garter, was an event of considerable importance to Henry VII. The Order of the Garter lay at the heart of the king's political and ceremonial thinking. Here was a device designed to boost his majesty, and the king was in the habit of extracting from it every ounce of prestige he possibly could.

So when Castiglione arrived at Dover, he found himself looking into the eyes of Sir Thomas Brandon, a senior Knight of the Garter and a close adviser to the king. Brandon sat resplendent in plumes and armor on a huge and gleaming horse. Behind him, stretched out in serried ranks, was a company of immaculately liveried servants mounted on the finest English horses, their colorful banners fluttering in the wind. It must have been a splendid sight. Rows and rows of mounted soldiers stood lined up to a fixed pattern behind their knight, waiting in silence as their horses stamped and whinnied, their swords glinting in the thin autumnal sunshine. To any ordinary English villagers, lying on their stomachs on the grass above and peeking over the edge of the cliffs, this was a glimpse of an exciting romantic ideal. To Castiglione it was a flattering display of the richest English swagger and bravado.

To the comforting sound of clanking armor and a rhythmic bass line of clopping hoofs, Brandon and his men rode with Castiglione and his companions to Deptford in Kent. Here they were met by Sir Thomas Docwra, lord prior of the Order of St. John of Jerusalem, and Sir Thomas Wriothesley, the principal Garter king of arms, and thirty more soldiers, all in new liveries and bristling with javelins, bows, and arrows. The three English Thomases and their men accompanied the Italians to their lodgings and the next day rode with them into London, arriving just as the sky turned a dark inky blue, with only a smudge of brightness still visible above the skyline of Westminster in the west.

London in 1506 was one of the great cities of Europe with a population of seventy-five thousand crowded within its walls and spilling out beyond them. Even from the center of the city it was an easy walk to get out into the country, which was just as well because the houses were closely packed together, with pigs and chickens to be found rooting around in most back yards. At its heart there were beautiful churches, public buildings, and large private homes owned by lords and wealthy merchants. An Italian visitor walking along Cheapside six years earlier had been astonished to find no fewer than fifty-two goldsmiths' shops and an astonishing range of other luxuries for sale. Erasmus, visiting London for the first time in 1499, was equally impressed and went into raptures about the peculiar English habit of kissing. The place was undoubtedly bustling with activity, its daily life punctuated with regular displays of civic pomp.

To the east, dominating the skyline, was the Tower, a huge, brooding presence, part palace, part prison. The Tower housed a great maze of offices and storerooms as well as the royal menagerie, where Londoners could view the lions and leopards. Not far from them was the office of the royal alchemist, an optimist of great daring and ambition who toiled away at his hopeless task, charged with solving the never-ending fiscal problems of his king.

Between the Tower and the Palace of Westminster, London's great highway was the River Thames. This was a glittering swath of movement, winding through the center of the city, and much wider than it is today. It was spanned by a single bridge, London Bridge, which was considered to be one of the wonders of the world. The river was perpetually alive with flocks of swans and other waterbirds that spent their lives weaving about among the dozens of little boats constantly carrying goods and people to and fro, from one landing to another, upstream to Oxford and beyond, and downstream to meet the grand galleon ships that sailed to the countries of Europe.

Downstream on a great bend in the river, freshened by clean estuary breezes, was Greenwich Palace, built by Henry VII as a very visible symbol of his wealth, power, and sophistication. If you were to go to Greenwich today, you would find nothing that bears any resemblance to the Tudor palace; most of it was swept away when Inigo Jones remodeled the house in the seventeenth century. But the sweep of the river is still unchanged, its bobbing waters accommodating ducks, moorhens, the odd police launch, and a few brave trippers on pleasure boats.

In search of a sense of the building as it had been in Henry VII's day, I made a visit to the Ashmolean Museum in Oxford, where, in the print room, I was shown two beautiful little watercolors of

Greenwich Palace by Anthonis van den Wyngaerde dated 1558. Although they were painted after Castiglione's visit and following some additions by Henry VIII, they give a sense of the palace, of its showy grandeur in a sea of rolling green fields and trees. A long, low, narrow block of public rooms sits on the waterfront, its towers topped with onion domes. The king's five-story donjon, or great tower, sits toward the end of the row, containing his bedroom at first-floor level and his most private chambers, perhaps his library and office, above. Although the donjon was a fundamental element of castle design from Norman times, Greenwich had no fortifications, no moat, and no visible sense of being a castle. With its rows of grand bay windows along the waterfront, it must have been more like a fashionable and extremely lavish urban house, in spite of its rural setting.

Even today, its sense of distance from central London still appeals, and you can imagine how in the sixteenth century it was a place of escape for the king and his court. Henry VII liked to spend much of his time here in winter, away from the crowded center of London with its fetid stinks and bouts of plague. And it was to Greenwich Palace that Castiglione was summoned, a couple of days after his arrival, to meet the monarch and to deliver his gifts. Very much the image-conscious Italian courtier, Castiglione probably put on his best jerkin, lined with red silk, under his heavy fur-collared gown. But he had to bully his cold, stiffened leather boots to admit his toes. By the time he had arrived on a barge rowed by a team of gaily dressed royal oarsmen, the chilling mist had lifted.

When Henry VII stayed at Greenwich, he could see right out over the water from his first-floor royal apartments, which gave him a sweeping view of the bending river and all the high-masted ships. He enjoyed watching these noble vessels, each one a pleasing symbol of wealth as it plied upstream carrying precious imports into London and back downstream filled with exports. Behind the royal apartments were great warrens of chambers and lesser rooms that accommodated his multifarious court.

And so it was that Castiglione, alighting with relief from his barge, was ushered into the presence of not just the monarch but also a full-blown contingent of courtiers and servants, a perpetually scurrying affirmation of the solitude of state. Here was a king who knew how to present himself. Every detail was designed to impress. Bowing courtiers reverentially referred to him as "Your Majesty," a new word that had recently entered the English language. He wore, perhaps, the same sort of clothes that he had worn to greet a recent visiting ambassador of the duke of Milan: a violet-colored gown, lined with cloth of gold, and a collar of pearls and jewels strung out in four dazzling rows. In fact Henry was often laden with jewels. On his fingers were jeweled rings, and on his cap he wore a large diamond and a beautiful pear-shaped pearl. Henry had a taste for diamonds, rubies, emeralds, and other gems. He had spent over a hundred thousand pounds on them in just twelve years, his appetite deriving from his view of them as easily transportable assets if ever he had to leave in a hurry.

Considering that he reigned five hundred years ago, you might be surprised to discover how many images and credible descriptions of Henry VII can still be found. There is a beautiful terra-cotta bust by Pietro Torrigiano, which is now in the Victoria and Albert Museum in London. There are coins, a death mask, and a realistic tomb effigy. But it is the portrait at the National Portrait Gallery, a small head and shoulders panel painting made in 1505 by an anonymous Dutch artist, by which I like to imagine him. He sits awkwardly, a forty-eight-year-old widower, large-nosed and without eyelashes, as if looking through a window. His lips are pursed tight, his cheeks sunken, and his eyes are narrow and shrewd. At the base of the painting, his long acquisitive fingers curl over and grip the edge of the inscription, as if ready to reach out and gather in more revenues from his people. The painting was destined for Margaret of Savoy, the daughter of the Emperor Maximilian I, as part of marriage negotiations. Although it succeeded admirably in conveying the king's astuteness with money, it did not persuade her to marry him.

A handful of foreign diplomats also left written descriptions of him. He was clearly a reserved character with little of Henry VIII's false heartiness or Elizabeth I's adroit condescension. "His appearance," wrote Italian scholar Polydore Vergil, "was remarkably attractive and his face cheerful, especially when speaking; his eyes were small and blue, his teeth few, poor and blackish; his hair was thin and white; his complexion sallow."

So this was the monarch, resplendent in his costume of majesty but daunting in his solemnity, who received Castiglione in a hall hung with handsome tapestries and arranged with gilt chairs covered with cloth of gold.

Bowing with appropriate deference, the Italian presented his credentials to the king and then delivered, as he later informed his mother, an eloquent—and much rehearsed—oration in Latin. The various gifts of horses and falcons were discussed and then, two months after he had set off with it from Urbino, Castiglione finally delivered the small painted panel into the long, jewel-carbuncled fingers of the English king.

Following any kind of mystery trail like this involves, by its very nature, encounters with deviations, detours, and blockages. And when dealing with events that occurred so long ago, and which have left such a meager paper trail, a certain amount of guesswork becomes inevitable. Obstacles add to the fun of the chase. All was going miraculously well on my trail following the Raphael *St. George* until I met Edward Chaney at a party in London. Chaney is professor of fine and decorative arts at Southampton University and has recently published an excellent book on English collecting. Naturally I began to ask him about the Raphael *St. George*, which had gone to Henry VII. Cheney look as pained as if I had just slapped him in the face. No, no, no, he said, shaking his head vigorously. Have you not read Cecil Clough's paper? The painting didn't go to England in 1506. No, no. A lot of people thought it did, but no, no. No, it's much more likely that it was given to Sir Gilbert Talbot, the king's envoy who visited Italy to perform the Garter ceremonies for the duke of Urbino.

This was turning out to be more complicated than I had expected. It was also turning out to be much more interesting. I had read Clough's 1981 book, *The Duchy of Urbino in the Renaissance*, in which he had repeated the same Henry VII theory and suggested that the Raphael *St. George* had been the first Renaissance painting to arrive in England. But then in 1984, Clough changed his mind and all sorts of arguments broke out. With some difficulty I rooted out a copy of his paper, published in the splendidly obscure journal *Report of the Society of the Friends of St. George's and Descendants of the Knights of the Garter.*

It had been assumed by Passavant that Henry VII had handed the painting on to his son Henry VIII, and that it had passed from that king, after his death, into the Pembroke family. There was one flaw in this theory: the painting does not appear in Henry VII's or Henry VIII's inventories. Having pondered this fact for ten years or so, Clough came up with a new idea. He proposed that the painting had been given not to Henry VII but to Sir Gilbert Talbot, the king's envoy in Italy. Talbot's great-great-granddaughter Mary Talbot had married the third earl of Pembroke, and it is possible that the painting could have been passed down and entered the Pembroke family at the time of her marriage. Unfortunately

Clough could find no wills or inventories that mentioned it. There was no documentary evidence to support this theory.

As a seeker of such treasure myself, I delved further and found myself face to face with June Osborne, an art historian who lives in the English seaside town of Rye. She is another passionate Raphael disciple who loves this painting and harbors evolving theories about its life. During the early stages of my research I had written an article in the *Times* about the painting and its journey from the court of Urbino to the court of Henry VII. In response June Osborne had written to my publishers, stating that this theory was incorrect and that I should revise my views in light of Clough's work. Copies had been sent to various art critics and reviewers of her acquaintance.

I didn't feel like being intimidated at one remove, so I made contact with her. We exchanged tentative greetings, and then a few months later, in a letter, she hinted to me that she had solved the riddle of the painting's disappearance. I took a train from Charing Cross and met June at Rye station. She is short and smiley with kind, elderly eyes that glow like a pair of modest chandeliers. Dressed in sensible khaki and carrying a clear plastic bag containing two wholemeal buns, she took me on a little tour of the old town, trundling up the hilly peak to the Norman church and down again before taking me back to her thatched cottage. Sunlight streamed in the windows and fell on the piles of books and papers and letters strewn in happy abundance around her sitting room.

As a young graduate she had worked at the Slade School of Fine Art for Ernst Gombrich, the doyen of art historians, and it was he, in a postcard from Urbino, who had first sparked June's lifelong interest in the magical city. Many years later she embarked on writing a history of Urbino, and after thirty years of research and thought, it was finally published in 2003. By then she had long been seduced by the beauty and mystery of the Raphael *St. George*, and for the last fifteen years, she has spent a great deal of time trying to trace the whereabouts of the painting during the first hundred years of its life.

We settled ourselves on comfortable low armchairs spilling over with cushions. For a while June chatted about her grandchildren and about her next trip to Urbino, when she hopes to find an Italian publisher for her book. I measured out a polite margin of small talk and then, wary of the train timetable, plunged into the subject of the painting. I explained that I was neither a professional art historian nor a scholar, but that this book was to be a kind of personal journey of discovery. I told her I would love to know where the painting had got to during its blank century.

She turned slowly to face me. "I know where it was," she said. A tantalizing look glinted in her eye. She smiled. I waited patiently. She stared down again at her sandals. After a while I broke the silence. "So where was it?" Again the seconds ticked emptily away. She was stroking a large cat, which had jumped up into her lap. I looked vaguely round the room, glancing at the bookcases full of art books. My years of sluggish conversations in Japan, where acres of silence float by unfingered, gave me the strength to sit this out. Eventually she spoke again. "It didn't go to the Tudors. But I know where it did go." June sounded insistent.

Half an hour went by while she explained her theory that the painting would not have been considered important enough as a gift for the king. We sat down to a delicious meal of salmon and salad. Still there was no answer. By the time we were drinking coffee, she was winding up the meeting. "Anyway," she said, "they had to give something to Talbot, and I think this was it. The painting was hung in a country house in England which is now a hotel." Unfortunately June declined to tell me which hotel, or how the painting had got there. It is possible she believes it was hung at Grafton

Manor in Worcestershire, where Gilbert Talbot lived during the reign of Henry VII. The original building was burnt down in 1710 and the house subsequently built on the site has been turned into a hotel. On the other hand, June offered me no proof. One day she may publish her theory. I went home exasperated.

Neither the Henry VII theory nor the Talbot theory can muster supporting facts. But then we cannot expect to have proof of everything. Those maddeningly elusive details of the distant past are blurred at the best of times. Hard-and-fast proof is a luxury that rests on the chance survival of a few ancient documents. Maybe one day a new piece of evidence will emerge and a fresh theory will be embraced. But in the meantime, I like to think that theories about the painting should not be cordoned off as the exclusive preserve of the academic elite.

I know I am going—crazily and eccentrically—against the views of the esteemed Edward Chaney, Cecil Clough, and June Osborne, but I still believe that the most plausible version of the story is Passavant's and that the painting did go to England in 1506, where it was presented to King Henry VII. I have not spent decades studying the subject, but I still find it hard to accept that the duke of Urbino commissioned a work of art of this quality (and its quality would have been appreciated in Italy even if not yet in England) from a fast-rising star in order to hand it over to an envoy. And after all, this was the story believed by many of those ruthlessly self-promoting men and women who acquired and treasured the painting during the various episodes of its journey.

Dozens of art historians over the years have agreed with Passavant in print. Russian empresses who happened to have the painting hanging on their walls agreed. The dealers and subsequent buyers all agreed, reproducing the theory in their writings and giving it the sheen of established fact. Even a director of the Washington National Gallery, which now owns the painting, still concurred with this theory, citing it on the first page of his 1972 guide to the collection. The Victoria and Albert Museum, which owns an engraving of the picture made in 1627, agrees that it went to Henry VII. And Chaney himself, I notice, hedges his bets by stating in his 2003 book, *The Evolution of English Collecting*, that the Raphael *St. George* "might have been presented to Henry VII." Actually, I was not in bad company with this theory.

Henry must have been stunned by the beauty of Raphael's little painting. It had traveled well and arrived undamaged, a feat by no means guaranteed given the length and dangers of the journey. This was the first great Renaissance painting ever to come to England, and it had been painted by the man who was to become the Renaissance master of masters. Henry VII was, however, singularly ill-equipped to appreciate all this. In any case, the word *Renaissance* was not used in England or, indeed, anywhere for another three hundred years.

At his palace at Richmond, Henry already possessed a painting of St. George and the dragon. It had been commissioned from a Flemish artist in 1503, and it portrayed Henry and his wife, Elizabeth of York, kneeling with their sons and daughters, all dressed in identical robes to give legitimacy to what was a highly dubious dynastic claim to the throne. Above their heads, St. George, who bears an uncanny resemblance to the king, gallops across the picture to finish off a dramatic flying dragon representing the turmoil of the Wars of the Roses.

And there were other representations of St. George too. Henry posed for his portrait kneeling in adoration of the saint. He had himself painted in vigorous action astride his mount as the embodiment of the saint. To our eyes today, many of these paintings look unintentionally comical. To Henry's eyes, having now seen

Raphael's sublime creation, they must have all suddenly looked desperately crude.

But it wasn't the Renaissance sophistication of the painting that caught his eye first, or the superbly worked delicacy of technique. What appealed to the king was its thoroughly pleasing subject. With his long fingers curled acquisitively around its edges, the king's heavily lidded eyes homed in on the little gilded garter, painted around St. George's left leg. Perhaps he permitted himself a small smile at this divine representation of his favorite subject, his courtiers nodding and smiling too and concurring noisily at the marvel of the thing.

Henry VII was devoted to the cult of St. George and the Order of the Garter, his commitment largely based on his need to legitimize his rule. As a minor Welsh lord with only tenuous links to the dynasty that gave rise to both the Yorkist and Lancastrian factions, Henry had a claim on the crown that was far from persuasive. In short, he was a usurper of the throne. In his efforts to unite England behind him, it is no wonder that he grabbed at St. George, England's greatest symbol of chivalry, as a unifying, popular, and suitably romantic figurehead.

Immediately after his victory, against the odds, over Richard III at the Battle of Bosworth, Henry had presented at St. Paul's the three banners carried in the field of battle. One of them was embroidered with an image of St. George. A team of seamstresses quickly set to work sewing six yards of crimson velvet into a huge cross of St. George for Henry's coronation. With the greatest of speed, before his shaky victory could be overturned, Henry presented himself, amid hastily choreographed displays of magnificence, for coronation at St. Paul's. Only two years earlier, the archbishop had lowered the crown onto Richard III's scheming head. Now, beneath the great red velvet cross of St. George, he repeated the procedure, anointing and crowning the no-less-cunning head of Henry Tudor.

A week later, Henry's first Parliament met to enact his craftily phrased declaration, which forced parliamentarians to "confirm" rather than "create" him king of England. He had dated his reign from the day before Bosworth, in a stroke turning those who had fought against him into traitors. Behind the scenes, Henry was quietly arranging for Richard III's nominated heir, the ten-year-old earl of Warwick, and anyone so much as rumored to be a supporter of his cause, to be rounded up and locked in the Tower of London. Any other claimants to the throne met the same fate.

Henry's devotion to the Order of the Garter was not surprising. Its appeal lay in its very function: to underpin the authority and majesty of its superior, the king of England. In essence, the Order of the Garter existed to empower Henry himself. It was an elite society whose membership included, apart from the sovereign and his heir, the most distinguished soldiers and peers of the realm, as well as foreign princes. It stood at the very apex of the English chivalric hierarchy and was supported with lavish ceremonial activities and splendid liveries. It encapsulated all that was most cherished in the lives of the noble classes.

The Order of the Garter soon became a cornerstone of Henry's court, a kind of superior gentlemen's club for the king and his closest intimates. These were men, knights from grand families, first drawn together in Henry's failed uprising against Richard III in 1483, who had shared exile with Henry and then been vindicated with him in the field at Bosworth, two years later. Men like Sir Thomas Lovell, Sir Richard Guildford, and Sir Reginald Bray ran local government, held key administrative offices, and strutted around at Garter ceremonies, dressed in gowns and chains, imagining themselves as the embodiment of chivalry. The elaborate charade of showpiece rituals and costumed ceremonies became an important part of the public demonstration of Henry's sovereign power.

Castiglione was to be given a taste of the theatricality of the Garter ceremony at Windsor a few days later, but first he was invited to discuss the affairs of Italy with the king. Sitting on his gilt chair, Castiglione regaled the king with news from Urbino. His first surprise was that the king could speak passable Italian himself. His second surprise was to discover that Henry employed a large number of Italians at court, and that he was well informed on the personalities and cultural and political affairs of the leading Italian courts. In truth, the king was well represented in Rome, with large numbers of highly placed Italian agents, handsomely paid to keep him informed.

During his twenty-one years on the throne, Henry had encouraged cultured Italians to settle in England, welcoming many of them to important positions at court. Giovanni Gigli had become bishop of Worcester, the poet Pietro Carmeliano was employed as Latin secretary to the king, and a clever entrepreneur named Gulielmus Parronus had managed to insinuate his way into the English court to become Henry VII's highly paid court astrologer. But the most famous Italian employed by Henry was Polydore Vergil, who happened to come from Urbino. He was named archdeacon of Wells and wrote a history of England, the *Anglicae Historiae*, which he had begun in the year of Castiglione's visit and completed three decades later.

Fighting widespread public prejudice against the employment of foreigners, scores of Renaissance Italians made careers for themselves in England with Henry's support. And they brought value with them, endowing England with new ideas in literature, science, and the arts.

England truly needed them. Henry's coronation in 1485 had marked the end of what later came to be known as the Wars of the Roses, a period of rumbling episodic violence that had seen the crown change hands five times in the space of thirty years. England had been in turmoil for an entire generation. Two of Henry's predecessors had been murdered, one had died in battle, and one had been driven ignominiously from the kingdom in the middle of his reign. Plots, rebellions, and battles raged all over the country, often centered around baronial feuding and rivalry for local dominance. The fundamental social, economic, and political problems that Henry VII inherited ran deep.

The civil war had also left a barren artistic legacy. England was an insular nation, most of its inhabitants marooned at an exceptionally low educational level. The average nobleman read little and wrote indifferently, with highly idiosyncratic spelling. There were no dictionaries, but even a merchant running a considerable business could only just make himself understood. The majority of the country gentry could neither read nor write, and the visual arts awareness of the average Englishman was negligible. Unlike in Rome, where there were supposed to be more classical statues than people, in the England of Henry VII, it was said that only sheep outnumbered people.

England was undeniably backward when it came to an appreciation of the arts. Had Henry shown his new painting of St. George to one of his noblemen, its subject would certainly have made an impact. Its highly crafted technical skills would probably also have impressed, reminding him of the beautifully wrought and minutely painted manuscripts that were popular at the time. But the average nobleman would not have registered much more than that. Raphael's name, in English upper-class circles in 1506, did not yet excite the kind of thrill and associated mad desire that it would in later centuries.

Henry himself, however, had considerably more knowledge of European arts than the average English nobleman. He had spent fourteen years in exile on the Continent before his accession, and this sojourn had opened his mind to outside influences. Once on the throne, he saw that he needed to attract great artists to magnify his court and enhance it in the eyes of posterity. So he became, although very unostentatiously, an important and influential patron of the arts. He built the great Savoy Hospital, modeled on the Ospedale di Santa Maria Nuova in Florence. He bought beautifully crafted Italian furniture and sent envoys to Italy to buy cloth of gold and the finest damasks. He commissioned gorgeous church vestments to be made and embroidered for him in Florence.

He established a permanent Royal Library at court and founded a school of illuminators, which soon gained such prestige that it began to attract miniaturists and artists from some of the highest-ranking posts in Europe. He transformed the office of the king's glazier, commissioning new stained-glass windows for his ambitious building projects at Richmond and Greenwich. For King's College Chapel in Cambridge, the windows begun in 1506 were to be acknowledged as the masterwork of Renaissance Flemish glazing.

Still anxious to bring his court into line with the magnificent art-loving courts of the Continent, Henry also built up a large collection of the finest and most expensive Flemish tapestries, which accompanied him wherever he went. They traveled to Calais in 1500 to be a lavish backdrop for his meeting with the archduke of Burgundy. In 1503, they went to Scotland for the marriage of his daughter Margaret to James IV. And when he wished to spend time at his newly built Richmond Palace or at Greenwich, the weary royal tapestry packers duly set to work, crating up and relocating these hulking great treasures once again.

Although many of his tastes were Franco-Flemish, Henry also built on his privileged access to Italian culture and became an important patron of Italian Renaissance arts, particularly sculpture.

In a culture that still priced sculpture by the foot, Henry's innovations were extraordinary. Against the odds, he managed to attract some of the most distinguished Italian sculptors to England. Guido Mazzoni, one of the greatest artists ever to work in terracotta, introduced the medium to England, and it was probably he who sculpted the small terra-cotta portrait bust of a laughing child, possibly Henry VIII, now in the royal collection. But the most important of the immigrant Italian sculptors was Pietro Torrigiano, a brilliant and ambitious but volatile artist who came to work on the tomb of Henry's mother, Lady Margaret Beaufort, in Westminster Abbey. He later designed tombs for Henry VII and his queen. The mercurial Torrigiano had his downside, though. Were it not for him, Henry might have attracted the brilliant goldsmith and sculptor Benvenuto Cellini to England. But when Torrigiano returned to Florence to recruit help for further "bold deeds among those beasts of Englishmen," he boasted of having broken Michelangelo's nose, and this so alienated the impressionable young Cellini that he refused to accompany him to England. London's loss was Florence's gain.

Henry had less trouble keeping his poets and scholars in line. In the new post of court chronicler, the first occupant was French friar Bernard André, who set the tone with his *Les Douze Triomphes de Henry VII*. This staggering eulogy celebrated the completion of Henry's first twelve years by comparing them to the labors of Hercules.

Such displays of flattery were necessary, for Henry was a spectacularly unpopular monarch who taxed his subjects down to their very fingertips. In order to pay for all this art and show of kingship, he needed large amounts of money. At his coronation, he had inherited royal coffers that were almost empty, so he honed every available procedure of government to secure maximum amounts of money from his people. Many of his methods were undignified; some were improper, others outright venal.

With conventional resources strained to the breaking point, Henry hunted for alternative revenues. A special council of his most intimate and trusted courtiers met weekly and came up with ingenious schemes to gather in more money from his people. He imposed heavy fines in place of imprisonment in the case of richer transgressors; his treasury benefited while at the same time he gained a reputation for clemency. He demanded imaginative premiums from anyone appointed to an office of profit. Dr. John Yonge was forced to pay a thousand pounds on his appointment as master of the rolls, and many others met similar demands on taking up new public posts. By the end of his reign, King Henry was hoarding huge sums of money and, with his increasingly efficient systems, extracting more and more from his groaning subjects.

Just as Richard III bore a reputation for centuries as an unredeemably wicked hunchback, so Henry VII has been remembered for his outstanding avarice. Bacon believed that he amassed treasure in gold and silver worth almost two million pounds and jewels valued at a hundred thousand pounds. Even the Venetian ambassador in London in 1509, a man used to tales of great wealth, was amazed: "The King ... was a very great miser, but a man of vast ability, and had accumulated so much gold that he is supposed to have more than well nigh all the other kings of Christendom."

Henry was undoubtedly cash rich, but cultivating the loyalty and awe of the people was an expensive business for any monarch. Accordingly he did, though with reluctance, let a great deal of money slip from his tight grasp to be spent on feasts, pageantry, tournaments, and general display. All of this outlay was designed to portray him as the stable, wealthy, and powerful monarch he liked to imagine himself to be.

The ceremonial splendor of St. George and the Order of the Garter consumed a large proportion of this expenditure, but there were other areas on which he conspicuously splurged. The surviving pages of his meticulous accounts, all initialed in the king's own tiny, florid script, paint a picture of lavish entertainments and festivals at court. Large numbers of professionals were hired—and seen to be hired—in order to keep him and his family in good humor. Musicians were paid to tootle and pluck, tumblers to tumble. Children were rewarded for singing in the garden; trumpeters were paid for loud fanfares whenever the king stepped off the royal barge. And a "young damoysell that daunceth" received the large and rather suspicious sum of thirty pounds for unnamed services in 1493.

The king hunted or hawked every day. He jousted; watched cockfights and bearbaiting; played chess, dice, and cards; and enjoyed archery and tennis. He paid for fools to make him laugh, dancers, minstrels, stilt-walkers, and fire-eaters. Cages full of growling, fluttering, and scaly beasts were imported for his delectation, strange and exotic animals such as lions, leopards, parrots, and wild cats. In 1507, a "dragon" made its appearance at court.

Raphael's evil beast of a dragon must have, if not charmed King Henry, certainly aroused his curiosity. Dragons were hugely fashionable at court, and the king came face-to-face with them with alarming regularity. In 1494, for example, Walter Alwyn, who was Henry VII's imaginative master of the revels, constructed a pageant based around "a terrible and huge red dragon, the which in sundry places of the hall as he passed, spit fire at his mouth." Halfway through a gentle interlude of singing by the King's Players, performed before the king, queen, and various foreign ambassadors, the fire-snorting dragon burst in, pursued by one of the musicians dressed as St. George, and trailed behind by a fair maiden dressed as a princess. Only after a theatrical pursuit and the bloodcurdling capture of the dragon did the King's Players deliver their lusty rendition of St. George's anthem. Fortunately for

Alwyn, the king expressed his pleasure at the performance with a slight smile.

But the most lavish and extravagant celebrations of the cult of St. George took place at Windsor Castle, which became filled with vigor, color, feasting, gorgeous clothes, and swaggering men on such occasions. These events, all laboriously listed in the statutes, were invested with an elaborate symbolism, often gratuitous and over-worked, but radiating the values of chivalry and righteous splendor with which Henry liked to be associated. Admission to the Garter represented the height of ceremonial flattery in England.

Castiglione, standing in as the Duke of Urbino's proxy, was to be accorded precisely the same chivalric indulgence as Guidobaldo would have received had he been there himself. Two days after his audience with the king, and accompanied on horseback by the king's lieutenant and his liveried servants, Castiglione set off in a magnificent procession from the City of London, heading west for Windsor. It must have been quite a spectacle. Large crowds of admiring onlookers had gathered to watch, pale urchins shouting in the rush for a good view, fathers carrying their children on their shoulders, small boys peeping through the legs of their elders. Senior Knights of the Garter led the procession on huge champ-ing steeds, followed by their various companies of servants dressed in brightly colored liveries, their polished steel swords and javelins bouncing around in a great jangling chorus as they rode.

As our world today is so very different from the London of 1506, it is hard to conjure up an image of such a scene. We are surrounded by high-rise buildings, by the roar of cars and buses and the trill-ing of mobile telephones, all of which distract from our mental image. But you can get some idea of the thrill of such an occasion at the Lord Mayor's Show, when thousands gather to line the pave-ments of Cheapside in the City of London to watch the spectacle of the procession. Giles and I went last year with our three young daughters, and I suppose because I was still pursuing the trail of "my picture," I instinctively transferred the scene in my mind. Children were scrambling through people's legs for a closer view, or sitting on their parents' shoulders. Men and women cheered as new, more spectacular visions rolled before their eyes. With the mayor in his golden carriage and the aldermen, the masters of the livery companies and the massed bands of dozens of regiments, the costumes, the music, and the spectacle were every bit as exotic to us as a procession of the Knights of the Garter would have been to Londoners of 1506.

Along the way, Castiglione was entertained to some hawking, and the company finally arrived that evening at Windsor, where Castiglione was taken to his lodgings at the dean's house. The next day, wearing his scarlet silk and velvet Garter gown, he was escorted, amid great blowings of trumpets and serenadings by boy choristers, on an elaborate route around the grounds of the castle, to St. George's Chapel. The chapel was decked out in its greatest finery for the occasion, groaning with fine tapestries, embroidered altar cloths, gold and silver plates and candelabra. All was minutely choreographed according to the formalities written down in the ancient statute books, and every move of Castiglione's role was mapped out.

During the delicate ceremonial dance of knights and courtiers, he was presented with a sword, a blue velvet mantle embroidered with a red cross, and, finally, the heavy collar and Great George, a jeweled pendant of St. George slaying the dragon. Marching about here and there in their billowing gowns and mantles, clanking under their load of chains and badges, the knights all seemed unaware of their absurdity, pacing through the ceremonies with somber faces of strained formality, looking as exotic as actors in a theater, decked out in glossy new costumes.

Now a Garter Knight proxy, Castiglione repaired to St. George's Hall for a magnificent celebratory feast. He took his seat at the top table among senior knights, the Marquis of Dorset Sir Thomas Grey, the Earl of Surrey Sir Thomas Howard, who was also Lord Treasurer, and Sir Gilbert Talbot, Earl of Shrewsbury and Steward of the Royal Household. As soon as they sat down, the first of a series of dishes began to arrive at their tables, fantastic concoctions featuring herons, cygnets, capons, venison, rich pies decorated like embroidery patterns, fresh salmon and pike, tarts garnished with the pastry arms of senior knights, and smooth ceramic bowls of custard decorated with garter designs. Morsels of these delicacies were washed down with wine, sack, ale, or all of the above. That was only the first course.

The cooks of Windsor had sweated for two days to produce this feast. Stripped to the waist and gleaming with the effort, they had plucked and hacked and broiled and garnished beasts and birds brought in from the countryside. They had spiced fruits and made jellies and brought dozens of crisp tarts tumbling out of their ovens. Pheasants, delivered cold and limp from the hills, had been vested with new plumages of apple and parsnip. Rabbits had been squashed with jelly into delicate pastry nests. Kid, quail, and venison joined sweetmeats and cakes on the tables where the guests noisily devoured their fill. That the bill of fare far exceeded the capacities of their bellies did not matter. The point of the exercise was to impress.

As the knights sucked at their bones and mopped up their sauces, they perhaps regaled Castiglione with tales of the hoard of valuable but grisly relics held at St. George's Chapel. There was the box believed to contain the heart of St. George, an object of intense worship. And there was the "right leg of St. George," sup-posedly a hunk of his thigh bone, which was encased in silver and had been presented to a delighted Henry VII in 1505 by Cardinal d'Amboise on behalf of the French king.

Back in London, Castiglione did the rounds visiting all the Garter Knights in the city, as was the custom, and then paid a final visit to the royal palace at Greenwich to see the king. This time, he wrote proudly to his mother, he was welcomed with "even greater kindness than before." Perhaps, like the Venetian captain Vin-cenzo Cappello a few months earlier, Castiglione was invited to dinner and was treated to a concert by Lady Margaret and the wid-owed Princess of Wales, Catherine of Aragon, playing the spinet. We know that he was presented to Henry, the fourteen-year-old Prince of Wales, and was so impressed by his Renaissance combina-tion of sporting prowess and intellectual eloquence that he wrote him into his book, *The Courtier*. "Look," cries Ottaviano Fregoso, in the book, "at my Lord Henry, Prince of Wales, growing up under his great father in every form of excellence, like a tender shoot in the shade, a fruit-laden tree, to become even more beautiful and fruitful in its time."

As soon as the Christmas festivities were over, Castiglione set off for home, bearing messages and letters for the duke, as well as valuable presents. The king gave Castiglione several horses and dogs as well as a gold chain of S-links from which hung two minia-ture portcullises and a golden rose with a silver center. The chain was a particular sign of royal favor. Castiglione treasured it for the rest of his life.

Seven years after his return to Italy, Castiglione settled down to write *The Courtier* and came close himself to becoming the model of the perfect courtier and universal Renaissance gentleman. He remained friends with Raphael, and together they spent many days on excursions in the Roman countryside, visiting newly unearthed

Roman antiquities. In 1515, Raphael painted the portrait of Castiglione that hangs today in the Louvre. It shows the thirty-seven-
year-old courtier, bearded and swathed in elegant black velvet and
gray silk, his cool, steely blue eyes calm as he levels a gaze of intellectual affinity and evident friendship at the painter.

One of Castiglione's great life achievements was his book, *The
Courtier*, an elegant and sometimes richly playful narrative codify-
ing the High Renaissance ideal of the "universal man." Four hundred years later it was still being widely read and still having its
effect. Friends of James Joyce, for example, reported that he had
become a lot more polite but a lot less sincere after reading it. But
Castiglione's other achievement was equally important: the safe
delivery of the first Renaissance masterwork onto English soil, Raphael's painting of St. George and the dragon.

This little painting offered the first hint in England of the massive artistic explosion, later known as the High Renaissance, that
was being unleashed in Italy. Raphael was its standard-bearer. His
St. George and the Dragon of 1506 would have outclassed every one
of the limited paintings in the English royal collection. Among the
portraits by Michael Sittow, and the assortment of crude, anonymous works celebrating Henry's magnificence, there was nothing
that approached Raphael's painting in terms of beauty and spiritu-
ality, even if the English did not yet see it that way.

When Henry VII died in 1509, after twenty-four years on the
throne, he had built, virtually from scratch, a reputation as a patron
of art and architecture and had established strong links with Renaissance Italy. Like all good monarchs he had also established a
reputation for splendor on the basis of the magnificence of his
expenditure. His son, Henry VIII, crowned that year at the age of
seventeen, set out to be more extravagant still, to win Europe-wide
renown for his magnificence.

He was well educated, splendidly sporting, and highly self-assured. Brought up to be bountiful and lavish, he expressed his desires for glory through elaborate rituals and spectacular ceremonies. Within a few years, his court resembled a medieval theater of pleasure, its days filled with hunting and hawking, jousting and tournaments, and its nights with revels by torchlight. Like his father, Henry well understood the propaganda value of ostentatious display. But there was a difference. While Henry VII had gone through the motions of lavish pageantry, usually as a remote spectator, his son relished every minute of it. He took part in tournaments, initially displaying his prowess incognito, and later openly participating, full of good fellowship and surrounded by favorites and friends. Soon he had become the glamorous star of a dazzling sequence of tournaments and revels.

Henry VIII shared his father's taste for romantic heroism and chivalry, and wherever possible, the pageantry at court incorporated these themes. Most popular were, of course, St. George and the Order of the Garter. The young Henry—and perhaps even more his advisers—appreciated the convenient sovereign appeal of St. George and the potential of the Garter to unite the faction-ridden nobles around the throne. He had been crowned on St. George's Day and had chosen the saint's day as his official birthday. Ever since the age of four, he had been a Knight of the Garter, and still now, as a teenage king, he took St. George as his unrivaled hero.

From the start of his reign, the elaborate games of knightly ritual surrounding St. George and the Order of the Garter continued to be acted out with an ever-increasing degree of artificiality and refinement. The Garter was still England's highest and most coveted order of chivalry, and Henry VIII, with his policy of accentuating his own magnificence wherever possible, made great play of this saint of knights and nobles.

The twenty-five Knights of the Order of the Garter, the "co-

brethren and confreres" of the sovereign himself, formed the innermost circle of Henry's Tudor elite. For them he devised elaborate new fancy-dress costumes, a "blue velvet mantle with a Garter
on the left shoulder, lined with white sarcenet and scarlet hose
with black velvet around the thighs." Each wore a light blue silk
garter with a gold buckle and embroidered Tudor roses around
his leg and a rich gold collar of twelve Tudor roses, interspersed
with twelve tasseled knots. From this heavy collar dangled the huge
jeweled pendant known as the Great George. The costume sounds
ridiculously fancy to us today, but in light of what Tudor courtiers
wore every day, it was far from outlandish.

The king did not stop at elaborating only his knights' costumes.
He had the saint depicted in the metalwork of one of his crowns
and then had several splendid suits of armor made, enchased with
scenes from the story of St. George and the dragon. Occasionally,
with the help of a team of gentlemen of the chamber, he would
clamber into one of these and clank around court, pretending to
be a great romantic hero, armed to do battle against pagans, her-
etics, and the French.

Dotted around his many palaces, at Richmond, Greenwich,
Hampton Court, Nonsuch, and Whitehall, he collected and
hoarded dozens of treasures associated with St. George or with
the Garter. More than thirty such items appear in the inventory of
his possessions drawn up after his death. Beautiful wooden carvings of St. George are listed alongside silver dishes engraved with
the Garter motto, embroideries, tapestries, paintings, and sculptures as well as his elaborate Garter robes and chains, the hoods,
mantles, posies, and jewel-encrusted pendants. There were also no
fewer than eleven garters, the symbolic little buckled ties so familiar from his swaggering portraits, fastened to glint just below the
knee, where they draw attention to the muscularity of his meaty
legs.

One of the highlights of the year for Henry VIII was the annual feast of the Order of the Garter, which took place on St. George's Day, April 23. These were astonishing extravaganzas. In normal circumstances, the king's hospitality bordered on the excessive: entertaining just thirty guests at Windsor, for example, the royal kitchen staff would be expected to produce fourteen varieties of meat, eight hundred eggs, ninety dishes of butter, eighty loaves of chestnut bread, three hundred wafers, gingerbread coated in gold leaf, and sufficient quantities of ale, wine, or sack for each guest to have twenty alcoholic drinks. But for St. George's Day, the stakes were raised far higher. Up to seven hundred guests might be invited, and two hundred and forty dishes were served on gold and silver platters. At the end of the feasting, a "prodigy dish," a magnum opus of the confectioner's art, would be served in the form of a "George on Horseback." This was a life-sized sculpture made of sugar and almond paste, painted and then gilded, and carried in by bearers on an enormous tray. Into this sickly sweet confection, renowned for being "an assault for valiant teeth," were compressed all of Henry's imperial ideals: stoic mastery of the great horse, sovereignty over the world, martial strength, philosophical composure, and Christian chivalry.

This was gourmet culture deployed as propaganda. Henry presided over these extravaganzas with one eye deftly cocked on his European rivals. Word of such displays, if extravagant enough, would inevitably spread; in many ways they were all about impressing and intimidating his fellow monarchs across the Channel and beyond. For the young Henry VIII was able to mobilize financial resources unmatched certainly by any Italian patron.

His coffers were overflowing and he attempted to intimidate with his expenditure. His tournaments and rituals were effective, but when it came to investment in art and architecture, he was not hugely discriminating in his tastes. He collected and built on a grand scale but failed to rival his fellow monarchs Charles V and Francis I. Even Holbein, who was recommended to the king when the painter was at the peak of his powers, was woefully underemployed, being more or less restricted to painting portraits of potential wives. For his walls, Henry preferred quaint battle scenes, painted by now long-forgotten German artists. The Raphael *St. George and the Dragon* would have appealed for its subject but not yet intrinsically as a work of art.

But the one act that did most to slow Henry VIII's progress in establishing artistic relationships with Renaissance Italy was the Reformation. And it was this, the break with the papacy and the stripping away of Catholic festivals, relic cults, and saints, that ironically may have led to Raphael's *St. George* migrating out of the hands of the royal collection and into the grasp of an English family of infinite ambition, guile, and growing power.

3.

B Y THE TIME HENRY VIII was fifty years old, his years of excessive
high living, debauchery, and feasting were catching up with
him. He was massively overweight. A portrait dating from around
this time shows him standing upright, full-bellied and florid-faced.
His head is a splendidly colored object: pink tremulous cheeks,
ruddy beard, and a neck bulging like a grub from his collar. In his
youth he had been acclaimed as a sporting hero, lithe and handsome. But now he was beyond the horseback feats of speed and
daring, the wild dancing, the elaborate masques and seductions.
He still loved the day-to-day life of the court, so as he grew older
and his waistline expanded, he surrounded himself with an elite
of new favorites. These were slim and handsome young bucks, the
cream of England's aristocratic youth, whose sporting triumphs,
elegant conduct, and amorous intrigues he relished vicariously.

One of these young men was William Herbert, whose family
was to become the next owner of the Raphael *St. George and the
Dragon*. William Herbert was to found a grand dynasty based upon
an earldom, establishing a massive fortune and an unrivaled power
base. He was also to build what was to become one of the grandest houses in England, a house which, at the peak of its fortunes
during Charles I's rule, resembled a Renaissance court in itself.

Like the Tudors themselves, the Herberts were Welsh arrivistes.
Although rather less successful, they were nevertheless deeply
ambitious. The mere smell of power was profoundly attractive to

them. Social position gnawed at their innards and burrowed under their skins as they slept at night. They dreamed of wealth and its display, the gaudy pomp of court life, its rich costumes and treasuries of jewels. They relished notions of elegance and chivalry, all those ideals of beauty, youth, grace, and talent embodied in the St. George of Raphael's painting.

The Herberts, who were later to become the earls of Pembroke, were clearly a powerful family in sixteenth-century England. All the evidence we have about them indicates that they invested everything, successfully, in building up and nurturing close relations with their sovereigns. This husbandry brought them a rich harvest of returns, royal handouts in the form of land, offices, networks, and gifts. We know that they were in possession of the Raphael *St. George* in 1627, because an engraving of the painting, now in the Victoria and Albert Museum, states that it is a copy of the painting owned by the earl of Pembroke at that date. This was the third earl, but what we don't know, however, is when it came into the family's possession.

This question was undeniably a bit of a roadblock. I had known I would come up against them. Such things are of course all part of pursuing a mystery trail. But as I circled, feeling my way around the edges of this one, I discovered that plenty of other people had come up against it too. June Osborne was one. Another was a young woman who began a master's thesis at London's Courtauld Institute of Art on the Raphael *St. George*'s missing century and was forced to abandon it for lack of material. The blunt fact is that nobody knows whether it was the first, the second, or the third earl who received the painting. The details of the lives of these three men, the papers and documents that record the contours and events that shaped their world, appear to have been lost. It is possible that they were burnt in the fire of 1647 that destroyed much of the interior of Wilton House.

In the maddening absence of such illuminating pieces of evidence, I suggest that the painting was transferred to the Herberts during the lifetime of William Herbert. I have no proof, but the custom of gift giving that was prevalent during the years of King Henry VIII's reign, to which I shall return, means that it was possible. There is also another potential explanation, which we shall come to later.

William's father, Richard, who was the illegitimate son of an earl, hoped to direct his son into the courtly circles he himself so admired and began by securing a position for him as a valet in the household of Charles Somerset, Earl of Worcester. It was an excellent choice. The earl was an accomplished soldier and diplomat, had been a prominent figure as lord chamberlain in the early court of Henry VIII, and was well acquainted with at least three of the greatest patron princes of Europe. His liveried entourage provided a perfect training ground for the boy. The teenage William began to hone his chivalric instincts and soon made a smooth progression into royal service himself. By 1526, at the age of nineteen, he was listed as one of the gentleman pensioners to Henry VIII, a splendid sinecure with few specific duties but incomparable access to the polish of courtly life. William's task was to groom himself to become a soldier and servant of the sovereign.

Unfortunately, the man who was possibly to become the owner of Raphael's *St. George and the Dragon* was not so easily polished. On Midsummer's Day in 1527, the twenty-year-old William joined a party of young Welsh noblemen in Bristol to enjoy traditional midsummer ceremonies, dancing, and sports. Boisterous rough and tumble was a traditional part of the festivities, and William, who was described by John Aubrey as "a mad young fighting fellow," had probably indulged in a certain amount of horseplay with his fellow Welsh bloods. The next day, he got himself involved in a very serious predicament. Perhaps he had drunk too much, but crossing Bristol Bridge he encountered a tailor named Richard Vaughan, who failed to display sufficient deference. This, at least, was what William thought. Voices were raised and violent blows exchanged. The tailor ended up lying dead in a pool of blood.

Street brawls were not uncommon in these times. Noblemen and knights would pitch in as readily as anyone else if they considered themselves slighted. Many courtiers had a brutish contempt for those not of their class. Some had appalling reputations for violent behavior. Fingers were frequently lopped off, noses bitten off and carried away as grisly trophies in the victor's pockets. But murder was something else altogether. With murder on his hands, William could not remain in England, let alone anywhere near the court. His thuggish act of violence would land him in chains. Years would be required to atone for this moment of madness.

Thinking quickly, he rushed from the bridge, escaping into the narrow Bristol back streets, out through the gate of the city, and into the marshes. Reaching the coast, he hired a boat and, with the luck of the tide in his favor, made his escape to France.

William remained in France for eight years. Clearly he had inherited his father's shrewd political instincts, for during his spell in exile, he managed to insinuate himself into the outer circles of the French court. Francis I was a magnificent knight, a cultivated man of pleasure, and a Renaissance prince par excellence. He was the epitome of the royal patron, a man in love with culture, whose massive treasury attracted the finest painters, sculptors, and scholars.

The sophisticated and highly perfumed life of the French court made a lasting impression on William Herbert, if we are to judge by the splendor of his own later lifestyle. Herbert's public world was to become ostentatious even by Tudor standards, and in his possible ownership of the only Raphael masterpiece in the country, artistically advanced too. His courtly skills had been sharpened there too, for by the mid–1530s, he had returned to England and worked his way back into the court of Henry VIII as esquire to the king's body (a very close personal attendant) and attorney general of Glamorgan. Around the same time, he also married Anne, youngest daughter of Sir Thomas Parr, who had been master of the wards during the early years of Henry VIII's reign. Although the Parrs were an ancient family, Anne had not been particularly well provided for at her father's death, and Herbert did not gain any great material or social advantage from this unremarkable marriage.

He might have ambled for years along the well-defined but drearily comfortable path of a minor court servant, had it not been for a chance event that no one could have predicted. On July 12, 1543, his wife's elder sister, Catherine Parr, became the sixth queen of Henry VIII, making Herbert the king's brother-in-law. It was an event that would alter the course of his life.

Herbert was tall, good-looking, and athletic. He was a fine horseman too and appreciated the advantages of displaying his talents at court. He was sixteen years younger than the king, making him a perfect companion to lure the bloated monarch toward flattering dreams of youthful fantasy.

With his new proximity to the king, William's ambition was ignited and he began calculating how to gain greatest advantage at court. In France he had honed his skills of monarchic flattery and had familiarized himself with the dark arts of court intrigue. Now he cast his opportunistic eyes around this English court of delicious patronage and power and, playing his cards carefully, was soon welcomed into the intimate inner circle.

He must have impressed the aging king, for he began to reap a rich harvest of royal favor. Within three years he had been knighted, appointed captain of the castle at Aberystwyth, and made a gentleman of the privy chamber, a role as close royal companion rather than servant. The king also appointed him the steward of extensive royal properties in the west of England and granted him the manor of Hendon in Middlesex and the crown lands and castle of Cardiff. In 1546, as a mark of Herbert's new status, the king also granted him the keepership of Baynard's Castle on the banks of the Thames, which became the main London residence of the family. Such were the advantages of being married to the queen's sister.

A man of reputation and a courtier as prominent as the now Sir William Herbert required a suitable country retreat. Grand houses built on large estates underpinned the aspirations of all upwardly mobile aristocrats. As a result, a rash of wildly extravagant palatial houses was spreading across the country to accommodate leading courtiers and their entourages. These country seats served a dual function: as havens from the tempests and bitter rivalries of courtly life, and as conspicuously lavish palaces for entertaining the king in great style. The life of a courtier was all about dazzling spectacle, particularly for one who recognized, as Herbert possibly did, the value of owning the only masterpiece in England by Raphael.

Country estates were much talked of in court circles, and Herbert, ever eager to better his rivals, would have gleaned every available detail before planning his own. A few years earlier, in 1514, Thomas Wolsey had been appointed archbishop of York, a promotion which demanded a magnificent residence to match. Ambitious and now fabulously rich, Wolsey had alighted on Hampton

Court, an existing country house used by the Order of the Knights Hospitalers, which he built up at prodigious cost into a sensational moated Gothic palace surrounded by formal parks and gardens and filled with six hundred of the best tapestries in the world. Here he lived and entertained, regularly receiving the king and queen, and hosting great diplomatic occasions such as the visit of the emperor Charles V in 1522, until he was forced to give up the house to Henry in 1528.

Then there was Richard Fermor, another close intimate of the king, and an extremely wealthy man who had made his money from provisioning the royal army throughout its campaigns. He had built himself a splendidly impressive country house in the 1530s at Easton Neston in Northamptonshire. Described as a "beautiful seat" by William Camden in his 1586 *Britannia* survey, the original house was an amalgam of Tudor pitched roofs, gables, arched doorways, and mullioned windows. The house was rebuilt in 1702 by Nicholas Hawksmoor, but it retained its role as power base for the Fermor family, who continued, after Richard, in succeeding generations to profit from large estate revenues and to entertain sovereigns and their traveling courts in style.

Herbert would also have been aware of Knole in Kent, a house so large that it looks from a distance like a medieval village or small town. This was built by the archbishop of Canterbury, Thomas Bourchier. And Herbert may have visited palatial Compton Wynyates in Warwickshire, designed in grand style to exhibit the wealth of Sir William Compton, Chief Gentleman of the Bedchamber to Henry VIII.

Herbert had these impressive precedents in mind when, in 1541 and 1544, a series of royal grants handed him the extensive estate and buildings of the abandoned Abbey of Wilton, just a few miles west of Salisbury. He immediately drew up plans for an ostentatious seat of his own at Wilton. The existing buildings were cleared and within a few years and at the enormous cost of over ten thousand pounds, a mansion was erected around a central quadrangle, fronted by a large courtyard and surrounded by a high wall. Such lavish expenditure was one way in which Herbert could give himself respectability. By building a grand country seat and filling it with artistic treasures, all discerningly selected, he could establish himself as a true nobleman, not simply the embodiment of "new money."

A strong element of competitiveness was of the essence in these house-building projects. Accordingly, everything about Wilton was designed to reflect Herbert's superior status at court. In the original inner courtyard, the Holbein Porch was designed in imitation of Hampton Court, with a great bay window providing light for rooms on a number of floors. Although Henry VIII's painter and designer Hans Holbein died in 1543, and is unlikely to have actually contributed to its design, the porch was named after him in a gesture of flattery to the king.

A garden was laid out and trees planted around the house. Some of the yews are still there today, looking like huge gnarled creatures, their long arms and stretching fingers reflecting the vicissitudes they have survived over the centuries.

One weekend in the summer of 2004, I made my first visit to Wilton. It was a hot day and the large playground just inside the entrance, filled with swings and slides, kept our daughters entertained for several happy hours. With Giles sitting on a gaily colored mushroom, monitoring the children while reading a book, I stole away to explore the place.

The house itself has changed almost beyond recognition, but the garden and parkland retain the bones of their original form. The riverbanks are still as velvety and mossy as they were in the days of Sir William Herbert. Willows dangle into the water, and the yews, planted in his day, are still young in the world of yew trees, for they can live for up to two thousand years.

Inside, the guard on duty took my ticket. Passing beyond and on into the house, I immediately sensed that special residual hush, the rich, refined, dry smell of a country house on a hot summer's day. The place seemed settled and seasoned with its own historic light and odor, an accumulation of centuries-old memories.

On this site, four hundred years of prosperity and power have been invested in one British family and in this, their showcase house. The place is as exotic as a giant box of treasures. You feel as if you have entered a huge reliquary containing an immeasurably precious bounty of beautiful works of art, furniture, and objects, which the family has drawn into its possession over the course of many generations. And it is strangely exhilarating to think that the Pembrokes, certainly the earls of the sixteenth and seventeenth centuries, collected these trophies in order to outclass their connoisseur peers and to establish a reputation for being cultured on the basis of the magnificence, or perhaps excessiveness, of their expenditure.

Today, in a world in which earls can expect little real power from their titles, Wilton is all the more extraordinary and enchanting. It is easy to lose yourself in its ancient, silent corridors and its intimate chambers, densely hung with portraits of earlier Herberts and the fine, detailed paintings of the house made over the years to show it off in its various incarnations. Between these hang more portraits of English kings and queens, many bestowed as a mark of favor or commissioned to demonstrate intimacy. And then there is the serious haul of paintings gathered by later generations, works by Holbein, Rubens, Van Dyck, Rembrandt, and many others, hung in the most lavish surroundings imaginable.

I did my tour off-piste, avoiding a guide, because I wanted to linger and try to imagine the house as it had been in its original form. This turned out to be harder than I'd thought. As in most houses of this age, the many layers of alterations made over the centuries have obscured the original layout and feel of the building. There was so much to absorb in that place. Eventually I went outside and sat down on the ancient stone terrace, warmed through by the heat of the day. I looked up at those old yew trees. They have already presided over such a huge sweep of time as to make all our short-term preoccupations seem inconsequential. Our shy, fugitive little panel, the Raphael *St. George*, may have hung in this house among the early portraits in William Herbert's time, as evidence of his intimacy with the royal family.

If it came to him, it would have come as a gift. Lavish gift giving was very common, for it was traditional for the monarch to reward his loyal courtiers with valuable objects from the extensive royal collections. They too gave gifts in return. But beneath the surface beauty of these exquisite books, paintings, and jewels lurked careful evaluations of what returns they might bring. Gift giving was part of a highly structured method of establishing networks of loyalty and personal indebtedness that could be called in at times of need.

According to Maria Hayward, fellow of the Society of Antiquaries, who writes about gift giving in the court of Henry VIII in the *Antiquaries Journal*, volume 85, 2005, Henry VIII exchanged gifts with the social elite in England as well as with members of his household. New Year's Day was the most important occasion for gift giving, and the style and value of the gift was determined by the social standing and current favor of the recipient.

But it is possible the Raphael *St. George* may have been given to Pembroke because the value of its imagery had been diminished. At the time of the Reformation, aspects of the old Catholic cults were stripped out of churches. Many of the festivals, relic cults, and shrines were abolished and saints and martyrs discredited. The number of saints' legends was drastically reduced, and George, among others, was eliminated, briefly, from the calendar before being restored in 1536. It is possible that Raphael's little painting of this discredited saint was considered better placed outside the royal collection.

Henry's daughter Elizabeth I also gave and received huge numbers of gifts and was later to keep careful records of the value of the gifts her courtiers gave her at New Year. Seemingly endless streams of embroidered and scented gloves, painted miniatures, portrait medallions, cameos, jewels, and silver drinking cups flowed into the royal storehouse. She also recorded the value of the gifts she gave in return, which were usually rather less costly. But during her lifetime there was no additional reason, from the point of view of the royal collection, to consider it appropriate to get rid of a painting of St. George.

With all this speculation going on as to when the painting had arrived at Wilton, I had to make do, in compensation, with the vivid portraits of its earliest occupants.

Whether he was a homicidal opportunist, as Aubrey makes out, or a calculating political player, Herbert was setting the tone for the family with his single-minded commitment to winning royal favor. He had outstanding abilities as a courtier. At his disposal was flattery, razor-sharp political instinct, ruthlessness, and a clear-eyed focus on total loyalty to the source of power of the day: the monarch. Herbert's descendants inherited these instincts, and for three generations, they clawed their way through the courts of six sovereigns, ruthlessly pushing aside rivals to ingratiate their way to monarchical favor and power.

By now Herbert had tangible evidence of what rich rewards proximity to the sovereign could bring. For him, the king and his court held an almost hypnotic quality. This lushly extravagant cocoon of power, constantly abuzz with intrigue, offered a heightened, intoxicating world where, as John Donne later explained, "At court the spring already advanced is, The sun stays longer up." It was at court, in the close company of the monarch, that the greatest rewards and favors were to be had. Herbert was ready to snap and snarl at any potential rival for the king's largesse.

He was now one of the most powerful noblemen in England. Some twenty years separated him from that day of brutal violence in Bristol. Few, if any, at court knew of it, and even if they did, they were wise enough to hold their tongues. Now he was not only re-building his name, he was rising in status far beyond what he had ever expected. The higher he rose, the more ambition clawed at his innards and burrowed under his skin.

Memories must have buzzed around Herbert's head of the riches and treasures he had seen in the French court, and the splendors of conspicuous consumption so beloved of Henry VIII. Herbert began to assemble the parts of a regal lifestyle that would mirror that of his own sovereign.

He did everything he could to emulate the king, styling himself as a perfect mirror of monarchic taste. Although he read little and badly—some say he could not read at all—he was gratified to find that playwrights, poets, and novelists flocked to dedicate their works to him. Even if Herbert could not appreciate their literary qualities himself, his prominent position at court was more than adequate compensation for the efforts of these men.

When it came to art, however, Herbert was rather more sophisticated. After all, he had spent several years observing the workings of the French court, a center of culture and patronage, where Francis I's courtiers mixed with the likes of Leonardo. Herbert was now gathering art works of his own for a collection that was to grow to an unusually extravagant and ambitious scale. It is possible that Henry VIII was aware of Herbert's interest in art and his growing collection of paintings.

Whether Herbert was perhaps being rewarded for some past act of loyalty, or in anticipation of his future support, we will never know. But he was undoubtedly close enough to the king to have received something as important as the Raphael *St. George*. It was eventually to hang at Wilton, but to Herbert's disappointment, the house was not completed in time for the king to visit.

On January 28, 1547, the bloated and exhausted fifty-six-year-old king collapsed and died. The news reverberated quickly around the court, and senior courtiers scuttled to cement new royal connections. Within a short time, as the nation began to hear the news and absorb the shock, Herbert found that he had acquired a new status: he had been named as one of the executors of the king's will. He had also been bequeathed the large sum of three hundred pounds and had been chosen as one of the twelve privy councillors to advise the future Edward VI. At the funeral, Herbert was one of two privileged intimates to ride in the chariot carrying the coffin. He had succeeded in ingratiating himself into the very heart of the court.

Herbert continued his policy of total loyalty to the sovereign. But he was not alone. The world of the Tudor court buzzed with newly enriched courtiers, acquisitive and competitive players who had gained status and vast wealth along with lands from Henry VIII. Every aspect of their lives was now bound up with showy spectacle: their houses, their guests, their banquets, clothes, and even their pastimes were designed to provide magnificent display at all times. This conspicuous consumption was a complicated, calculated, and functional affair, a combination of pleasure and investment, shrewdly judged so as to maximize the public impact of their resources.

Herbert achieved all this on a par with the best of them, but he was also unusually astute politically. Playing his cards carefully, he succeeded in currying rapid favor with the young Edward VI.

His rewards came thick and fast. In 1548, he was made a Knight of the Garter and master of the horse, responsible for all matters relating to the stables, whether for travel, war, or hunting. On October 10, 1551, he was raised to the peerage as Baron Herbert of Cardiff and, the following day, he was created earl of Pembroke. Then in August 1552, the young king honored the earl with a visit to his princely seat at Wilton.

The greatest honor a monarch could do a subject was to stay at his house and use it as his own. Thomas Lovell at his house at Enfield provided a complete set of lodgings for the king and queen, separate from his own. At Compton Wynyates, Henry VIII's favorite, Sir William Compton, erected the royal arms above the entrance and in an inscription dedicated his mansion to the king. So for Pembroke, as we shall now call him, Edward's visit was a seal of approval from the highest rank.

Traveling with the usual ceremonial pomp, attended by Pembroke himself and fifty of his liveried horsemen, the fifteen-year-old king and his enormous, rambunctious traveling court settled like a flock of garish and demanding birds on Wilton for the night. Naturally, the best of everything was laid out for him. Pembroke would have furnished Wilton in the style of the grandest establishments of the day. Up to a hundred tapestries and gorgeous silk and gold hangings were displayed on a scale available only to the superrich. Paintings were shown prominently along with choice pieces of furniture from France, Italy, and the Netherlands. The linen in the bedchambers was as fine as silk, the plates and goblets were silver, and the food and drink that graced them were exquisite.

A display of this sort was the equivalent of exhibiting one's bank balance in public. Pembroke bowed and scraped with carefully studied dignity, flourishing a hand here and there to expound upon issues of the moment.

The king's visit to Wilton was a success. Within a year, Pembroke was appointed to new and lucrative posts and was granted as a gift the manor of Dungate in Somerset and other land and possessions. By now he controlled a very large number of offices and, in terms of cash, he was said to be receiving a larger share of the crown's bounty than any other member of the court. His prestige was very high, and it was around this time that the Spanish king's ambassador, stationed in London, noted that the earl of Pembroke, along with the earl of Warwick and the marquis of Northampton, ruled "in such sort that no one in the Council dares to oppose him."

In matters of state, as in the continuous low-level court disputes of the day, Pembroke was cunning. He acted like a weathervane, turning with every fresh blast. Shamelessly he would drop his support for, or even sabotage, the losing faction, backing the more likely winners to secure his own future. His success rested on his ability, of which he often boasted, to lean "on both sides the stairs to get up." Shrewd, calculating, and well-informed, he used his wits to survive at court. Others did the same. The marquis of Winchester, for example, when asked about the secrets of his survival, is said to have replied, "I am made of pliable willow, not of stubborne Oake." But Pembroke's tactics were particularly effective, and they ensured his survival, with many changes of direction, through the reigns of four successive sovereigns.

His approach to politics is worth recounting not only for its remarkably clear-eyed ruthlessness, but also because it mirrored his approach to personal extravagance in a supremely extravagant age. At the heart of this desire for display lay his estate, Wilton House, its expensive decorations and its fine paintings, the finest of which was perhaps the Raphael *St. George*. According to the curious machinations of the day, a display of great wealth seemed to justify receipt of yet more wealth, and Pembroke went out of his way to dazzle the king and his rival courtiers with his wealth and sophistication, just as he went out of his way to weather the political storms at court.

His turncoat approach to politics became brazenly clear in 1553 when the frail Edward VI died at the age of sixteen. On hearing the news, Pembroke immediately rushed off with the duke of Northumberland to Syon House to announce to Lady Jane Grey her succession to the throne under the terms of the king's will. Treating Mary and her sister Elizabeth as illegitimate, Pembroke, we are told, knelt to kiss Jane's hand. In preparation for her accession, Northumberland had already married his son to Lady Jane, and Pembroke had married his eldest son to her sister.

But within a few days, Mary had asserted her right to the throne in a powerful letter, and thousands were flocking to her support. Anticipating what was coming, Pembroke quickly changed sides and summoned a meeting at Baynard's Castle, where a plan was hatched to sabotage Northumberland's ambitions. A few days later, with the country on the brink of civil war, a second meeting, this time of the Privy Council, was called at Baynard's Castle. There, on his own territory, and in the presence of the lord mayor, aldermen, and other city magnates, Pembroke rose to declare his support for Mary. If words should not be enough, he cried, drawing his sword from its scabbard, "this blade shall make Mary Queen, or I will lose my life."

Pembroke, who only a few days earlier had kissed the hand of another putative queen, read out the proclamation of Queen Mary, and as the crowd shouted out "God save the Queen," he ostentatiously tossed his jeweled cap, filled with coins, into the air and flung his purse into the crowd.

Such was Pembroke's style. During the months and years that I was pursuing the extraordinary and bizarre story of this painting,

I couldn't help feeling at times that no novelist, however imaginative or inventive, could possibly have made it up. For five hundred years the painting had ricocheted around the world, acquiring layers of enriching patinas, its journey anticipating the rise and fall of the great powers of the Western world. It had driven kings, dukes, empresses, and exceedingly wealthy men mad with desire. People accustomed to having everything they wished for assumed they would have this painting. Perhaps I too, in following its story, had assumed I could piece together the puzzle of its whole life. Now I had got to the Pembrokes, and I had reached an impasse. But somehow, this Pembroke, the man who had murdered a stranger, fled justice, and then over the years had cunningly crept right up to a position of enormous power in the English court, seemed the right character to assume ownership of the painting. Given the ruthless scheming that characterized its later owners, Pembroke fitted the family of collectors perfectly.

Always with the interests of himself and his dynasty at heart, Pembroke adapted himself readily to the prevailing expectations at court. When Mary made the unwelcome announcement that she was to marry the Catholic Philip of Spain, Pembroke, the wily Protestant, remained silent. Soon he found himself being offered the very handsome pension of five hundred pounds by Charles V's envoy, to persuade him to support the marriage. Pembroke complied and in 1554 laid on a spectacular welcoming party at Wilton for Philip's ambassador, the marquis de las Novas. It is likely that the art collection, and in particular the Raphael *St. George*, was viewed and appreciated by this envoy from one of Europe's collector kings, adding weight to Pembroke's name in ever-widening circles.

By the time of Mary's wedding in Winchester Cathedral, Pembroke was so well ensconced at court that he was one of four peers who gave away the bride in the name of the realm. Spanish envoys reported back that Pembroke was one of the most powerful courtiers in England, with a "very grand establishment" at Wilton and more than a thousand men clad in his livery. One reported that "since the new queen succeeded, he has always been about the palace and does not leave her side."

When Mary died, three years later, Pembroke characteristically rushed straight off to Hatfield to inform Princess Elizabeth of her accession. Within days, she had set off on her procession to London, attended by hundreds of nobles. Pembroke was of course at the front, carrying her sword. Less than six months after her coronation, Pembroke hosted a dinner for her on St. George's Day at Baynard's Castle. After dinner she took a boat and with Pembroke by her side rowed up and down the river. Hundreds of boats and barges flocked toward her, and thousands of people cheered her from the riverbanks.

True to form, it had not taken Pembroke long to ease his way into high favor with the new monarch. He flattered her, subtly. He supported her loyally on matters of religion, politics, whatever court battles she was expected to fight. And then displaying his means, he entertained her lavishly at Wilton, which was by now an estate fit for a queen, complete with royal apartments and accommodation for the enormous retinue that traveled with her.

So what else could the boastfully illustrious Pembroke do to promote himself and his family's fortunes and ensure his own immortality? There was one thing he still had to do, something that all the subsequent owners of the Raphael *St. George* also did, and that was to commission a formal portrait of himself. Now well into his fifties, he had put behind him his reputation as a murderer and had established himself as one of the most powerful noblemen in the country. Gathered around him were all the symbols that in sixteenth-century England represented pure power. His country estate was one of the grandest in the land. He had the largest of London houses. He also had great swaths of offices of state and their enormous related incomes. He had liveried retinues, a growing art collection, the literary dedications, and of course the all-important heir to continue the line. The time had come, he mused, to record his status for posterity.

To carry out this important task, he chose Hans Eworth, a Dutch painter who had been living in England since 1545. Eworth's great skills with the brush had won admiration from Queen Mary, who had made him her court painter, and he had retained this eminent position in the court of Queen Elizabeth. He was certainly the most fashionable choice of the day.

Eworth's portrait shows Pembroke standing in front of a pale blue satin curtain, which glimmers with a voluptuous sheen. He is half turned toward the painter, his chest thrust out, one hand holding his white staff of office, the other a pair of fine leather gloves and the gold hilt of his finely tapered rapier sword. He wears a new black brocade coat, richly embroidered with gold thread and tiny pearls, and a black velvet hat. On his long legs he wears his gold embroidered Garter ribbon, from which a single elegant pearl dangles. He has combed his beard and waxed his mustache into points, and his head sits on a deep and snowy white ruff that seems to detach it from his body, as if it is being served up on a platter.

Pembroke looks every inch the powerful nobleman. He stares sternly at Eworth, his ruddy cheeks glowing, his heavily hooded eyes trained like laser beams on the artist, as if defying him to deviate from the agreed promotional arrangement. Eworth's job was to glorify Pembroke, and in this, over the course of a few hours of sittings and a great deal more detailed work in the studio, he succeeded handsomely.

Pembroke's position and wealth are evident from the ostentatious costume and the staff of office. He looks appropriately handsome and athletic—Eworth's brush has drawn a discreet veil over his sagging face and bulging waistline—and yet of an age and disposition to imply political weight and wisdom.

The portrait joined a considerable hoard of impressive paintings at Wilton House, for Pembroke's eye had been well trained in Renaissance art. During his years at the French court, he had seen works by the finest Renaissance masters—Raphael, Titian, Tintoretto, Michelangelo, and da Vinci—alongside the best that Northern Europe could offer. With this kind of collection in mind, he had been gathering gems of all sorts over the years. Collaborating with a small coterie of other English noblemen, and before it became fashionable to do so, he had employed an agent to acquire marble sculptures from the Continent. He had bought fine carpets, gold and silver plate, rich fabrics, and furniture from France and Italy. And his collection of paintings ran to just under sixty works.

Collections of up to a dozen works were not uncommon at this time, and a few noblemen owned up to twenty paintings. But having a collection that numbered some sixty works was exceptional for a Tudor nobleman. It was surprising in some ways that this man who had escaped trial as a murderer by fleeing to France had turned into a sensitive and important collector of fine art, but this transformation fitted with Pembroke's story.

A large part of his rise from murderer to powerful courtier involved the display of wealth and sophistication, a theme that was to become common among owners of the Raphael painting. Pembroke already had the houses, the titles, the portrait, and the entourage, but what better way to cement that status than by collecting the best European art he could lay his hands on?

Most of his paintings were portraits, as was common at the time. He had paintings of all the Tudor monarchs, boasting of his close association with the four he had known personally. He had portraits of his own family and their circle of political allies, and of other noblemen who were members of Pembroke's own faction at court. He had portraits of important European figures such as Catherine de' Medici and a beautiful full-length Holbein of Christina of Denmark. Pembroke also owned a range, unusual for its time, of other paintings—religious scenes, a still life, and a landscape—as well as drawings and a map of London.

All these works of art, displayed among the gold and silver vessels, the tapestries, and the fine furniture, were designed to convey the impression of the "very grand establishment" that the Spanish and Italian envoys so frequently described to their employers back home.

By the age of sixty-eight, Pembroke had become frail. He was still politically active, still trading on his wits to steer a safe course through the perilous world of the court, but his physical strengths were waning. Fittingly, he was at Hampton Court with the queen when he died, and he was buried with great ceremony at St. Paul's. At his death he was one of the five wealthiest peers in England. In his will he left the queen his finest jewel and his richest bed. She wrote a long letter of condolence to his widow.

Pembroke had achieved a great deal. He had established his family with an earldom, built up a stupendous fortune, built a house at Wilton that was one of the grandest in England, a miniature court fit for a monarch. He had begun a significant art collection, boosting his family's grandeur and status, and it is possible that he had acquired our jewel, Raphael's *St. George and the Dragon*.

Under his son Henry, the second earl, Wilton House became more important as a center of cultural and literary affairs. Beyond the royal court, Wilton was the closest thing to a Renaissance court England could offer. The great stone house, with its central courtyard and four towers, and its maturing garden laid out along the banks of the River Nadder, turned into a kind of small-scale Urbino under the Montefeltro dukes. Poets, writers, artists, and playwrights flocked to associate themselves with the house and to win patronage from the family.

By the time Henry married the sixteen-year-old Mary Sidney, the daughter of the powerful Sir Henry Sidney, in 1577, Wilton was flourishing as a center for the arts as well as a meeting ground, often suspected as a center of intrigue, for political discussions among the Pembrokes, the Sidneys, and the Dudleys, the three leading courtier families of the day.

Wilton was a large aristocratic household, frequented by Pembroke relatives and friends, distinguished political and diplomatic guests, and filled with scores of scurrying servants. Smart carriages rumbled on most days toward Wilton on the road from London, over the sloping green hills of the Wiltshire Downs and along the straight, tree-lined avenues, carrying important personages to be entertained lavishly by the dazzlingly rich Pembrokes.

The second earl had inherited his father's ambition, and his sights were firmly set on seeking royal favor and powerful friends. When his first son, William, was born, Henry must have been gratified that Elizabeth I agreed to be the child's godmother. Never mind that she already had more than a hundred other godchildren.

Mary's brother was Philip Sidney the poet, and he spent many months in the house in her company, working on his most famous work, *Arcadia*, which is set in the grounds of Wilton and dedicated to the Countess of Pembroke. Dozens of other poets, including Ben Jonson, were invited to spend time in the congenial surroundings of Wilton House, and many of them dedicated works to the countess.

The second earl spent much of his time at court or managing his other estates and offices, his shrewd, calculating mind constantly at work currying ever more favors, building stronger political alliances, and carrying out his duties in a manner that would best cement the Pembrokes' powerful position at court. He set up marriages that would bolster his own family; he promoted those who could be relied upon to offer their loyal support. But he also spent time at Wilton, in the company of the poets, artists, playwrights, including Shakespeare, and players, and with the art lovers whom his wife gathered around her.

Like his father, Henry had a rough underside. He was renowned as a blunt and impulsive man, with an imperious manner and little polish. But all this was hidden from posterity when in 1590, at the age of fifty-six, he commissioned a portrait of himself. True to the exhibitionist style of the period, he dressed in massive splendor for the event. His doublet is embroidered all over with tiny pearls and gold thread, his silk sleeves slashed in hundreds of places to show the contrasting color beneath. His shoulders are padded, his waist is narrow, and his ruff a fulsome pillow in pristine white. Behind him, painted as if suspended on the rich velvet drapes, is the Pembroke coat of arms, surrounded by the motto of the Order of the Garter.

He gazes out of this swaggering costume with the shrewd eyes of a successful aristocrat, a man confident of his place in society. But in spite of the swagger and bravado evident in this portrait, within ten years, Pembroke was seriously ill. He was suffering from pains in his head, able to relieve them only with the constant use of tobacco, the weed recently imported into England by Sir Walter Raleigh. He died in 1601.

The next to inherit the title, the house, and perhaps the Raphael painting was his eldest son, William. He also inherited all the advantages at court, the cushioning networks and fruits of his forebears' political gamesmanship. William was soon granted an audience with the aging Elizabeth, but with all the rebellious foolishness of a privileged eldest son, he failed to charm her.

In a world where the public prestige of a nobleman played a large part in determining his advancement at court, William was not living up to the family tradition at the time of his father's decline. He had failed in the all-important task of securing favor at court. He was a licentious spendthrift, and he was running out of money fast. The possibility loomed of his father's precious offices being awarded at his death to aspiring individuals outside the family circle.

A few days before his father's death, William woke up to the realization that he might lose all that he had assumed would come naturally to him. In a series of begging letters to Robert Cecil, Elizabeth's secretary of state, he pleaded to receive his inheritance undiminished. He was treated kindly but was seen to have abused his position.

For William had repeatedly refused to marry the various young ladies suggested by his parents. Worse still, he had seduced the beautiful young Mary Fitton, a lady-in-waiting to the queen, and made her pregnant. To compound the scandal, he had refused to marry her. The queen, who was always concerned with the honor and welfare of her court ladies, was furious. William was dumped in Fleet prison, left to cool his heels there for a few weeks, and then banished from court.

He spent several months traveling around Italy, and by the time he had returned, he had squandered a large amount of his inherited fortune on extravagant living. In some ways, however, he had matured. He had come to understand the paramount importance of currying favor at court. And a stroke of luck made this currying possible.

In 1603, Elizabeth died and King James of Scotland acceded to the throne, giving William the chance to put the Mary Fitton scandal behind him. James was attracted to handsome young men, and his roving eyes soon alighted on the twenty-three-year-old William and his nineteen-year-old brother, Philip. Both were tall and strikingly good-looking, certainly among the best-looking at court. Both were also fully aware of the advantages of proximity to the monarch.

William was quickly brought into the inner sanctum of the court. Just weeks before the coronation, the king created him a Knight of the Garter. By the time of the coronation itself, William had become uncommonly intimate with the new king. The Venetian ambassador recorded how the peers of the realm kissed the king's hand and touched the crown. And he added, with some astonishment, that "The Earl of Pembroke, a handsome youth, who is always with the king and always joking with him, actually kissed His Majesty's face, whereupon the king laughed and gave him a little cuff."

Soon after, another opportunity arose for further cementing the relationship. Plague broke out in the late summer, and a royal progress was planned that took in a visit to Wilton House. King James and his court spent several nights at Wilton that summer. He returned again to spend much of the autumn there.

More than in the impressive artworks, the furniture, the sophisticated decoration, and style of the house, the king was interested in the two handsome brothers. Soon he began to settle in at Wilton for long periods at a time, sometimes bringing his own entertainment. During one of his sojourns at the house, the King's Men, the acting company to which Shakespeare belonged, were summoned to perform. And there, in a large hall, possibly hung with the Raphael painting, they performed *As You Like It* for their royal patron.

William's brother Philip was an exceptionally good-looking young man. He was wily too, and he exploited his appearance to the full; Philip knew he could hold James's roving eye. The relationship proved to be productive. Before the coronation, he had been made a Knight of the Bath. A few months later, he received a stash of very lucrative grants and was created earl of Montgomery.

The marriages of William and Philip further strengthened their positions at court. After prolonged negotiations, a match was agreed between William and Mary Talbot, the daughter of the acrimonious but extremely wealthy seventh earl of Shrewsbury, and a descendant of Sir Gilbert Talbot, who had been Henry VII's envoy to the court of the duke of Urbino. Mary Talbot was, according to contemporary reports, "dwarfish and unattractive," but this did not discourage Pembroke. She was the co-heiress of the vast Shrewsbury estates and her immense fortune would do nicely to patch up his own diminished finances. She would also provide him, through her powerful father, with some useful connections. The wedding was celebrated at Wilton with a great tournament attended by the king. And some historians believe, although they too have no evidence to substantiate it, that this is when the Raphael *St. George* arrived at Wilton, as part of Mary Talbot's dowry.

Two months later, in December 1604, the handsome court favorite Philip Herbert married Susan Vere, the daughter of the earl of Oxford. The wedding was celebrated in lavish style at Whitehall, the bride given away by the king. Beautiful gifts were bandied about, large tracts of valuable land given to the couple, and generally much royal attention lavished on the young man. The next morning, according to a letter written a few days later by Sir Dudley Carleton, the king visited the chamber of the newlywed couple "in his shirt and nightgown" and gave them a "reveille matin before they were up and spent a good time in or upon the bed, chuse which you will believe."

Drunkenness, fornication, brawling, and vomiting were all part of life at court under James I. Those close to the king made it a point to be seen to enjoy such behavior, and the third earl was no exception. The custodian of one of England's finest country estates spent his time in facile horseplay with the monarch of the day. He did whatever was required to remain in favor with the king.

But within a few years, James was dead, and Charles I succeeded to the throne. Under Charles, the tone and flavor of the court was to change dramatically. A new appreciation of Italian Renaissance art was to develop at court, bringing with it a new knowledge of art among senior courtiers. And it was this new awareness and learning, this broadening of English artistic horizons, that was to change the fortunes of Raphael's masterpiece once again.

4.

ON SUMMER EVENINGS, AFTER Wilton House has been emptied of its ravening daytime hordes, the place is transformed. The crowds of T-shirted day-trippers have melted away. The sticky-fingered children have fled, and the elderly couples masticating gently on cream-laden scones have all packed up and gone home. At last Wilton yields itself to the gently enveloping arms of a soft English heat. The air smells faintly of cut grass. The house looms golden and silent out of a sweet mist. In the incomparable light of an English summer evening, the scene plucks at all the senses. These very same sensations must have greeted Charles I when he arrived at Wilton with his queen, Henrietta Maria, on his annual private visit in the summer of 1627.

Winding his way west from Whitehall, the king must have felt his head clear, released of the demands and exigencies of London court life. On private visits such as this, he traveled with a pared-down retinue. As his small carriage jolted and squeaked along the bumpy roads, his mind must have focused gratefully on the escape that Wilton represented for him. Here in this beautiful part of Wiltshire, he could climb into a womblike privacy, a cool grotto of a house rich with layers of culture and the safety of three generations of accumulated sovereign support. Wilton offered him a rare and relaxed intimacy in whose embrace he could escape the feeling of being devoured by his dependents.

At Wilton, Charles and Henrietta Maria wandered in the flower gardens and along the banks of the Nadder. They were entertained to concerts and plays performed by the earl's players. But the one aspect of Wilton that the king enjoyed more than all others was the art collection. The Pembrokes had by now accumulated one of the greatest family collections in the country.

On the evening of the king's arrival, the house glimmered with candles, animating the walls with amber pools and fluid shadows. I like to imagine the king in this sensuous light, wandering off to find the Raphael and standing before it, drinking in the flavors of its beauty, admiring the grace of its lines and the deep glow of its colors, delicate as a butterfly's wing.

This small painted panel held inestimable appeal to the king. Bound up within its frame, Charles's interests in art, religion, and the Order of the Garter all came together in an irresistible combination. He desperately wanted to have it. And it was during this visit, hosted by the third earl, that a swap was discussed: his prized "great booke" of Holbein drawings for the Raphael.

The earl was a cultured man. He understood the value of the Raphael within his own collection. It was still probably the only masterpiece in England by this now-recognized genius of Italian art. This fact alone conferred on it enormous value. It was also the finest depiction in the country of England's greatly loved patron saint. The earl was well aware of the king's status as the head of the Order of the Garter, and of his desires to promote this cult of chivalry to support his position. He knew too of the king's powerful devotion to the church, and his desire to elevate St. George as a Christian hero. And of course, as a collector himself, he knew the king's own art collection and his intense interest in the great Italian paintings of the sixteenth century. The earl could see why Charles longed to have this gem for himself.

William Pembroke came from a family line of courtiers who among them had given a hundred years of loyal support and service to their sovereigns. In return they had gained enormous wealth and power. The king's proposal made absolute sense to him. The "great booke" of Holbein portrait drawings was a superb collection of delicate studies in ink and colored chalks. It was highly prized, but Pembroke appreciated Charles's willingness to swap. There were already many fine Holbeins in the king's collection, as well as works by other northern artists, by Dürer, Brueghel, and Rembrandt. Pembroke could see that in Charles's eyes, Raphael held far greater appeal.

The earl did not hesitate. He agreed to hand it over, but first he had an engraving made by Lucas Vorsterman, the Flemish former apprentice of Rubens. Naturally, Pembroke's chosen artist was one of the most fashionable engravers of his day.

A print from this very engraving now hangs in the British Galleries of the Victoria and Albert Museum in London, labeled by Vorsterman as an engraving of the painting in the possession of the earl of Pembroke. You approach it through the Henry VII gallery, kept splendidly dim for preservation reasons, with small torches provided for visitors to illuminate for themselves the tiny carved gems or beautiful painted writing boxes of his day. Henry VII sits at the center of the room inside a glass box. His life-size head and shoulders were recreated by Torrigiano with almost photographic accuracy from a death mask. The painted terra-cotta face, with its flesh color and dimpled skin, seems eerily suspended between life and death, and the king seems to follow you, observing everything with his coolly scrutinizing eyes.

On you go, escaping the dead king's gaze, through the dazzling Elizabethan galleries of Hilliard miniatures, jewels, and portrait cameos and eventually into the Jacobean gallery. Just beyond a cabinet full of lace collars and gloves embroidered with tiny pearls, you are greeted with the sight of the Raphael *St. George and the*

Dragon. This is the Vorsterman engraving, the image reversed because Vorsterman did not redraw it before he engraved his plate.

At the base of his engraving, Vorsterman recorded the date, 1627, and the fact that the painting from which it was made belonged to the third earl of Pembroke. This gives us the painting's first definitive sighting in England.

Back in 1627, the third earl of Pembroke must have had some regrets as the Raphael painting was taken down from the wall, wrapped in protective covers, wedged inside a sturdy wooden container, and sent off to Whitehall. He clearly did not think much of the book of Holbein drawings he got in return, because soon afterwards, he passed it on to Lord Arundel, a known Holbein collector, presumably in exchange for another work of art. No record survives to tell us what this was.

That summer of 1627, the twenty-seven-year-old monarch, just two years on the throne, had been a man in search of a Raphael. He was already a sophisticated art connoisseur, with a broad knowledge of the visual arts and a particular liking for the Italian masters of the fifteenth and sixteenth centuries. His interest in art went back to his childhood, when at the age of eleven, he had inherited from his brother Henry a collection of paintings that included a large number of works by Venetian masters. In 1615, he had commissioned three paintings by the English artist Isaac Oliver, and two years later, his mother had left him her collection of one hundred and sixty-one paintings.

Charles had grown up surrounded by fine works of art. All around him buzzed the throngs of collector aristocrats who frequented the court and made it their business to impress King James and his son, Charles. Although the king had not been particularly interested in art himself, Charles was fascinated by the huge canvases on the royal walls. Gradually, with the benefit of knowledge and guidance from collector courtiers, he built up a comprehensive understanding of art. At the same time he was developing an appreciation that was showing signs of the passions that were to come. By the time he was twenty, he was very well-informed; so well-informed, in fact, that he returned the *Judith and Holofernes* he had commissioned from Rubens, because he could tell that it was largely the work of an apprentice. Rubens was so impressed by the prince's knowledge, and embarrassed by his sharp eye, that he admitted it was a "terrible" picture and promised another one, "entirely of my own hand."

Long before I came under the contagious influence of Raphael's *St. George* and succumbed to the urge to follow the trail of the painting, I had spent some time in Antwerp. I saw many of Rubens's enormous canvases and visited the house in which he had lived. It is a handsome and beautifully preserved town house, generously decorated with works by him or associated with him, with a charming formal garden filled with wisteria at the back and a series of marvelously dark, ground-floor rooms, their walls covered with stamped and colored leather that looks strangely like slabs of chocolate. Apart from the Flemish portraits and drawings, the one oil painting that has always stuck in my mind described a room belonging to a courtier collector during the first half of the seventeenth century. Many of these kinds of paintings exist, but in their riot of color and visual excitement they present just the kind of room you might have found in an aristocratic English town house of the period. Paintings, objets, and curiosities fill every inch of wall space. They spill over every furniture surface and ooze in a gently spreading tide over the wooden floor. As I read about Charles's growing interest in art and passion for collecting, it was to these images that my mind often returned, relishing the mad abundance and excess of the scene.

⌘

In 1623, a few years before he received the Raphael *St. George*, Charles's knowledge of art had exploded during a trip to Spain to win the hand of the Spanish Infanta Maria. With the sanction of his father, and accompanied by his father's favorite, the duke of Buckingham, he traveled in romantic incognito, the two men wearing false beards and riding on horseback over rough mountains. Although the marriage proposal came to nothing, the fantastically well-stocked galleries of the Escorial made a deep impression on Charles.

He reveled in the collections of Philip IV and soon realized that the connoisseurship of this eighteen-year-old monarch was far greater than his own. Resolving to learn more, Charles spent his time studying the paintings and sculptures in the Spanish royal collection. He saw many of the great Titians for the first time, and so admired his *Jupiter and Antiope* that the Spanish king promptly had it taken off the wall and presented to him. Charles acquired more Titians for himself, sat to the young Velázquez, and visited the leading collectors in Spanish court circles. Wherever he went, he bought all the paintings he could lay his hands on, paying on some occasions with money lent to him by Buckingham. When he finally came home, he was accompanied by an impressive haul of Correggios, Titians, a Holbein, and many other fine paintings, as well as other gifts from the Spanish king, including four asses, five camels, and one "ellefant," which created a great stir on its arrival in London.

Charles's art-collecting eyes had been opened wide by his Spanish trip. And it was perhaps this trip that established somewhere in the psyche of Charles I the act of art collecting as an incurable addiction. Now he was determined to build up a collection of his own that would dazzle not only his noble friends but also eclipse his rivals in Europe. All over the continent, a network of scouts fanned out in search of treasures to adorn Charles's palaces and residences. Ambassadors, friends, agents, and diplomats were put to work hunting for paintings and other treasures. Once spotted, these artworks had to be verified; then they were purchased, packed up, and shipped off to England in crate after crate, following an endless northward trail of booty.

Diplomacy and art collecting began to blend together. Reports of acquisitions arrived in London mixed in among the highest-level diplomatic communications. In the Netherlands, Dudley Carleton and Balthazar Gerbier acted for the king, buying paintings. In Germany the marquis of Hamilton was his key agent; in Spain it was Michael de la Croix and Henry Stone. But by far the largest team was at work for him in Italy. Charles, like his friend Philip of Spain, had developed an incurable passion for the Italian old masters, and he viewed Italy as a storehouse to be ransacked for gems. His Italian team was therefore his most important. Sir Henry Wotton, Nicholas Lanier, and Daniel Nys searched for treasures, and papal envoy Gregorio Panzani became one of the intermediaries for their import into England. The agents were assisted in their efforts by Cardinal Barberini, who vainly hoped, by flattering the tastes of the king of England, to win an important convert to Catholicism.

As Charles's collection grew, the courtiers closest to him shared, or made it their business to share, his aesthetic and cultural tastes. Swaggering in their plush costumes, their hands compressed inside white gloves, their nostrils bristling at fragrant pomanders, they swarmed around the young king, swapping news of finds, buying and selling for their own collections, and complimenting the king on his impeccable taste. For most of these courtiers, the business of collecting art was a social and political necessity. By imitating their sovereign, they found that they could flatter him.

The duke of Buckingham enjoyed an affectionate rivalry in connoisseurship, vying with him for the best works on offer. And the Scottish duke of Hamilton also appreciated the king's tastes and cooperated in acquiring for Charles what he most coveted. But by far the most scholarly patron and genuine aesthete collector was Thomas Howard, Earl of Arundel, who spent more than a year traveling in Italy in the company of Inigo Jones, acquiring his connoisseurship at first hand. He had already developed a passion for the works of Holbein, but he also owned works by Rubens, Van Dyck, da Vinci, and Dürer. Howard must have been delighted to receive the book of Holbein drawings which came his way, via the earl of Pembroke, when Charles acquired the beautiful Raphael *St. George.*

It was around the time that he secured this picture, his first Raphael, that Charles's compulsive appetite for collecting art was transported to a yet higher level. A few months after his triumphant swap at Wilton, Charles, with stealth and quiet glee, and to the astonishment and fury of his European collector rivals, successfully clinched the greatest art coup imaginable: the purchase of one of the most stupendous art collections in Europe, that of the dukes of Mantua. It sent shock waves throughout the continent.

For two hundred years the Gonzaga dukes of Mantua had been building up one of the finest collections of art in Europe. For generations, successive dukes had extended the shrewd hand of patronage to some of the finest of the great Italian masters, and between them they had accumulated a bounty of works by Mantegna, da Vinci, Perugino, Correggio, and many others. More superb paintings had come their way after the plunder of Urbino by Cesare Borgia in 1502. As they gathered in more artworks, the collection became famous, and at the same time, the dukes of Mantua prospered. They spent their wealth on successively grander palaces, decorated with this astonishing array of artworks, offering visible evidence of their great prosperity. Enjoyed with pride by the people of Mantua, known and envied throughout the length and breadth of Italy and increasingly admired from abroad, the Gonzaga art collection had become the symbol of their strength.

It was to Charles's good fortune, but to the great loss of the people of Mantua, that in 1628 the dukes found themselves in severe economic difficulties. The silk industry, the basis of their prosperity, had been in decline for fifteen years, and the dukes could no longer maintain their lavish court lifestyle. They had already been reduced to pawning their jewelry. Unfortunately for Mantua, the two dukes who reigned during the silk industry decline—Vincenzo II and his cousin Carlo—were not self-respecting Renaissance princes in the traditional mold. They did not understand that the treasures of their art collection were more than mere adornments. They did not appreciate the prestige and status that lay in the ownership of great paintings. Instead, these two former cardinals led disreputable lives ruled by food, drink, mistresses, and their fashionable collections of parrots.

A few years earlier, one of the dukes had dropped a hint to the visiting countess of Arundel about his idea for an art sale to raise revenues. Naturally, word of this thrilling possibility raced back to England, and before long, a mysterious merchant named Daniel Nys arrived from Venice at the Mantuan court for confidential talks with the ducal grand chancellor. Ostensibly, he was there to sell rare perfumes, vases, mirrors, furs, and other exotic paraphernalia to the dukes, but behind this front he had a much more important job to do. He was acting secretly as an art agent for Charles I, for the Arundels, and for the duke of Buckingham. Nys was an experienced hand in the murky world of international art dealing, and he straightaway sensed the vulnerability of his target. The incumbent duke's main interests, he realized, lay far from his works of art.

Within a short time, Nys was joined by Nicholas Lanier, master of the king's music, and together, the two men negotiated for the sale of the collection to Charles I. Inevitably word began to leak out, and at once voices of protest were raised. A senior former treasurer to the court, Niccolo Avellani, warned the duke that "if it is true that these pictures are to be sold, being such that the whole world has not the like, all friends of the house of Mantua will grieve." The duke responded by demanding greater secrecy, and then in the late summer of 1627, the deal was clinched. Nys bought the bulk of the pictures including Titian's *Twelve Caesars*, Raphael's *Holy Family*, an Andrea del Sarto, two Correggios, a Caravaggio and many others. The price for this extraordinary haul was fifteen thousand pounds.

As soon as the news broke, there was a deafening outcry in Mantua. "What is done is done," cried out the ex-treasurer, Avellani, "but God pardon whoever proposed such a sale." Nys was of course overjoyed with the outcome and reported back that all of Mantua and all of the princes of Europe were astonished that the duke could have done such a thing. The outburst against the duke was so terrible that, momentarily, he wavered and considered raising a loan to buy the whole lot back. He did not consider it for long. When he discovered that a particularly ravishing female dwarf had come on to the market in Hungary, that decided him. The paintings would have to go in order for his personal needs to be satisfied. Lounging on his cushions in the ducal palace at Maderno, he sought respite from the terrible fury of his people in some exotic new perfumes. These fragrant salves had been obligingly sold to him by that stealthy, silver-tongued merchant, Daniel Nys.

Nys was especially delighted with his deal because he had beaten off fierce competition from the grand duke of Tuscany to bag the Mantua collection for Charles. Of all his deals, he reflected, this had been the most difficult. "I myself am astounded at my success," he pronounced. The paintings are "so wonderful and glorious," he assured the king, "that the like will never again be met with;

they are truly worthy of so great a king as His Majesty.... In this business I have been aided by divine assistance.... To God then be the glory!" But as he celebrated, Nys sensed that the opportunities in Mantua had not yet been fully exploited.

The duke had held back nine great paintings from the sale. They were the pick of the whole collection, Mantegna's *Triumphs of Julius Caesar*. Word soon trickled into Charles's ear that "he who does not have them has nothing." There were still some statues too, Cupids believed to be by Praxiteles and Michelangelo. "Believe me, all the statues in England are bagatelles compared with these," Nys wrote to Charles. The king barely needed any persuasion, but as an added incentive to act quickly, Nys informed him that Cardinal Richelieu was after them, as was the queen mother of France and a determined grand duke of Tuscany who had been beaten to the punch the first time around.

Charles, with the itching fingers of a true collector, gave his enthusiastic consent. Nys closed in again on the duke, armed with more exotic perfumes and other snake-oil offerings besides, and tied up the second deal, buying the lot for just over ten thousand pounds. Again a terrible outcry went up in Mantua, and this time it reverberated all over Europe. Rubens protested that the duke should have died rather than let such a thing happen. The sale was regarded as a European scandal.

Charles was of course jubilant. His short reign to date had been lackluster, but now, with the sensational acquisition of the Mantua art collections, he had at last a triumph on his hands. But it had not come without sacrifice. With this acquisition, Charles had crossed some sort of psychological threshold. He had succumbed to the competitive greed of his era and was now demonstrably addicted to collecting art at the expense of politics. For at the time of the Mantuan negotiations, the duke of Buckingham was leading an expedition of the king's men to the Ile de Ré to relieve the Huguenot citadel of La Rochelle from Cardinal Richelieu's armies. Buckingham desperately needed more supplies to achieve his objectives. Just as his urgent request for fourteen thousand pounds arrived, the king's financier received the bill for fifteen thousand pounds for the Mantuan pictures. Horrified at the cost of the pictures, he informed Charles that he did not have sufficient money for both and asked him to make a decision. Writing a disingenuous letter of support to Buckingham, Charles calmly sacrificed his troops and opted for the paintings. Buckingham's expedition, thus starved of supplies, collapsed.

Charles had got what he wanted. In many ways he was glad to be out of the war too. And, as luck would have it, the diplomat sent to England to negotiate the peace on behalf of the Spanish king was none other than the painter, Peter Paul Rubens.

There was no coincidence in the selection of Rubens for the job. The Belgian artist-diplomat who arrived in England was well known to Charles as a painter of the first rank. The two men had much in common, and their friendship and mutual interests probably did much to achieve a satisfactory outcome. During the months that it took to negotiate the peace treaty with Spain, Rubens was able to familiarize himself with Charles's art collections. And he could barely believe his eyes at what he found.

Only a few years earlier, one of the yardsticks for European art collections had been that of the Habsburg emperor Rudolph II, an outstanding art gourmand of his time. His collection in Prague, put together in the last years of the sixteenth century, constituted the ideal upon which the royal and noble dilettanti of Europe based their aspirations. His hoard contained not only pictures and statues of the highest celebrity but bronzes, gold and silver plate, precious stones, curiously wrought rock crystals, ivory carvings, faience, medals, coins, and mathematical instruments. Sculptors, tapestry makers, clock makers, and astrologers came from all over Europe to enjoy his patronage. The Titians, da Vincis, Raphaels, and Dürers that he bought were joined by works from contemporary artists that had been specially painted to suit his eccentric tastes: the zoological fantasies of Brueghel, the sinuous sculptures of Giambologna, and the animated vegetables of Arcimboldi. Isolated in his enormous palace of Hradschin in Prague, Rudolph wandered the corridors disguised as a groom, reveling in his riches, the finest collection in Europe. It was an art collection so fascinating that it excited the wonder—according to contemporary accounts—of the entire world. But Rudolph's collection had now been broken up and plundered during the Thirty Years War, its spoils scattered as war booty among the victors.

This realignment of art riches had resulted in a new hierarchy of collections. The Spanish royal collection was still one of the finest, but now King Charles, just ten years after his trip to Madrid, had built up a collection of his own that could easily rival the Spanish. Rubens was staggered at the range and the quality of Charles's artworks. He wandered up and down the royal galleries, inspecting and admiring the Tintorettos, the Caravaggios, the Titians, and the da Vincis. Never, he exclaimed, had he seen so many fine pictures in one place. Charles, he reckoned, was probably one of the best-informed art connoisseurs of all the European princes, and probably the best judge of a canvas. Some years earlier, he had written to a friend, "*Monsieur Le Prince de Galles est le prince le plus amateur de la peinture qui soit du monde.*" Even allowing for the hyperbolic style of the professional diplomat-courtier, this was high praise indeed.

Unlike many of his voracious but incurious royal rivals in Europe, who generally bought indifferently, Charles was not merely following the widespread fashion for extravagant collecting. He had a genuine love of art. The papal agent in London and Van Dyck himself both agreed—in private letters with no necessity for flattery—that Charles had "a good nose for pictures" and that he had "a perfect understanding of painting." By now genuinely admired for his taste, the king was enjoying his own connoisseurship, trailing like magical dust his familiarity with the works of the greatest European artists.

When it came to grand and glorious art, the princes and monarchs of Europe, as well as their wealthiest ministers and collectors, were increasingly driven by competitive greed, their lives shaped by a desire to plunder the continent for its finest art works. Charles was no different. His appetite for art was already insatiable. He bought everything of quality he could lay his hands on. Diplomats and courtiers, turning the king's love of art to their own advantage, commissioned foreign artists to make gifts for him. Foreign rulers also took advantage of the king's susceptibilities. Cardinal Barberini remarked that he would "not hesitate to rob Rome of her most valuable ornaments, if in exchange we might be so happy as to have the king of England's name amongst those princes who submit to the Apostolic See."

There is a depiction of Charles I in the National Gallery that I find utterly absorbing. It's the portrait of the king on horseback, painted about 1637 by Van Dyck. The canvas is enormous, about three meters high and almost as wide, showing the king sitting elegantly astride a magnificent full-chested horse beneath a stormy sky. He is dressed in armor, wearing the medallion of a Garter Sovereign, and riding as if at the head of his knights, surveying the horizon with an air of consummate authority. There is something special about the power of the horse too, the smooth curve of its muscular neck and its long and feminine mane and tail, contrasted with the slightly fragile dignity of the king. Van Dyck's work confirmed what Charles's supporters wanted people to believe: that the king was in control. But it was painted not long before the outbreak of the civil war that was to lead to the king's execution.

Giles and I sometimes take our children to look at it, and they love its power and the overwhelming sense of its sheer physical presence. They always start off far too close, straining their necks and standing open-mouthed as they peer up the legs of the huge horse, trying to put the king's distant head into some kind of perspective. From close up and below, if you get down to their level, the view does actually reveal how small the king is, giving us a truer reading of his real power.

Charles's appetite for art was being fed from all directions. Every time a consignment of pictures arrived at Whitehall, he would hurriedly summon the queen and his connoisseur friends, the earl of Pembroke, Inigo Jones, and others, and together they would unpack the artworks and examine them by candlelight. Sometimes he would have the labels covered and they would challenge each other to guess the painter by the style. You can just imagine these aristocratic aesthetes circling the fabulous, freshly opened canvases, bending and stretching to get a closer look, their sword tips flickering like wagtails, and slapping their thighs in enthusiastic agreement at each other's suggestions.

These magical paintings, pouring in an apparently ceaseless stream into his possession, provided the king with fabulous adornments to his life and his palaces. Of course, as they accumulated around him, they gave him an escape from the pressures of the court, and a shell to protect him from the distant reality—which he could only imagine—of his ordinary, disorderly, and seldom-washed subjects. He probably never saw or smelled the squatters who lived in shacks and sold fish around the edges of the palace walls.

Given his splendid isolation, it is only natural that paintings became one of the chief pleasures of Charles's life. Their range and quality would have pleased anyone brought up with even the slightest understanding and the dimmest appreciation of art, let alone someone in his position. But for Charles, they also had another, different function. This was to bring order, truth, and meaning to the confusions of life, to illuminate the will of God. As he saw it, these paintings were there to project an image of virtue and majesty, to give substance to the divine right of the sovereign.

His collection was growing at an extraordinary rate, and its quality was outstanding. But among the rows and rows of superb old masters, the sculptures and the gorgeous jewels, there were naturally particular favorites. Rubens had noticed and admired these favorites, "the marvels of the cabinet of his Majesty," as he had toured the vast collections. These were the choicest of all the paintings, which Charles kept in a kind of inner sanctum, open only to his most cherished and important visitors.

Of all the hundreds of paintings in his collection, there were eight that pleased him most, and one of these was Raphael's *St. George and the Dragon*. In 1628, Charles had begun employing Peter Oliver, son of the miniaturist Isaac, to make small copies, mostly in watercolor, of his favorite pictures. There were about a dozen in all—eight favorites from his own collection, and four others that remained beyond his reach. The *St. George* was one of his copied paintings, as well as Raphael's *Holy Family*, which had come with the Mantuan collection. There were four Titians, of which two belonged to him, the other two being unavailable. There were three Correggios, one of which belonged to the duke of Buckingham; two Holbeins, one belonging to Lord Arundel; and a portrait by Isaac Oliver of Prince Henry. These holy of holies were arranged in cupboards in one of his rooms in Whitehall, as intimate tributes to the beauty of those paintings Charles most admired.

So among these riches, among these hundreds of great paintings, sculptures, tapestries, and jewels, why was it that the king prized Raphael's little *St. George and the Dragon* so highly? Without documentary evidence, the precise reasons will never be known for sure, but I believe there were several reasons for Charles's special love of the painting. One of these was Raphael's name.

In the minds of the ruthless collector princes of Europe, the great art gangsters who were slowly gathering in all the masterworks of sixteenth-century Italy, paintings by Raphael had emerged as among the most sought-after treasures. An admiration for Raphael was considered a hallmark of noble collecting. And you can see why. Raphael's paintings were sophisticated. They were religious in a time of religious fervor. And they were exquisitely beautiful. Charles declared that Raphael was his favorite painter, but there were plenty of others on the hunt for his works too.

Queen Christina of Sweden, in a letter written a few years later to fellow art lover Paolo Giordano Orsini II, declared of her vast collection of pictures in Stockholm that it contained "an infinite number of items, but apart from thirty or forty original Italians, I care nothing for any of the others. There are some by Alberto Dürer and other German masters whose names I do not know, and anyone else would think very highly of them, but I swear that I would give away the whole lot for a couple of Raphaels, and I think that even that would be paying them too much honor."

Christina of Sweden was a glutton for culture. With an appetite as insatiable as Charles's, and no apparent restraint, she had agents in London, the Hague, and Rome constantly on the lookout for acquisitions. She bought libraries wholesale and had them shipped back to Sweden. She bought pictures, manuscripts, and jewels, and the loot came, in crateload after crateload, winding its way northward toward her palace in Stockholm.

Another reason for Charles's fondness for the Raphael *St.*

George was a more personal one. It lay in the artist's exquisite rendering of St. George, patron saint of the Order of the Garter. Ever since his earliest days on the throne, Charles had appreciated the role of the Order of the Garter as a symbol of honor, chivalry, order, and propriety. On his succession as king, he had taken over from a bibulously dissolute, bisexual father for whom court life revolved around hunting parties, orgies, and ribaldry. In reaction to this precedent, Charles had already emerged as an earnest and dour moralist who some say took after his mother, Anne of Denmark. He was chaste, temperate, and serious, and once he was on the throne, the fools, mimics, and catamites of his father's court quickly drifted away.

Charles was determined to rule according to a new rulebook, insisting on decorum and formality to the letter. Greater reverence and ritual surrounded the king, and rules were drawn up for behavior at court in which swearing and innuendo were not tolerated. Gentlemen who offended the king were immediately demoted. Such changes in court style and substance were felt within days of Charles's succession.

In all this general moral tightening up, the Order of the Garter was an obvious symbolic tool. For the king it represented all the virtues his father had lacked: manliness, chivalry and piety, honor and propriety. And in its public ceremonies and rituals, in the religious ceremonies associated with the inauguration of new knights, it offered a form of dedication and worship.

Under Charles's direction, St. George himself, following his demotion under Henry VIII at the time of the Reformation, was remolded as the Christian hero. He appeared in pictures in St. George's Chapel at Windsor and was woven into a tapestry for the altar alongside the Virgin Mary. The Grand Feast of St. George, which had migrated to other locations during the reigns of Elizabeth and James, was permanently restored to Windsor and reinstated in all its solemnity and splendor. It became less of a public spectacle and more of a dignified religious occasion, an elaborate showpiece of Anglican ritual.

Few monarchs had a greater sense of their duty and accountability to God than Charles I. It was natural, therefore, that he wished the Garter to return to the purity of its supposed origins—founded to the honor of almighty God. Ceremonies became more dignified, less showy occasions. Soon after his succession, Charles added to the regalia by ordering the cloak of every Garter Knight to be embroidered with a large cross within a garter, with a "glory" of silver rays emanating from the cross. But the Garter regalia were not only for ceremonial occasions. Every morning on getting dressed himself, he put on his Lesser George under his shirt. This was a locket suspended from a blue ribbon. Inside it, he kept two pictures: one of St. George and one of his wife, Henrietta Maria.

St. George lay close to the king's heart. But the saint was also in his mind. Volumes about St. George and the Garter accounted for two-thirds of his personal library. He also owned hundreds of objects associated with the saint—plates, bronzes, medals, and of course his prized Raphael painting. On his windowsill he kept a small bronze of St. George slaying the dragon, made by the Florentine sculptor Francesco Fanelli and based on the Lucas Vorsterman engraving, which the earl of Pembroke had commissioned before the painting left Wilton for Whitehall.

The cult of St. George gathered steam over the early years of his reign, and the king did not hide his delight at being portrayed—in paint or in verse—in the image of his favorite saint. The poet Sir John Denham earned praise, and possibly a financial reward, for his poem equating King Charles with St. George:

> *In whose Heroic face I see the Saint*
> *Better expressed than in the liveliest paint,*

That fortitude which made him famous here,
That heavenly piety, which saints him There,
Who when this Order he forsakes, may he
Companion of that Sacred Order be ...

Other courtiers enjoyed flattering comparisons with St. George too. The duke of Buckingham was depicted in a beautifully crafted, colored drawing as a handsome saint, leading a small, well-behaved dragon on a fine blue cord, a Garter hung prettily around its neck. But the most successful artists knew better whom to portray as St. George. Rubens, during his spell in London, succumbed happily to Charles's cult of St. George. In 1630, he painted a large canvas, *Landscape with St. George and the Dragon*, now in the royal collection, glorifying Charles as England's patron saint. In the painting, the king stands in glistening armor with one foot resting on the dragon's head. He faces the maiden, who bears a strong resemblance to Henrietta Maria, and declares his victory to her. Behind the victorious knight is a broad and peaceful scene spread out along the banks of the Thames. London can be seen in the background, with Lambeth Palace in the distance, and in the sky are angels ready with George's martyr's crown, soon ironically to be earned by Charles himself.

If you let your eyes drop down from this idyllic English pastoral scene, you find the foreground littered with the carnage of bodies and slain corpses around the dragon, representing the slaughter of the Thirty Years War. Charles is the saint who has slain the dragon of war and brought peace to his realm. The king liked the painting enormously and presented the artist with a large diamond ring from his own finger and a diamond-studded hatband, as well as the ceremonial sword with which he had knighted him.

Rubens must have been delighted with his time in England. He had been showered with gifts and honored with a knighthood; he had won commissions from many important courtiers, and he had painted the ceiling of the king's Banqueting House with a series of great propagandist scenes commemorating James I.

Some years ago, the Banqueting House returned to its full Jacobean splendor when Simon Thurley, then curator of the Historic Royal Palaces, hosted his birthday party there, a full Jacobean costume extravaganza. Giles and I attended, and the scene that evening was magnificent. The place came alive as several hundred people arrived, all authentically dressed to recreate a ball of the era. Silk dresses rustled and fans flapped. Modern-day bankers, historians, and journalists, with mobile phones secreted about their persons, adjusted their wigs and their corsets as they imagined themselves transported back nearly four hundred years. Gentlemen in silk breeches wove through the crowd bearing edible delicacies as we stood staring up at the superb ceiling festooned with garlands of chubby putti exposing their pink bottoms. In its day, the Banqueting House was an astonishing piece of virtuoso architectural design by Inigo Jones. Its monumental ceiling by Rubens, in nine panels, was a demonstration of all the power and sophistication of Charles's reign. As we stood looking at it that night, we realized how enduring its power has been over the centuries. Apart from the flashing cameras, Rubens would have felt entirely at home.

The painter perhaps attended just such a celebratory ball himself, for he had successfully negotiated peace between England and Spain and had won the friendship of Charles with a painting that not only glorified the monarch but also signaled the success of his own negotiating skills. The serenely beautiful Thames-side fields symbolized the peace, prosperity and success of Charles's reign.

But the reality was quite different. For Charles and other courtiers close to him, there was another, equally self-deluding way of reading the picture. For them the allegory of triumph over evil could be read as the victory of a cultured court over barbarity. The natural enemy of Charles's court was no longer the Catholics in Spain. It was the Puritans at home.

Charles had begun to rule without Parliament. There were numerous aspects of his personal rule that engendered opposition from a growing and increasingly voluble body of Puritans. Censorship of the press and control of the judiciary were just a couple. But the one that was most visible, and which also concerns us most closely, was the king's aristocratic temperament, from which the excessive extravagance at court resulted. By the 1630s, Charles I had instituted a scale of spending and splendor at court that elevated him and his circle far beyond the reach of his subjects. This development was to lead, as we know, to disaster.

Life at court was conspicuously extravagant. As Rubens wrote home, "All the leading nobles here live on a most sumptuous scale and spend money lavishly.... Splendor and liberality are the first considerations of this court.... In this place I find none of the crudeness that one might expect from a place so remote from Italian elegance." The tone for such grandeur was of course set by the monarch, and Charles's day-to-day lifestyle was astonishingly grand.

Charles and his queen took their meals in public, served by waiters on bended knee (he was the only monarch in Europe to insist on this) and amid so much ceremony and deference that they hardly ever ate their food hot. A vast team of servants, a little over three hundred, supported the upstairs world of display; below stairs there were twice as many. Fifty-eight gentlemen pensioners stood in ceremonial attendance on the king, 210 provided his bodyguard, and 263 members of the royal stables attended him on his ceaseless travels and hunting expeditions, along with the officers of the bears and mastiffs, the harriers, and the falconers. There were hundreds more miscellaneous members of staff, musicians and instrument makers, clock keepers, physicians and chaplains, perfumers and painters as well as the teams of cooks, laundresses, scullions, and cleaners who ultimately kept the royal household running smoothly. The queen had 172 servants in her household and by the end of the 1630s, there were 200 more attending on the five royal children. In all, the royal household employed a team that at times ballooned to 2,600 people. With all their dependents, this population amounted to a large town.

Then there were the nineteen palaces, castles, and residences to keep up, all of which required constant renovation and repairs as well as a permanent core staff. In London, the largest was Whitehall, the effective hub of the kingdom, spread over some twenty acres and consisting of fifty-three buildings and courtyards ranging from the small beer buttery to the sublime Palladian-style Banqueting House. Across the park from Whitehall was St. James's Palace, built by Henry VIII as the residence of the heir to the throne. Henrietta Maria had her private Roman Catholic chapel there, although her official residence was Somerset or Denmark House, situated on the north bank of the Thames a mile downstream from Whitehall. Further downstream was Greenwich Palace, one of Henry VII's favorites, and a few miles upstream from Whitehall was Richmond Palace. Hampton Court required another hour's rowing upstream, and then it took a further half a day to reach the royal castle and palace at Windsor, home to Charles's beloved Order of the Garter.

Further afield were Nonsuch, a day's ride to the south from London, Oatlands in Surrey, Theobalds in Hertfordshire, and Royston near Cambridge, set in some of the finest hunting grounds in England. Northeast from Royston was Newmarket, one of his most comfortable private homes. And if he grew tired of his own houses, the king could always visit those of his subjects. In the summer of 1634, for example, Charles and his retinue were on the move for months on end, staying at the country seats of favored courtiers. He spent six weeks hunting in Leicestershire, Northamptonshire, and Huntingdonshire. The king and queen then gave up their pleasures for two weeks for a state visit to Nottingham, for which the corporation spent two hundred pounds, a third of their annual revenue, on cleaning and repairing the city center. Unfortunately the house they chose to store the royal wardrobe collapsed under the weight of the king and queen's clothes. Charles and his queen quickly packed up and moved on and were soon safely installed privately in the more comfortable and lavish Bolsover Castle in Derbyshire, where the earl of Cavendish spent a reputed ten thousand on entertainments, which were attended by gentry from all over the north of England.

Such traveling was not unusual for an English monarch, although Charles did sometimes travel to excess. In one three-month period, he moved from house to house twenty-seven times. For centuries, English kings and queens had moved around the country like nomads, settling in a residence or castle, eating it clean and hunting its game, and then moving on like a swarm of locusts to the next. Elizabeth used her progresses to show herself to her people and to win their loyalty. But Charles hated publicity stunts. His official visits became increasingly rare. As he traveled, he devoted more and more of his time to his own private pleasures.

The luxury of his lifestyle, and that of his father, depended on a predominantly rural population of whom at least half were desperately poor, plague-stricken, and often undernourished. For them, bad harvests and high prices meant malnutrition. Even employed laborers and apprentices got only ten pence a day, while the king could spend as much as four thousand pounds on a single night's entertainment. These evenings, filled with masques and dancing, often designed by the brilliant Inigo Jones, relied on elaborate and fanciful costumes and stage sets and portrayed an increasingly unrealistic view of a rapidly disintegrating reality.

It was not as if Charles could afford all this either. In addition to cripplingly expensive wars with France and Spain, the costs of the huge royal households were immense. Between 1631 and 1635 they averaged £260,000 a year, something like forty percent of the king's income. This figure would have been far greater if the king had not been allowed, according to a long-standing and highly unpopular tradition, to requisition horses, wagons, and supplies as the court traveled the country, paying for them at well below market prices. On top of his vast expenses, corruption at court was rife, and much of the king's already dwindling income was being wasted or embezzled. By 1635, the king was £1,730,000 in debt. Crown lands and woods had been sold off, royal jewels had been pawned, and the debt was still spiraling.

Even without these huge debts, how could Charles make ends meet without the subsidies that only Parliament could sanction? Charles himself tried to economize, but he was not good at it. It did not help matters that Henrietta Maria refused to economize on her household and wardrobe expenses. The king achieved some economies in dress, but he still indulged himself, buying a three-hundred-pound ring, set with a large square diamond. And in 1634 he was seen fondling a "great round rope of pearls," which had been imported duty-free for his inspection. He wanted to establish order in the accounting systems and restraint in expenditure, but because the example was not set at the top, little was achieved.

Charles could not help spending money. To counterbalance his expenditure on himself, he was always giving others lavish presents. He presented the Savoy ambassador with a gold tablet set with diamonds. He gave horses worth five hundred pounds to Henrietta Maria's brother, the French king, and the same to her sister.

But more significantly, he was still commissioning vastly expensive building projects. He drew up schemes with Inigo Jones for beautifying the capital, including the restoration of St. Paul's Cathedral. He also commissioned Jones to build a new house for the queen at Greenwich, a new palace at Whitehall, and a triumphal arch. He spent money improving his manor in York, he converted a tennis court at Somerset House into a chapel for the queen, and he created a deer park between Richmond and Hampton Court, alienating hundreds of poor people who had common rights to the land.

One of the king's biggest personal extravagances remained his picture buying, still a central psychological prop in his pressured life. In 1629, he had sent Orazio Gentileschi, of the Italian father-and-daughter team of painters, to Italy with the task of buying a picture collection subject to the approval of his adviser Nicholas Lanier. Fortunately for the Exchequer, Lanier advised against the purchase. But nine years later, Charles bought another collection of twenty-three Italian works including six grisailles attributed to Caravaggio and paintings by Titian and Guido Reni. He also bought, on the recommendation of his friend Rubens, a set of Raphael cartoons, the *Acts of the Apostles*, and sent them off to be made into tapestries at Mortlake. In addition to these major purchases, he was constantly picking up other paintings or commissioning new ones from his circle of favorite artists.

The reality of a commission from Charles I, however, was less glamorous than it might have appeared. Many of those commissioned found that they were not being paid on time—or at all. Rubens was still owed three thousand pounds in 1638, a year after delivery of the Banqueting House paintings. Van Dyck was owed money, as were the Gentileschis. The king began to slice chunks off the bills presented for paintings, reducing the fee for a half-length portrait from thirty-two to twenty-six pounds, and a full-length portrait from fifty to forty. Van Dyck had been deservedly raking in money from the nobility, for whom he painted dozens of portraits, but in 1638, he found that the king had slashed his latest bill for twenty-four works, halving the price of *Le Roi à la Chasse* from two hundred to one hundred pounds. In 1639, his annual pension of two hundred pounds was five years in arrears, and the modest claim he had made for his superb portrait of the king's three children (now at Windsor) was cut to one hundred pounds. The bills for at least nineteen of his portraits of the king and queen were still unpaid.

Although his advisers urged the king to rein in his expenditure, he disregarded them, in the high-handed way in which he was conducting all his affairs. He demanded more and more money, and eventually he was refused by the Treasury.

Charles was an addict when it came to art. Picture buying was, quite simply, his chief preoccupation. It took up much of his time, energy, enthusiasm, and money during the period in the 1630s when he was not inclined to expend much energy governing England. While he forced himself to economize on the sums he spent, simply by squeezing painters' earnings, he found he was unable to control his desire to acquire more. The Mantuan collection had cost him just over twenty-five thousand pounds, the Rubens ceiling had a price tag of three thousand. And the many other treasures, still being scouted, purchased, and gathered in from all over Europe, were costing him thousands more.

Reading about Charles's growing obsessions and passions to gather ever more artworks into his possession, I kept returning in my mind to the Raphael *St. George*. It had been a relatively early acquisition for him, perhaps one that whetted his appetite for more. And it was one of his favorites too. I wondered whether he ever took it with him when he traveled. As we know, he did have a copy made. I kept a reproduction of Raphael's painting on my desk, but no reproduction can do it justice. When you look at it in a book, it sits snugly within the confines of the page, and you have no true measure of its impact. I can still remember the shock of entering Room 20 at the National Gallery in Washington and seeing this painting. It contained reams of stories and histories, enough to fill a whole wall, all fitted within this impeccably detailed panel of wood no larger than a sheet of letter paper. A great reckoning in a little room.

Although the king demonstrated exquisite tastes, judgment, and patronage of excellence, it is not surprising that his extravagant collecting upset many people. Few dared say it at the time, but later the condemnation was to become savage, one critic thundering that "great sums were squandered away on braveries and vanities; On old rotten pictures, on broken-nosed Marble."

But there was a darker fear associated with Charles's connoisseurship. The style in both painting and architecture that the king favored was identified with the Renaissance courts of Italy and of the Spanish and Austrian Habsburgs. Puritan sensibilities were offended by such taints of Catholicism. The king, they reasoned, had tried to marry a Spanish Habsburg. He had then married a Catholic queen. What was more, they saw associations between Queen Henrietta Maria's aggressive Catholicism, the king's extravagant and propagandist use of the arts, expressive of most un-English ideas, and his political and legal search for ways of governing without recourse to Parliament.

It is not surprising that Charles's personal galleries of artworks, gathered with so much ambition and catalogued and cared for with such undeviating zeal, became a special symbol of excess to the more philistine Puritans. As they saw it, the king was sacrificing politics and the proper governing of the country in favor of his own personal art collection. Opposition was growing at a furious rate among those who were ultimately paying for Charles's extravagance. But the king neither knew nor seemed to care what passions he was antagonizing.

He continued his pleasurable life, searching out and buying works of fine art, commissioning buildings, traveling and hunting with his friends, and staying in the beautiful country houses of his favored courtiers. He dressed, as did his courtiers, in a raffish Cavalier style, setting new extremes of personal display with his long curling wigs, cascading lace, shoes decorated with large floppy rosettes, and hats so flamboyantly plumed that he might have been celebrating victory in a war against ostriches.

Already in 1628, the irrepressible William Prynne, a barrister and a prolific Puritan agitator, had denounced the lifestyle at court. In his treatise entitled *Unlovelinesse of Love Lockes*, or a *Summarie discourse proving the wearing, and nourishing of a Locke or Love-Locke to be altogether unseemly and unlawfull unto Christians*, he had witheringly declared long hair for men to be idolatrous, lascivious, and unnatural. He railed against "English hermaphrodites" and declared that any man sporting long curls had hair "frizzled like a Baboone."

Although prodigiously clever, Prynne was himself no beauty. According to Aubrey, he had a "strange saturnine complection and the countenance of a witch." Portraits of him show wide, sensual lips curled down in a permanent sneer. He was the son of a tenant farmer in Somerset on land belonging to Oriel College, Oxford. He had been educated at Bath and at Oriel and had become a barrister at Lincoln's Inn. He was a compulsive writer and a rabid Calvinist, and much of his energy was devoted to the comprehensive denunciation of life's pleasures. In one voluminous treatise he damned drinking and carousing. In his next one, he moved on from the bodily pleasures and launched an attack on masques and stage plays, in which he included a mocking reference to St. George. This was aimed as a critique of a recently published history of St. George, written by a staunch supporter of the king, the established church, and St. George.

Charles's precarious world was unraveling. In the rapidly polarizing England of the 1630s, a patriotic attachment to St. George had come to be seen as a mark of allegiance to the court and the established church. The king's faction decided to take action. In 1633 Prynne's book, which was said to contain passages derogatory to the queen, was banned and Prynne was arrested. The following year he was tried. His accusers declared that "this book may justly be called libellous, scandalous and seditious." During the trial it was claimed that he had written in opposition of St. George. Naturally, Prynne was found guilty. His university degrees and membership of the Bar were withdrawn; he was fined five thousand pounds and imprisoned for life. For good measure, his ears were cut off.

The king's identification with St. George was becoming increasingly explicit. The Order of the Garter was now identified as a Royalist symbol and Prynne's attack was seen to be political by nature. Soon others were being taken to court for supposedly derogatory remarks about St. George.

The more the opposition rose against the king, and the more he worried about parliamentary agitation and Puritan clamorings, the greater was his desire simply to step away from it all and retire among the riches of his art collection. Isolated and lacking support, he wished more than anything else to gaze upon his soothing and seductive Raphael *St. George*, to banish self-doubt with the reassuringly majestic portraits of himself by Van Dyck, to lose himself in the grand allegorical canvases by Titian and Correggio that hung in his huge, echoing galleries. His collection provided him with the escape, the fantasy, the protection that he sought when he found he was losing his grip on power. But his art could not save him.

On January 10, 1642, Charles I fled with his wife and three eldest children, leaving London and its terrifying, clamoring mobs. During the next three nomadic years, he spent time at many of his palaces in the country, but he never again, until the very end, saw Whitehall and his favorite paintings.

On the run and increasingly forced to focus his mind on civil war, the king turned to the martial, chivalric spirit of the Knights of the Garter for backing. Lacking any authoritative central court, he made the ceremony and rituals of the Order of the Garter the focus for reaffirmation of loyalty to himself and the crown of England on the part of his senior nobles.

And even after war had erupted, and his forces were doing increasingly badly, Charles still seemed to cling to the charmed, ceremonial Order of the Garter as his secret military weapon. Perhaps he imagined himself as St. George, valiantly fighting the dragon, the evil forces of the Parliamentary cause, to protect the maiden, England's sovereign tradition.

The angry people of London would have scoffed loudly at such an idea as they wandered around inside Whitehall Palace. The place had been left empty for months after the royal family had fled. With no guards on the gates, streams of curious men, women, and children came to gaze in astonishment at the royal apartments, and to gawk innocently at the pictures.

As they traipsed up and down the long gallery and the other great rooms, few would have had any idea of the value of the twenty-eight Titians, the nine Raphaels, the eleven Correggios, sixteen Van Dycks, eleven Holbeins, the Veroneses, Giorgiones, Tintorettos, and the almost five hundred other beauties that were arrayed in the various apartments of the palace. Some even climbed onto the king's throne to try it out for size, barely containing their glee as they spread their common rumps on its velvet surface.

Works of art had been in danger for some time at the hands of iconoclasts, Puritan zealots, and Parliamentary troops. Already in 1640, the queen's chapel at Somerset House had been threatened by a mob planning to deface its "superstitious" monuments and pictures. A few years later, a House of Commons committee was sent with a body of soldiers to Somerset House, where the chapel was "licentiously rifled." An altarpiece by Rubens was thrown into the Thames. Altars were smashed, images broken and defiled, ornaments and books burnt.

The adverse decision of the tribunal to which Charles had rashly carried his quarrel with the English people cut short his career. But even to the last, he clung to the hope of regaining power, his mind still occupied with thoughts of his cherished possessions. On the day of his escape from Hampton Court, the letter which he left on his table, addressed to his custodian, contained orders to protect the "household stuff and movables of all sorts." He also specified three pictures there which, not being his own, he wished to restore to their rightful owners. Even in captivity, in 1647, he summoned Inigo Jones to Carisbrooke Castle, where he scrutinized the architect's plans for a new palace at Whitehall twice the size of the Escorial, the seat of his Spanish royal art-collecting rival.

In the end, St. George and the Order of the Garter failed him. Charles's last act, just minutes before his execution, as he stood in full view of his subjects on the scaffold at Whitehall, was to hand his gorgeous, diamond-encrusted Great George, which hung around his neck, together with his Garter cloak, to Bishop Juxon, who stood beside him to provide spiritual comfort at the end.

The act was richly symbolic. Returning the George and Garter mantle to the reigning sovereign was the final official duty expected of any Knight Companion of the Garter. Although Bishop Juxon would not have admitted it publicly in these politically dangerous times, these two most powerful Garter symbols were to be given to Charles's son. The hope was that one day they might become a part of the restoration of the monarchy.

After a short pause, the king stooped and knelt down and laid his head on the block. The executioner lifted the axe and, with one blow, severed the king's head from his body.

Within days of the king's execution, Parliament was facing demands for considerable sums of money that Charles owed in debts and wages. The new administration worked quickly, and an act was passed providing for the sale of the contents of the royal residences. The royal palaces, castles, manors, and lodges were stuffed with famous paintings, tapestries, furniture, statues, and jewels along with all the goods and chattels of the king and his family. The sale of all of these would raise huge sums.

But the art treasures of the king were not being liquidated simply to pay off debts. There was something far more symbolic about this sale. These works of art had become the sacrificial victim of a moral and social as well as a political movement. Over the course of more than twenty years, hundreds of treasures had been collected, at the expense of politics, for the king's personal art gallery. And in the course of gathering in these gems from all over Europe, the king had withdrawn into an exclusive circle of international connoisseurs, intellectually elevating himself far beyond the reach of his subjects. To the reforming zealots, these art works had become the visible symbols of a loathsome social system.

The Puritans had already cut down the great cross of Cheapside in London. They had desecrated the chapel of Henry VII at Westminster and voted to sell off the English cathedrals for scrap. They had decapitated the effigies in England's parish churches.

Once Charles I had been decapitated himself, they voted to sell his unique collection of pictures. The gallery of Whitehall was judged appropriate to pay the price of Charles's failures. The Commonwealth Sale, which began in October 1649 at Somerset House and continued over the course of two years, was the greatest sale of art treasures of all time. The inventories of the sale offer a poignant record of vanished luxury.

Last year I went to visit Jerry Brotton, the senior lecturer in Renaissance studies at Queen Mary College, University of London. Brotton had just completed his book *The Sale of the Late King's Goods,* a fascinating account of how the king's collection was put together and how it was then dispersed at the Commonwealth Sale. I was roughly halfway through my own story at the time, increasingly driven by the quest to track the Raphael *St. George* and experiencing a strange empty and excited state, feeling alternately haunted by it and blessed by it. Brotton kindly invited me to discuss the sale, so we met at his rooms and then went on to trade ideas and clues in more depth over a bowl of noodles.

He described to me the logistics of the sale, how merchants and traders were asked to inventory the royal collection and put prices not only on the royal pots and pans, tapestries and carpets, but also on the late king's Titians and Raphaels. Inevitably corruption was rife. For the first time in history, ordinary people began to traipse through the palaces that had been designed specifically to exclude them. There they were invited to pick up and assess some of the most cherished and personal belongings of their dead monarch.

By the autumn of 1649, workmen had collected together all the hastily labeled and priced items for sale from all the royal residences and brought them to Somerset House. There they were laid haphazardly down in a kind of arbitrary clutter for viewing.

Chamber pots were clumsily jumbled together with beautiful porcelain and sculptures. Piles of carpets and tapestries mounted up in obscure corners, and the paintings were hung randomly all over the walls. Some just stood stacked in corners. Just over thirteen hundred paintings were up for sale, as well as hundreds of carpets, tapestries, statues, and other miscellaneous pieces.

A Dutch diplomat visiting the sale reported, "We went to Somerset House again and saw a number of beautiful things, among them the most costly tapestries I ever saw. One room was valued at three hundred pounds. In that same room were many antique and modern statues, although nearly all damaged. There was also a unicorn cane as thick as an arm, with a large crystal knob. In the gallery above, we saw a very large number of beautiful paintings, but all so badly cared for and so dusty that it was a pitiable sight."

Some of the artworks were given away privately to settle old debts or claims. Oliver Cromwell reserved for himself the *Triumphs of Caesar* by Mantegna and the Raphael cartoons, along with plate, tapestries, and furnishings of all sorts. He gathered these together to decorate his apartments at Hampton Court, where he lived in great splendor.

But the rest, several thousand items, including many of the finest and most valuable paintings in all of Europe, the most exquisite sculptures, jewels, plate, and silver, were all put up for sale. Of course the event was carrion to the meat flies of Europe. All those kings and magnates, the rival collectors whom Charles had so often undercut or outbid, immediately saw their chance for revenge. Expressing their horror at the Puritan act of regicide, they quietly dispatched their agents to London to pick hungrily over the remains of the dead king.

All the old predators were there, hiding behind their chosen representatives, just as Charles had hidden behind Daniel Nys for his triumphant Mantua acquisitions. Philip IV of Spain sent his ambassador, Don Alonzo de Cardenas, to recover the Titians that Charles had carried off twenty-one years earlier. Acting ostensibly for the royal favorite, Don Luis de Haro, he acquired the paintings, along with cartloads of other booty. Haro, keeping up the pretense, received the paintings and then, declaring them too grand for a mere subject, subserviently handed them over to the king. Cardinal Mazarin dispatched his agent, who spent his time trying to outwit the Spanish ambassador. The agent nevertheless managed to secure a handsome share for his master, acquiring busts, tapestries, and paintings. Queen Christina, still unsatisfied even after her looting of Prague, sent her agent to bid for jewels. The Habsburg Archduke Leopold William, governor of Flanders, seized his chance to add to his own splendid collection. And the fifth big buyer at the sale was Everhard Jabach, a Cologne-born banker, resident in Paris, and a man of apparently inexhaustible means. He was buying for both Mazarin and himself, and he scooped up so many pictures, tapestries, sculptures, and other treasures that he returned to Paris at the head of a convoy of wagons, "loaded with artistic conquests, like a Roman victor at the head of a triumphal procession." Most of his goods were later sold to Louis XIV, and they ended their travels in the Louvre.

Edward Hyde, the earl of Clarendon, English ambassador to the court of Spain and of the exiled Charles II, was withering in his scorn of the European monarchs, all weakly protesting the murder of a kinsman while at the same time aggressively plundering his spoils. But at least the monarchs were not as indelicate as this upstart banker Jabach, he wrote. Clarendon was tactfully sent away from Madrid on the day the train of eighteen mules entered the city, loaded with twenty-four crates filled with the treasures of his murdered monarch. Among the gems in those crates were Raphael's *Madonna della Perla*, Mantegna's *Dormition of the Virgin*, and Titian's *Portrait of the Emperor Charles V with a Dog*, which are today considered to be three of the principal masterpieces of the Prado.

Many more of Charles I's paintings have ended up in the Prado and other major public collections. In fact, to reassemble his art collection would require the stripping of the principal galleries of Europe and America of their finest treasures. He had the best, and in vast numbers.

The scene of the sale must have been extraordinary. As well as genuine creditors and opportunistic buyers, there were swindlers, forgers, confidence tricksters, men gifted in all the subtle arts, who swarmed to the scene in hope of nourishment.

Many of the king's creditors organized themselves into dividends or syndicates, and their leaders negotiated on behalf of the group, acquiring royal goods in lieu of debt repayments. The dividend leaders, who were probably working secretly on behalf of the prowling agents of those European buyers, then handled the reselling of the goods and the distribution of profits.

One of the creditors and dividend leaders was a man named Edward Bass. During Charles's reign he had been a minor courtier. He had joined the Parliamentary cause and become a major in the army during the Civil War. At the end of the war he had worked as a bounty hunter, searching for possessions of the king that had been stolen and hidden during the upheaval of war and its aftermath. Bass must have made considerable sums of money in his pursuit of stolen goods, because we know that he caught out the unfortunate Sir Henry Mildmay, who had concealed "a parcel of the king's plate" among his own belongings. Bass was awarded nine hundred pounds for this discovery, while Sir Henry was fined double this amount.

Bass was in charge of three of the fourteen dividends, and on behalf of his various members, he managed to acquire some of the finest art works in the royal collection. Paintings were acquired by drawing lots, and Bass was extraordinarily lucky with his takings. On October 23, 1651, he acquired the most expensive painting in the entire collection. Valued at the almost inconceivable sum of two thousand pounds, it was the *Holy Family* by Raphael, which Charles had bought some twenty years earlier from the dukes of Mantua. Then, almost two months later, on December 19, another Raphael came up for sale, this time our seductive gem, *St. George and the Dragon.*

The painting was valued at £150, a sum exceeding the price of many other paintings in the royal collection. We don't know why Bass ended up with this painting. It may have simply been drawn in a lot, although it is more likely that he placed a quiet inducement in order to secure it. But it would have held particular interest for him personally. Bass was obsessed with the Order of the Garter. He had already bought privately, under his own name, the books from the king's library that concerned the Garter and its history. They were beautiful volumes, many of them kept in red velvet cases and bound with exquisite decorative covers and motifs, enriched with mounts and clasps of silver gilt and bindings of velvet and stamped with the coat of arms of the Prince of Wales. He had also bought the king's valuable ermine-lined coronation robes and his Garter robes, as well as some twenty-four paintings for himself and a further forty-six jointly with another creditor, John Hunt, who had been linen draper to the queen.

Those creditors grouped behind the figure of Edward Bass must have done very well indeed out of the Commonwealth Sale. Quite apart from two of the finest Raphaels ever painted, many other important works came into their possession to be resold, including a Rubens self-portrait. Altogether, his three dividends acquired seventy-one pictures, valued together at £3,323 and 10 shillings.

They then, in common with other creditors, set up shop informally, creating makeshift salerooms in houses dotted around

London, to resell the goods for profit. Large numbers of the king's pictures, many of them of the highest quality, as well as fine antique sculptures, were seen scattered around the homes of former members of the king's staff. At a wharf near Somerset House, the home of Edmund Harrison, the king's embroiderer, was stuffed with treasures. Magnificent paintings and other treasures had been handed over in lieu of debts to Grynder, the king's upholsterer; Baggley, the king's glazier; John Embree, the king's plumber; and many other ordinary tradesmen. And in the house of Emanuel de Critz, the king's copyist, there were said to be three rooms packed full of the king's pictures as well as the famous Bernini bust of the king.

Snooping furtively on the sidelines were the agents from abroad. They kept their ears to the ground, listening for the rumors, claims, and counterclaims. At a moment's notice, they were ready to snap up bargains for their masters, who were waiting, avid for good news, on the Continent.

Bass must have sold the two Raphaels almost immediately. The *Holy Family*, already famed across Europe, was snapped up, probably by arrangement, by the Spanish ambassador and joined the enormous shipment going back to Madrid. The *St. George* was not so well-known, but it would have appealed enormously to Bass—as it had done to Charles—both for the genius of its brushwork and for its poignant subject matter. Even though he held it in his hands for only a very short time, and even then, on behalf of a number of other people, he must have felt reluctant to part with this beauty.

But by necessity a deal was done, and very quickly. Once again Raphael's little painting was carefully packed up for another journey, one which this time would take it beyond England's shores for the next stage of its adventures.

5.

RAPHAEL'S PAINTING WAS TO find its way across the Channel and into a magnificent house in Paris, a kind of private
museum that sat at the center of France's exclusive fine-art world.
The house belonged to a man of immense wealth and ambition
and a great deal of lust, less for the flesh than for important paintings and the power they conferred. Pierre Crozat was a discerning
and respected cultural connoisseur who presided over the power
games of France's art circles. He was the third-richest man in the
country, but he was also the son of a commoner, and in the France
of the early eighteenth century, this fact constituted a distinct drag
on his social advancement. Crozat had worked all his adult life
to conceal humble origins. He had built a lavish Parisian home
and filled it with spectacular artworks. He had cultivated a crowd
of aristocratic and intellectual friends and a convincing air of lei-
sured wealth. He had even published a history of art collections,
the *Recueil Crozat*, in which he classed himself, to some degree justi-
fiably, alongside the monarchs of Europe. All the trappings of the
nobility were his. But Crozat was running away from something
else too. His all-enveloping cloak of cultural sophistication was designed also to disguise the disgrace of a half-buried scandal that
had branded him a thief.

The story of how Pierre Crozat, the son of a provincial trades-
man, came to own the superb Raphael *St. George*, property of kings,
dukes, and earls, is the story of one man's extraordinary journey to

satisfy his ambition and greed for power. It is all the more astonishing that he achieved it in eighteenth-century France, in a society that traditionally divided humanity into three inflexible classes: kings, noblemen, and peasants.

But the Raphael *St. George* did not tumble straight into Crozat's eagerly outstretched hands after the Commonwealth Sale. For a few years it lay low, first in the possession of Charles d'Escoubleau, the marquis of Sourdis, and then in the home of a goldsmith and banker, Laurent Le Tessier de Montarsy. For a short time it hung in the long gallery of de Montarsy's home near the Louvre, nestled among other paintings by the old masters. When de Montarsy's collection was sold in 1712, the bulk of it was bought by Louis XIV to add to the royal collection. Crozat, with his extensive networks of informers, had heard early whispers of the sale and hurried to the house for a viewing. What he saw, as he stood before the Raphael *St. George*, was an exquisitely beautiful masterpiece by the acknowledged genius of the Renaissance. Here was a representation of the triumph of strength of will over adversity. As a historical narrative it appealed instantly to Crozat's image of himself as a noble man winning his own battles against ignorance and malice.

But, of course, by now the painting was also much more than that. It had acquired a patina of ownership so rich that it was irresistible to this aspiring aristocrat. Crozat had an extravagant passion for objects with royal or noble pedigrees. He recognized in the *St. George* not only a magnetic beauty and historical significance but also great value. A familiar sensation of overpowering desire came over him. He was determined to add this glittering prize to his name.

It is possible that Crozat already knew the painting before he saw it. He was a dominant figure in the fine-art market and a regular visitor in the homes of other collectors, viewing, assessing, and frequently buying. He was also a shrewd financial operator who kept a large part of his funds liquid. When something came up that he desired for himself, he could hand over payment in cash and remove it the same day.

This time he made an offer for the *St. George* before the king's agents could get near it. The painting, wrapped once more against the elements, made the short journey from the cul-de-sac St.-Thomas-du-Louvre to Crozat's grand palace in the Rue de Richelieu. Hung in his intimate Cabinet Crozat, it was to attract admirers from all over the country and beyond, members of the royal family, aristocrats and connoisseurs, and all the leading collectors and artists of early eighteenth-century Paris. This was precisely the return Crozat had envisaged from his investment. The painting had quickly become a crucial part of the fragile façade of superiority and nobility with which he liked to disguise his less-than-fragrant past.

At the time he laid his hands on the Raphael, Crozat was massively wealthy. Only the king and his own older brother were richer. He was single, forty-seven years old, and already in the grips of a lifelong obsession with art collecting. But he was unusual. In early eighteenth-century France, the typical art collector was either a member of the royal family or a wealthy aristocrat. Occasionally, one might find a powerful government minister who had enriched himself sufficiently to acquire airs and graces and material possessions on an aristocratic scale. But Crozat belonged to none of these categories. Yet he owned the finest art collection in France after that of the royal family.

Crozat was an anomaly. He was descended from a lowly trading family from the provincial town of Albi, but when he died in 1740 he left, in his palatial Parisian home, collections of art on the scale of a prince. He had twelve paintings by Titian, eight by Correggio, ten by Veronese, works by Rembrandt, Michelangelo, Van Dyck, Holbein, Rubens, Tintoretto, and Poussin, as well as the now famous Raphael masterpiece. In all, he owned more than five hundred old master oil paintings, of which three hundred were very fine and a hundred were considered exceptional. On top of that he owned some nineteen thousand drawings, four hundred sculptures including works by Michelangelo and Bernini, fourteen hundred engraved gems, forty-seven diamond rings, and a collection of curiosities that included exotic shells, rhinoceros horns, and rare stuffed animals as well as two Egyptian mummies, which he kept in his boudoir.

What kind of man, living by himself, would keep Egyptian mummies in his boudoir? My hunt for clues about Pierre Crozat began frustratingly slowly. The British Library had precious little about him even though, as I now know, he was a very important collector. Even the wonderful London Library, staffed with irrepressibly imaginative librarians and groaning with volumes of splendid obscurity, threw up few crumbs for me to chew on. At the French libraries in London I met with polite blanks from the expensively dressed staff. Then I came across a reference to Cordelia Hattori, who had written a thesis on Pierre Crozat at the Sorbonne in the 1980s. Where could I get a copy? The British Library turned me away saying they no longer had the funds to do international interlibrary loans. My local library said that they could arrange it, but that it would take a year. I searched for her on the Internet. I contacted likely sources in Japan, but all to no avail. There was honestly no choice. As I booked my ticket to Paris, I began to suspect that the writing of this book had become a sort of private sin of mine. Following the trail of the Raphael *St. George* was turning into a quest far more thrilling and far more fun than I had imagined it perhaps should.

I went straight from the Gare du Nord to the Sorbonne, where I found the PhD thesis reading room. It turned out to be no more than an empty corridor opening directly onto the street and furnished with a couple of tables and a few chairs. Reference books sat untouched on shelves. A thin man was reading a musical score so intently he didn't notice me stumble in dragging my heavy bag. Eventually I found a member of the staff in a nearby room, and ten minutes later I held the thesis in my hands and was plunging into the world of Pierre Crozat, my French dictionary at my elbow. I am indebted to Hattori and her excellent thesis for much of the material on Crozat in this chapter.

A portrait survives from around the time he bought the Raphael *St. George*. It shows a proud figure of a man, corpulent and richly dressed. He sits on a sofa of scarlet silk with his long, tapering aesthete's fingers clutching at the gold braid of his coat. Arched eyebrows soar over a pair of deeply hooded eyes, and his boiled-plum lips are pressed together in a tight little pout, no doubt considered becoming at the time. Pierre liked to dress in the finest and most expensive clothes. When he died, in his house vast wardrobes were discovered filled with silk, satin, and embroidered garments, mountains of voluminously curled wigs, and twelve pairs of slippers. His companion, a small, elegant dog, was found curled up beside his bed in a basket lined with vermilion silk.

Liberal doses of ambition must have swum in the Crozat blood, because Pierre's older brother, Antoine, had already become a brilliant financier and was known as the richest man in France outside the royal family. Along with a string of châteaux outside Paris and a house in the Place Victoire, Antoine owned the two houses in Place Vendôme which have since been turned into the Ritz Hotel. Given his astonishing wealth, estimated at twenty million livres (something like one hundred twenty million pounds today), Antoine was known as Crozat le Riche, while Pierre was nicknamed Crozat le Pauvre, in spite of his fortune of at least eight million livres (some forty-two million pounds today), his huge Paris residence in Rue de Richelieu, and his château in vast landscaped grounds at Montmorency, north of Paris.

The rise of the Crozat family was one of the most spectacular examples of ambitious French bourgeois families clambering up the eighteenth-century social scale. First they achieved great riches. Next they began to acquire titles, along with land. And finally, through a string of strategic marriages, they achieved what they had yearned for: recognition as members of the aristocratic nobility.

The process had begun some time before the two brothers were even born, when their father, also named Antoine, had left his home in Albi. He moved to Toulouse as a young man and married the daughter of a powerful Toulousain lawyer. With his new wife came a large residence in the center of Toulouse, the grand Hôtel du Silence, right next to the Gothic Augustin church and monastery buildings. It was here that Pierre was born in 1665, the fifth of six children.

Pierre arrived in the world just as his father's considerable social and financial aspirations were beginning to bear fruit. After years of buying and selling property and using the surplus to buy government posts, the elder Crozat maneuvred himself into a position of local influence. Like many socially aspiring commoners of the period, he dressed in gaudy silks, sported a sword, invented a genealogy, and purchased lands with accompanying titles from impoverished noblemen. In 1653 he became seigneur de Barthecave after buying the property of a local minor aristocrat brought low by debts. So ruthless was his social ascent that he was charged with the offense of usurping the nobility and exploiting privileges and occupations formerly reserved for the aristocracy. None of this slowed him down, however, and a few years later, he was busy inventing a suitably aristocratic coat of arms for the family with silver chevrons and three silver stars. Soon he had bought the Hôtel du

Silence from his in-laws and had a clutch of local civic positions to his name. Then in 1682, he was elected chief officer of the stock market. This was the crowning glory of his career, for it was well known that the incumbent was chosen from among the richest and most powerful Toulousains.

Antoine senior had become a fiercely ambitious petit bourgeois. His rapidly acquired wealth had brought with it a yearning for the social status to match, and this he passed on to his two younger sons. But when Antoine and Pierre set off for Paris, no one could possibly have guessed how far up the social scale they would leap. Both would ruthlessly exploit a contemporary culture that allowed wealthy men to gather about them the rich raiments of the nobility.

When Pierre Crozat was seventeen years old, his father gave him the large sum of twenty thousand livres and fixed him up with his first job as tax collector for the Toulouse diocese of St. Papoul. It was a highly remunerative sinecure—the first of many—which he held for more than twenty years.

Within a couple of years, Pierre had bought his way into a job in Paris as an assistant to Pierre-Louis Reich de Pennautier, a brilliant financier, also from Toulouse. Pennautier had himself bought a senior post in the bureaucracy, as controller of the taxes of the entire clergy and treasurer of the bourse of the states of Languedoc. He was wealthy, powerful, and close to the court. Crucially, he was also one of the cronies of Jean-Baptiste Colbert, Louis XIV's administrator and finance minister.

Pierre moved on through the bureaucracy, becoming a financier, a much-desired role that brought with it not only security of tenure and no taxation but also the opportunity for huge profits. The salaries of these bureaucrats were relatively unimportant. It was the payments made by the public for every act of justice or administration carried out for them that made the positions valuable. Crozat's position was one of the most powerful and lucrative positions available. The financiers were agents of tax collection who staked everything on making a fortune from the antiquated system of revenue collection. Such was the scale of embezzlement at all levels that the treasury saw only a trickle of the revenue due to the king.

With Pennautier as his mentor, Pierre learned the intricate ways of extracting personal gain from the tax system. He moved in the circle of powerful dignitaries and came into regular contact with members of the court of Louis XIV. Pierre was enthralled by the grandeur of aristocratic life. But of course, no aspiring aristocrat could live grandly without very serious amounts of money, and this necessity was what Pierre addressed first.

As a guide to self-enrichment there could have been no better example than his brother, Antoine. A few years before Pierre left Toulouse, Antoine had moved to Paris and joined the bureaucracy as a financier. Antoine possessed an almost Midas-like talent for making money, and he had rapidly built up sufficient wealth as a tax collector to begin exploiting foreign trade. He began to reap stupendous profits in various speculative ventures, particularly military supplies and overseas trade. As the principal director of numerous trading companies, Antoine became master of almost all French maritime traffic. In 1712 he was granted a personal monopoly over trade with the Louisiana colony, which earned him one hundred to three hundred percent profit on the contents of every ship that bobbed on the waters between France and Louisiana, and another one hundred to two hundred percent on the goods it brought back. His approach neither encouraged long-term growth nor attracted settlers. Eventually the colony was suffocated. Had Antoine Crozat been less greedy for profit, the French might have remained in Louisiana and Americans today would probably be reading this in French.

Antoine's vast fortune was larger than those of Richelieu or Colbert, and with it he set the tone for the Crozat family in terms of advertising their wealth. In 1702 he built the biggest house in the new Place des Victoires, the charming square at the heart of the financiers' quarter of Paris, constructed around an oval centered on a statue of Louis XIV. Two years later, Antoine built one of the first houses in Place Vendôme, number seventeen, following this with a further house, number nineteen, in the corner. This he loaned to the impoverished young comte d'Évreux, a man soon to be pulled tighter into Antoine's net through marriage to his daughter.

This kind of social inversion was indicative of the rapid and unsettling social changes going on in France. Within the old, medieval hierarchy of king, nobleman, and peasant, an entirely new class had appeared. This was the urban bourgeoisie, which made its living from industry and commerce. In terms of power and financial muscle, these ambitious men, the town traders and professionals, were matching and often overtaking the members of the nobility. The landed gentry, who lived exclusively off the fixed incomes from their estates, were being hit hard by rising prices in the new monetary economy. Many nobles had become dependent on the favors and pensions of the king, and this dependency required frequent attendance at the court at Versailles, sometimes even full-time residency there. In their absence, the new opportunities for business, created in the wave of reforms introduced by Colbert, were being scooped up by the emerging bourgeois elite.

Colbert had introduced a kind of industrial revolution. Shipbuilding was developed; the army was modernized and expanded. Mines, foundries, mills, and refineries grew up and thrived, canals were built, and the wool trade flourished. France went to work in earnest, and the ambitious bourgeois financiers, lending and pocketing slices of funds here and there, made unimagined profits.

But any pleasure the financiers allowed themselves in amassing such great wealth was quickly stifled by the social derision that came with it. Naturally, the bourgeoisie and its quick profits were regarded with contempt by the members of society's uppermost echelons. And working on their side was the Catholic Church, which endeavored to propagate the view that acquired riches were neither legitimate nor ordained by God.

The French aristocratic ideal was resolutely antimaterialistic and antibourgeois. As their incomes dwindled, France's titled aristocrats clung all the more tenaciously to their cultivated lifestyles. Divided between their massive châteaux and the court at Versailles, their lives were defined by a scrupulous display of leisure, through occupations strictly without practical or commercial function. Aesthetic activities such as music and poetry or letter writing, sketching, and artful conversation became an important part of demonstrating a life without the low material concerns of the bourgeoisie.

Having made his enormous wealth, Antoine Crozat of course longed to cross the gulf between the classes. This meant cultivating an aristocratic lifestyle, displaying behavior that unquestionably demonstrated nonproductive leisure. The trend was widespread, as recorded in an official report on trade from 1701: "We know that the great contempt for trade and traders which reigns in France has for many years prompted them to retire from it as soon as they have gained sufficient wealth to assume a social position in which they enjoy more pleasure and approbation, greater eminence and distinction."

Just as Antoine was building his elaborate town houses, luring the comte d'Évreux into his debt and starting to cultivate an appropriately leisured lifestyle, Pierre was beginning to acquire wealth on the kind of scale that would allow him to do the same. But there was a difference. While Antoine carefully hid his massive personal gains beneath the cloak of service to the state, Pierre Crozat made the mistake of allowing himself to be seen stealing.

A few years earlier, Cardinal Mazarin and other ministers had set a pattern in the discreet but systematic fleecing of the crown's financial resources. Richelieu became one of the wealthiest men in Europe while serving the king, and Mazarin acquired a fortune without precedent in the history of the French monarchy.

There were many schemes by which money could be made, and it was common for the minister's family and cronies to benefit too. Colbert was not clean either. He had a reputation for being unable to distinguish between his own private purse and that of the king. His successor, Nicolas Desmaretz, who also happened to be his nephew, ran a scheme for reminting the nation's money in which the gold and silver content of coins was reduced. Desmaretz quietly pocketed the difference. Of moral scruples, these men had none.

The venality was so widespread, it is not surprising that Pierre too devised some underhand money-making schemes for himself. But for some reason, perhaps sheer hubris, he failed to disguise his vast embezzlement.

As right-hand man to Pennautier, Pierre had been considered his certain successor. But in 1708, he was suddenly expelled from the treasury and removed from the succession. Pierre had been responsible for the collection of taxes from the clergy, and he had been caught lining his own pockets with the takings. He had been seen dabbling his fingers in the swap between silver bars and paper money. On top of that he had been caught using tax receipts for his own private gain and lending clergy money to third parties as if it were his own. The scandal spiraled and official complaints were made. Letters from members of the clergy made it clear that they no longer trusted him. The controller general of finances, in a letter to the intendant of Languedoc, referred to Pierre as having pocketed an illicit fortune of three million livres during his tenure under Pennautier. This was probably only a tiny fraction of the true figure.

The number of complaints and their gravity rose until Pierre was in danger of being made a scapegoat. It was probably only the financial clout of his brother that allowed him to escape trial and imprisonment. Antoine was well plugged in to Colbert's network of cronies and highly important to the crown in terms of loans. His carefully targeted inducements helped the most aggrieved members of the community to forget about his brother's disgrace. Nevertheless, a shameful shadow still hung over Pierre in the world of finance.

It was fortunate for Pierre that by the time of the embezzlement scandal and his expulsion from the treasury, he had already built his palatial house, filled it with art, and established himself as an authority at the center of a growing circle of connoisseurs.

As a would-be aristocrat, Pierre naturally required a grand Parisian residence. He needed a luxurious forum in which to receive visitors and display his aristocratic manners and deportment, his sophisticated conversation, and—most tangibly—his art collection. The residence that Pierre built for himself in the Rue de Richelieu embodied the height of bourgeois ambition. In 1703 he had purchased eight blocks, a quarter of a kilometer in length and as deep again, at the northern end of the street. Pierre's highly attuned social antennae ensured that his home was comfortingly close to Mazarin's palace and not far from the Palais Royale, the home of the duc d'Orleans, the king's nephew and the future regent. Pierre's land extended over some nine thousand square meters, a plot that, it cannot have escaped his greedy eye, was roughly the same size as that of the Palais Royale.

On it he built a luxurious and ostentatious *hôtel*—the contemporary term for a large town house. It was described by some as the finest in Paris. His architect was Jean-Sylvain Cartaud, who had precisely the pedigree to appeal to someone of Pierre's background. He had already worked for the duc d'Orléans and the duc de Berry. What was more, his brother-in-law was the curator of the king's paintings.

Cartaud designed a Roman palazzo arranged around a small interior court. The visitor arrived from the street into a large courtyard, facing the house. Stables were to the left and a low wing was built along the right side of the courtyard to house the kitchens and offices. The main façade of the house was designed in the Italian classical tradition, bristling with pilasters. The Crozat coat of arms, created only a few years earlier by Pierre's father, smiled down on the visitor, from its niche above a pair of huge double doors.

A year ago, during my thesis-reading trip to Paris, I wandered onto Crozat territory searching for a hint or a smell of the thieving art collector. I had booked myself into a small hotel on Rue de Richelieu, and I set off on my first evening, imagining myself in the Paris of Pierre Crozat. I was delighted to be on the trail, and as I paced down the Rue de Richelieu, I tried to figure out which of the façades ahead of me was going to turn out to be his residence. The problem is, once you are on an investigative trail, it usually lengthens, and you find that the gods have put you down, with a certain arbitrary glee, in the wrong place. The Hôtel Crozat, I soon discovered, is gone. I was hugely disappointed.

His house and garden, the courtyard and the stables were all demolished long ago, replaced by a grid of streets lined with handsome, late-eighteenth-century buildings. These are now occupied by the rather mundane offices of insurance companies and travel agencies, by restaurants and hotels. I walked into a Lyonnais restaurant that sits on the site of Crozat's old stables. Luckily I was early, because the place filled up very quickly, bustling with local families, elderly couples, and at least one evidently illicit tryst. My spirits rose and my tastebuds rejoiced as wave after wave of fatty, salty pork arrived, tricked up in various guises.

Fueled by a glass or two of wine, I went back out onto the street. Where Pierre's house once stood is now the Opéra Comique and its large courtyard. Kids in sneakers played football on the paved space in front of the entrance steps, and teenagers stood around in little knots, chatting and winding their long scarves around their necks against the chill of autumn. The wind whistled up and down the canyons created by the surrounding streets. Perhaps the grid mimics the neat rows of limes, walnuts, and birches planted in Crozat's garden, positioned to create long cool paths for summer promenades in the shade. Here beautifully dressed ladies and gentlemen would have sauntered up and down the parterres, listening to the birds and the gentle plashing of water in the fountains, as they discussed the intrigues of the day and indulged in cultural one-upmanship.

As you wander up and down these streets, crisscrossing back and forth from the Rue de Richelieu to the Rue de Graumont and beyond, it becomes clear just how large Crozat's Paris residence must have been. I returned again and again in my head to an imaginary eighteenth-century *hôtel*, whose functional topography was acquiring detail with every new, fancied visit.

I imagined entering the house and walking through a series of increasingly impressive rooms leading, in a crescendo of ornamentation, to the long gallery built at the back across the entire width of the house. The gallery was majestic in scale and prospect with a series of French windows opening out onto the huge formal gardens. The gardens were designed according to the plans of "a little Roman palace." Crozat had extensive lawns and flower beds built up to form several different levels, and beyond these he had a stone gate with pillars simulating a triumphal arch, tree-lined paths, a covered walk, and an orangery. From this last an underground passage joined the garden to the market garden just outside the city walls. Here he had his *potager* and gardener's house, with vegetables, fruit trees, and all the other culinary requirements of a household aspiring to join the nobility.

In 1704, word of a sumptuous house being built in the Rue de Richelieu reached Versailles. Pierre was gratified to discover that the king immediately dispatched an envoy to the head of police demanding to find out who owned the plot and what would be built there.

In essence, Pierre's house was a boastful exhibition of his wealth, sophistication, and cultured intellect. If he could not lay claim to aristocracy by birth, he was going to create an aristocracy of the eye. Inside the house, Pierre brought to bear all his passions and his power, much of it in blatant imitation of the duc d'Orléans, to show the world that he could live like an aristocrat. The fine house, decorated with taste and luxury, and filled with what was to become the finest art collection outside royal hands, was part of Pierre's plan to kick over the traces of his origins as a commoner and his dubious past. The place was all about polish.

The interiors were decorated to the height of Parisian aristocratic fashion. The ceiling of the long gallery was painted with allegories and mythical scenes of the birth of Minerva by Charles de La Fosse, the most fashionable artist of the day. De La Fosse had painted the salon d'Apollon in the grand apartments at Versailles for Louis XIV. He was the only choice for the Hôtel Crozat.

The soaring grandness of the long gallery was further embellished with a series of huge mirrors, almost four meters high, cleverly arranged to repeat indoors the arcadian spectacle of the garden. The room was so large it could accommodate twelve red leather sofas and four large tables laden with various marble busts and bronze figures. But the most important element of the room was the art. In this, his largest gallery, Crozat hung sixteen of his biggest showpiece paintings: a Titian, a Veronese, a Rembrandt, two Rubenses, three Van Dycks, one of them of the English royal family, a Tintoretto, and many more. Here Crozat pictured himself as the northern counterpart of a Roman cardinal, walking guests through his gallery of paintings, extending a smooth white hand from a scarlet sleeve to point out this or that treasure.

It was a heart-stopping display, and any visitor who left having seen the acreage of painted canvas in this room would have gone home impressed. But there was more upstairs. Here the more intimate gems were arranged for the quiet appreciation of genuine connoisseurs, dealers, and sufficiently titled visitors. And here lay Pierre's demonstrable power. As an onion peels away to its eye-watering core, so one progressed in his house through layers of value, and Pierre conferred status or revoked it by granting access to his upstairs cabinets. Whoever attained the innermost chambers glimpsed the heart of Pierre's obsessions.

Fanatical art collecting had become the driving force of Pierre's life. He understood very clearly the social value of patronizing the arts. Great ministers like Richelieu and Mazarin, who had made fortunes in the final years of Louis XIV's reign, had set a pattern in the collection of works of art that others were quick to imitate. If he had the wit and the resources, any ambitious merchant could start buying his way up the social ladder with an art collection. Mazarin, whose *hôtel* was just a few yards along the Rue de Richelieu from Pierre's, had the resources to put himself in a class above most. He had built up a collection of over five hundred paintings and had a staff employed full-time to clean, restore, and preserve them. It was Mazarin who had sent an envoy to London to sniff out the bargains at the Commonwealth Sale. And he had agents all over Europe, hunting for treasures for his collection. In spite of his reputation as a miser, Mazarin loved his paintings, and not merely for their value. The report of his deathbed farewell was probably genuine: "Goodbye, beloved pictures which I loved so dearly and which cost me so much money."

France was one of the greatest powers in Europe, Paris the unrivaled capital of European politics, culture, and fashion. In such a sophisticated society, the ability to collect, appreciate, and talk knowledgeably about art was the mark of an elevated and noble sensibility. Collecting art also satisfied, for a member of the bourgeoisie, the twin obsessions of avarice and investment. Pierre stood to gain a huge amount, not only from the active promotion of certain artists, but also from the sheer fame and prestige of his art collection.

He had begun early. As a boy in Toulouse, he had started by buying drawings. Then as a teenager, he had been asked by his father, who had been elected municipal magistrate for the second time, to select and negotiate to buy some paintings for the gallery of the Toulouse town hall. Pierre chose works by Antoine Coypel and Jean Jouvenet. He must have been buying fast during the intervening years, for he already owned thirty drawings by these two artists.

But even as early as 1692—less than ten years later—soon after he had arrived in Paris as a clerk to Pennautier, Pierre's collection was mentioned among the *"curieux de Paris,"* installed at Pennautier's house, where he lodged in Rue Coq Heron. In 1706, another connoisseur mentioned the Crozat cabinet, *"extremement garni,"* and the fact that Pierre was making regular and considerable purchases to add to it.

Unmarried and undistracted, his passions undiluted by domestic affairs, Pierre's acquisitive instincts were focused almost entirely on his art, and his life revolved around its display. His house had evolved into a kind of public museum, before such places existed, open for the invited elite and designed, beyond all else, to impress.

The innermost core of this display was to be found upstairs in his cabinet rooms. Here, in a series of chambers arranged around a small central court, were his more intimate galleries. There was the Cabinet Octogone, a top-lit octagonal chamber, decorated with sculpted plaster figures representing the arts and sciences. This was designed to imitate the sixteenth-century Tribune built by the Medicis in the Palais des Offices, also known as "the Uffizi," in Florence. Here the Medicis kept some of their most precious pieces, and Pierre too stored his treasured collection of nineteen thousand drawings in his Octogone, along with his collection of engraved gems, arranged in specially made display cases.

Pierre's engraved gems were among his most loved possessions. His friend and fellow collector P. J. Mariette noticed his obsessions: "Like a jealous and passionate lover who cannot be apart from his loved one, M Crozat seemed to believe that his *pierres gravées* would disappear if he lost sight of them. He kept them carefully in his room, displayed in two magnificent marquetry chests, decorated with bronze ornamentation."

But the absolute pick of his collection was in the Cabinet Crozat, and this is where he hung the Raphael *St. George*. Walking into this room in the 1720s must have offered a truly dazzling spectacle. The walls were covered with blue satin. You would not have seen much of it, however, because arrayed from top to bottom, packed from eye level to the distant ceiling were Pierre's most enchanting paintings. The room was awash with color, gleaming varnish, and teeming imagery.

Raphael's great work was hung among some venerable names. There were two Veroneses, three Titians, a Michelangelo, three Giorgiones, and two other Raphaels, *The Four Evangelists* and *The Cardinal*.

But among these jewels, the *St. George and the Dragon* leapt out as one of Pierre's favorites. It is easy to imagine Crozat, slightly satiated by the opulence of his grand gallery with its vast Titians and Correggios, retiring gratefully upstairs to his intimate Cabinet Crozat, finding his Raphael *St. George* and kissing it like a lover and whispering, as it were, into its ear, "You alone please me." It was easy to be smitten with this beautiful painting.

As a connoisseur, Pierre could recognize its exceptional artistic qualities. But its story and journey as an art object appealed as much to his snobbery. The painting had already acquired a provenance that overshadowed everything else in his collection.

It was typical of Pierre that he was one of the first collectors to take provenance into account in his assessment of artworks. After all, grandeur by imitation and grandeur by association were the driving forces in his life. He corresponded regularly with the second duke of Devonshire, another enthusiastic collector, asking him the whereabouts of certain paintings, particularly those that had belonged to Charles I.

Pierre himself possessed works that had been previously owned by Vasari, by Van Dyck, Mazarin, Rubens, the Medicis, and by the dukes of Mantua. But none matched the gilded trail of his *St. George*. Owning a painting by Raphael, one of the greatest of all the Renaissance old masters, which had been commissioned by an Italian duke and owned by English kings and a family of English earls, was high-class indeed. For Crozat, the prestige conferred by this history was unsurpassed.

Naturally, as a dedicated collector of art, Pierre was constantly in touch with other collectors, artists, dealers, and connoisseurs, and with his tradition of a weekly open-house salon, he became famous as the center of an artistic circle. Every Sunday afternoon assorted members of the art world could be seen arriving at the gates of the Hôtel Crozat in Rue de Richelieu. Disembarking from their carriages, they would enter the house and wander, in a gradually un-folding ritual, around the elegant ground-floor salons. Then when everyone was assembled, they would all go upstairs into the Cabi-net Crozat or into the Octogone, depending on whether they were going to study paintings or drawings. As with any ritual, whether it takes place in a temple, an arena, or a theater, the setting is part of the experience, and Crozat's magical gardens and the wonder of his large-scale showpiece paintings built up the anticipation of what was to come.

Pierre must have been delighted, one Sunday in late 1712, to unveil before this elite circle of guests his newly acquired master-work, the Raphael *St. George*, and to explain its prestigious prove-nance.

A delicious satisfaction with the material world saturates our image of Pierre Crozat. One is struck not only by the elegance and opulence of his lifestyle but also by the unconcealed relish with which he, rich, vain and self-consciously cultivated, showed it off.

The regulars at the salon Crozat were an all-star roster of ar-tistic bluebloods, a mixture of titled aristocrats, ambassadors, in-terested amateurs, connoisseurs, artists, writers, and dealers who together made up an informed, intellectual artistic community. There was the comte de Caylus, a former military man turned author, draftsman, and connoisseur, who rejoiced in the full name Anne-Claude-Philippe de Tubières-Grimoard de Pestels de Levis, Comte de Caylus. He was related to Madame de Maintenon, one of Louis XIV's mistresses, and later wrote a respected biography of Watteau. Then there was Cardinal Melchior de Polignac, a wealthy collector and a member of the Académie Française. There was Jean de Jullienne, another big collector who had a particular in-terest in Watteau, and John Smith, brother of Joseph Smith, who had been Canaletto's patron. There was Richard Boyle, the third earl of Burlington. And in the early days Roger de Piles, an influential critic and theorist, was also a regular visitor. Pierre paid him a generous annual pension of fifteen hundred livres to contribute to the general artistic erudition of the Crozat circle.

Antoine Coypel, first painter to the duc d'Orléans, was another regular guest, and his son Charles, destined for equal success, also joined the famous weekly reunions at the Hôtel Crozat. Pierre's friend Mariette, who later became an influential connoisseur, wrote of these sessions, "I owe what little knowledge I have acquired to the works of the old masters that we examined there and equally to the conversation of the noble persons who made up the company."

Pierre's *hôtel* served as a kind of international clearing house for advanced artistic ideas. Acting as a shadow academy of arts, an entire generation of critics and art historians were nurtured there. Pierre and his circle became the arbiters of taste, taking over as the recognized authority on art from the august body of the Académie.

Modeling himself as a patron on Lorenzo de' Medici, Pierre also nurtured artists in his home. As soon as his Rue de Richelieu residence was built, he invited Charles de La Fosse to come and live with him and work on decorating his interiors. De La Fosse was already a celebrated painter with a long and distinguished career. He had worked for Louis XIV, he had painted the ceilings and walls of Montague House, the London home of the duke of Montague, and he was a member of the Académie Royale. In 1706 he moved into the Hôtel Crozat with his wife and niece. Pierre did not welcome them particularly graciously, making them pay two thousand livres a year for board and lodging. For six years, Charles and his family occupied an apartment on the first floor, while he painted the ceiling of the grand gallery and worked on two other paintings. Given his tenant's pedigree as painter to the king, Pierre believed that his work would have a guaranteed value. Nothing escaped the calculating mind of this bourgeois businessman.

The Venetian painter Rosalba Carriera also lodged in Pierre's house for a year in 1720. Crozat had met her in Venice and wrote generously offering her an apartment and carriages to take her on promenades—"all for nothing, as I would have the pleasure of having you lodging with me." The *Mercure de France* announced her arrival, explaining that she had been commissioned to paint a portrait of the king. During her stay with Pierre, she wrote in her diary of an incessant stream of high-ranking visitors to the Hôtel Crozat, many of whose portraits she painted. The list reads like a who's who of the art and social aristocracy. There was the prince de Conti; the prince de Carignan; Dezallier d'Argenville; Coypel, the curator of the king's pictures; Claude Audran, the concierge de Luxembourg; Hyacinthe Rigaud, who painted the famous portrait of Louis XIV in coronation robes; Jean Ranc, painter to Philip V of Spain; Giovanni-Antonio Pellegrini, Rosalba's brother-in-law, who came to Paris to paint the ceiling of the Banque Royale; Sebastiano Ricci, who went to England to decorate the home of Lord Burlington; Françoise Boucher; Louis-Michel van Loo; and Jean Chardin. In visiting the Hôtel Crozat, these people bestowed much-desired status on Pierre. All would have been invited upstairs to see the Raphael *St. George.*

François Boucher was a regular visitor to the Hôtel Crozat in the 1730s, finding his way upstairs to the Cabinet Crozat and to the Octogone, where he spent hours studying Pierre's collections of drawings and paintings. Another distinguished guest was Pierre Le Gros, the French sculptor often compared to Bernini, who lived in Rome most of the time but regularly stayed with Pierre in Paris for extended seasons.

But his most famous lodger was the young Jean-Antoine Watteau, who moved into the Hôtel Crozat in 1712 and stayed for four years, studying Pierre's collections and copying many of the sheets belonging to him. The comte de Caylus, in his biography of Watteau, wrote that he "profited avidly and he knew no greater plea-sure than examining and copying all the works of the old masters." During his time with Pierre, Watteau met many of the members of the Crozat salon, made use of the extensive library, and painted a series of four paintings, showing the four seasons, inlaid into the paneled walls of Pierre's dining room. His *Summer* panel is now in the National Gallery in Washington.

Watteau was to become a very influential painter. As a young man, observing life in the Hôtel Crozat, he absorbed the luxuries of his surroundings and became one of the first artists to record in paint the social changes going on in France. Watteau noticed how, as the bourgeoisie clambered up the social ladder toward the nobility, they appropriated rather exaggeratedly feminine aristo-cratic ideals in their behavior. He watched all this going on around him, painting the artful sociability of his host, the pointedly lei-sured lifestyle and elevated caprices that Crozat laid on as a sign of his privileged status. It was the beginning of the new rococo style, focused on sensual pleasures. Crozat's household, with its artis-tic gatherings, its decadent parties, concerts, and other displays of ephemeral pleasure, became a model for this new style of paint-ing, a kind of forcing house for the rococo style.

For Pierre, the concepts of investment and improvement were never far from his mind, and Watteau was consciously managed and promoted within his coterie. His graceful paintings became very well known. The beau monde dressed itself *"à la Watteau,"* the salons and boudoirs of Paris were appointed *"à la Watteau,"* and young ladies and gentlemen adopted a carriage and pose *"à la Wat-teau."* He was the leading painter of the merriment and flirtation of the age. Love and charming coquetry were his themes, and in his celebrated *fêtes galantes,* even nature rejoiced and assumed an air of frolic. His sensuous paintings depict opulent arrangements of tall windows opening onto the garden, sculptures and pillars, the rustling of silks, the flutter of fans, and chamber music on the afternoon breeze. Beautiful promenaders, music makers, dancers, and flirtatious lovers inhabit the paintings together, displaying an ambiguity of status deliberately sought by Crozat and his like.

Being in Paris, on the trail of a painting and its French eighteenth-century aesthete owner, I naturally went to the Louvre. Walking around this colossal treasure house, I found fabulous portraits of grand French connoisseurs of the period, men like Crozat, whose beautiful houses were crammed with billowing profusions of statuary, paintings, wall hangings, carpets, and drawings. Most of these men seemed to spend their lives lounging on gilt and velvet chairs dressed in long silk brocade robes, their stockinged feet, encased in elegant soft leather slippers, their long, aesthete's fingers extending elegantly from silk sleeves to point out some new acquisition. But it is the careless scattering of treasures, the marble bust knocked over on the floor to make way for some other statue, the grisaille drawing creased under a porcelain vase, which combine in these portraits to give us an overpowering sense of the profusion and wealth of the era. After about a dozen, I found I could take no more.

In modeling himself on the grand aristocrats of the age, Crozat obviously needed a large country residence. So in 1709—the year of the great winter famine in France and only a year after his disgrace—he doubled the size of his already huge country estate at Montmorency, north of Paris. Here in the early 1660s, Charles Le Brun, painter to Louis XIV, had built a fanciful building and a superb garden with grottos, cascades, pools, and fountains. Pierre had kept Le Brun's colonnade and commissioned Cartaud to build a vast new château on the model of a Roman palace. It was a magnificent building, with a basement and two stories, topped with a balustrade and statues. A giant order of Corinthian pillars decorated the front façade, as on Michelangelo's Capitoline palaces.

Inside, the principal room was the Oval Salon, the Salon à l'Italienne, for which La Fosse painted the domed roof of the cupola. A chapel, built above the entrance vestibule, was elaborately decorated in the rococo style with marble and stucco by another of his resident artists, Pierre Le Gros. But the gardens were, if possible, even more magnificent, with terraces, flower plantings in the shape of stars, and swirling geometric patterns of avenues bordered with lime trees. For his networks of fountains, pools, and ornamental lakes, Crozat ordered the diversion of the source of the Sainte-Valerie River. The inhabitants of the village of Montmorency were enraged, but being mere peasants, they had no redress.

Watteau set his famous painting *Le Perspective* at Montmorency. In the foreground, beautifully costumed ladies wander and gaze, or sit and talk on the grass. Behind them, an avenue of towering trees leads to a tantalizing glimpse in the distance of a classical façade, a part of the château.

Pierre regularly journeyed to Montmorency from Paris in his Berlin carriage pulled by four black horses. Some of the seventeen members of the staff who cared for him in Paris went ahead, joining his Montmorency staff to prepare for the elaborate events planned. Pierre invited his friends, some fifty at a time, to stay at the château and enjoy concerts, plays, and recitals there. During the day, they walked along the avenues of the park, strolled under the trees, and watched the fountains cascading. In the evenings, as the huge chandeliers and wall sconces of the château were lit with masses of tall white candles, they dressed for performance and wandered around the gardens, listening to music, displaying their costumes, and indulging in wine and revelry in a setting of flamboyant beauty.

Pierre's most important concerts were held in his Paris residence, and after 1720, these concerts as well as his art salons became regular events in the city's social calendar. Pierre was deeply honored by the attendance at these events of the duc d'Orléans and by John Law, the powerful Scottish financier who had been brought in by the regent to set up a royal bank.

It is interesting to see how the two Crozat brothers—Antoine *le riche* and Pierre *le pauvre*—reached the top of the social tree in France in their own distinct ways. Antoine made it through the application of sheer financial muscle. He purchased estates and titles, becoming baron de la Faulche, marquis de Mouy and de Thiers, baron du Châtel, and propriétaire du domaine de Tugny. His wife was the daughter of a powerful banking family, and his three sons and daughter were all guided toward prestigious marriage alliances, integrating the Crozat name into the ranks of the *haute noblesse*. His first son, who became marquis du Châtel, had two daughters who both married dukes. His second son had no children but made a prestigious marriage. His third son became baron de Thiers, married the daughter of a marquis, and had three daughters who married, among them, a count, a duke, and a marquis.

Antoine reached a new social peak with his daughter, Anne-Marie, who married Henri-Louis de la Tour d'Auvergne, comte d'Évreux, cousin of the duc de Vendôme, and son of one of the grandest families in France. When this marriage was announced, Antoine could barely contain his delight. Everyone knew that it had been forced through with the brute fist of money. The comte d'Évreux's finances were in ruins. Anne-Marie brought with her a widely advertised dowry of two million livres, prompting her putative mother-in-law to give her the nickname "my little gold ingot." The young countess d'Évreux was presented to the king on April 5, 1707. Watching this ritual, Antoine must have been in agonies of joy.

But Antoine himself achieved the absolute acme of his dreams when in 1715, after offering a three-million-livre interest-free loan to the king, he was appointed treasurer to the Ordre de Saint-Esprit. This was France's most socially exclusive club. Founded in 1578, it consisted of one hundred members, each from the highest ranks of the nobility. Every member was close to the king and his family. Antoine was invested on September 28, 1715, and the honor gave him the right to wear the Cordon Bleu. His fellow members were affronted, pointing out Antoine's commoner origins. But the king's financial needs were pressing, and with the emollient value of his bank account, Antoine slipped through the net.

Immediately he booked the most fashionable portraitist of the day to paint him in the robes of the order. He sits, exuding an almost comical degree of pleasure, dressed in his pompous gold-embroidered costume, one hand holding a magnificently feathered hat, the other gripping the spangled cloth-of-gold robes. A faint smile plays on his lips as he gazes, slightly downward, at a crowd of imagined humbler folk arrayed in awe at his perfumed feet. Beneath the bloated, ill-gotten wealth and the haughty, aristocratic airs, the delicate skeleton of the commoner barely twitches.

While Antoine's entry to high society was powered by pure cash, Pierre's was—once his bureaucratic career had been scuppered—the result of a calculated gathering and exploitation of knowledge and expertise in the arts.

The key to his success was his friendship with the duc d'Orléans, to whom he was probably introduced by Antoine, provider of cash to the stretched royal coffers. The duke had a keen interest in art and had heard about Pierre's famous collection and his magnificent house. The two men had much in common. They both appreciated the lusher reaches of the Italian art world, and it was through art that Pierre became an intimate of the duke, mixing in court circles and becoming a beneficiary of royal favors.

Although he was a serious patron of the arts, the duke was also known as Philippe the Debauched, a ruler who favored the company of actresses, courtesans, and rakes. Philippe was forty-one years old when he became regent at the death of his uncle, Louis XIV. He looked much older. Excessive revelry and too many drunken evenings had taken their toll. His left arm had been smashed by a cannonball in the wars, and his eyesight had deteriorated to the extent that he had to peer so closely at his documents that his quill pen became entangled in his wig. Yet he was voraciously well read, in literature and philosophy, and gifted with a remarkable memory. (When he died in 1723, worn out by his debaucheries, a grisly story circulated that, at his postmortem, one of his Great Danes jumped up and ate his heart.)

The duke recognized in Pierre the perfect adviser for his art collection. He was knowledgeable, experienced in the ways of the art market, and extremely well connected financially with access to bankers and financial agents all over Europe. Over the years Pierre became very useful to the duke. But the duke was, of course, much more useful to Pierre.

In 1714, the duke asked Pierre to go to Rome to negotiate to buy the magnificent art collection of Queen Christina of Sweden. She had died in Rome in 1689, and having changed hands several times, her collection was now in the penurious hands of Baldassare Erba-Odescalchi, duc de Bracciano, and Cardinal Erba-Odescalchi. Both men were carrying heavy debts.

Crozat was delighted at the commission. On arrival in Rome in October 1714, he found that his reputation had preceded him. He was immediately whisked off on a tour of the city's finest private collections, being royally entertained in between. As winter tightened its grip on the city, Pierre had still not seen the collection. When he eventually set eyes on it, three months after his arrival, he was stunned by its magnificence. There were pictures by Correggio, Veronese, Titian, Guido Reni, and Bassano and a superb Raphael, the *Madonna del Passeggio*, which is now in the National Gallery of Scotland.

Crozat was also impressed with the collection of drawings. "Messrs Odescalchi," he wrote, "have a very large jumble of drawings, among which there are a hundred which I would be very happy to have and which I am hopeful they will give me." After failing to reach an agreement, Pierre set off for Naples to buy some paintings on his own account. Returning to Rome, he found still no sign of an agreement. The Odescalchis wanted more money than the duke was prepared to pay. In an attempt to force the French to raise their offer, they pretended that the emperor himself was interested in buying.

Pierre quickly confirmed that there was no such rival offer and departed in disgust. He had seen some of the finest collections in Italy and had augmented his own collection in the process. He had bought antique busts and statues, engraved gems and terra-cotta models, and masses of drawings, buying several major collections in Rome. On his way home, he stopped in Urbino and bought many of Raphael's finest drawings from the descendants of one of his pupils. He bought more drawings in Bologna and picked up a Titian in Genoa. The duc d'Antin wrote about Pierre's collecting habits: "I know his taste. I'm sure that he only buys the best and at reasonable prices."

After prolonged negotiations from Paris, an agreement was finally reached in January 1721 for the sale of Queen Christina's collection. The duc d'Orléans bought two hundred fifty-nine paintings for ninety thousand ecus and one thousand louis d'or. Pierre set off for Amsterdam with his nephew and sold diamonds on behalf of the duke to raise funds to buy the paintings. Pierre went again to Rome to supervise the packing—he was extremely fussy about this—and saw that the paintings were rolled up carefully, not too tight, and packed with maximum protection in fifteen crates. They set off by boat on September 16, 1721, along with seven more crates filled with treasures for Pierre himself, and reached Paris exactly three months later. Twenty-seven of the finest works from this purchase were hung in the salon d'Oppenord in the Palais Royal. With the addition of these paintings, the regent's collection was now the finest in France. Pierre had earned his gratitude.

Now established as the French regent's key art adviser, and the man at the center of the Paris art world, Pierre was, if anything, even more obsessed with the size, provenance, and quality of his own collection compared to its European counterparts. With the help of a network of well-paid informers, Pierre made it his business to keep track of exactly what his rival collectors owned. The three most fabulous collections of the past hundred years—those of Charles I, the dukes of Mantua, and Mazarin—had all now been dispersed, and Pierre eagerly followed the trails of the works among them which were still on the move. But by the 1720s, there were just two collections which Pierre dreamed of matching: the French royal collection, owned by his new friend the duc d'Orléans, and the collection of the duke of Devonshire in England.

Pierre's all-consuming fanaticism led him to propose, with the duc d'Orléans, a major art history project. The two men planned to put together a comprehensive history of the major collections in Europe—those of the duke himself and a handful of others. This was to be the first comprehensive history of art, a record of the most beautiful examples of paintings, drawings, and sculptures. Descriptions of each work and a short life of the artist were to be published, and the collections were to include those of the Barberini family in Rome, the duke of Parma, the king of Spain, the emperor, as well as the duc d'Orléans, and, of course, Pierre himself.

The project was announced in the *Mercure de France* in February 1721. Two years later the duke died, but Crozat refused to abandon the project. He wrote to his friend the duke of Devonshire, saying he knew it would be *"goûtze des princes, des grands, et du public"*—to the taste of princes, nobles, and the public.

Plenty of other collectors had put together similar self-aggrandizing volumes, but Pierre's, the *Recueil Crozat*, was different. None of the others included text and descriptions of the painters. Pierre personally supervised the engraving of one hundred seventy-nine paintings, of which thirty-three belonged to himself. One of these was the Raphael *St. George*. The first volume was published in 1729, the second in 1741, just after Pierre's death.

Pierre's publishing effort was all about ambition. It reflected precisely the lifelong yearning for social position that had fueled him ever since boyhood. Surely he had exceeded his father's wildest dreams of social advancement and easily matched his brother's social success.

Pierre was less active as a patron and collector toward the end of his life, when he suffered many years of illness. Months passed when he was incapable of doing anything much. His close friends, with the exception of the art connoisseur Pierre Mariette, had died. His loneliness was increased by the fear that his superb collections would not remain intact after his death.

There is a story told of a Paris collector under the Second Empire who used to dream of witnessing an auction of his collection on the last day of his life. He would have given much to know what material sacrifices his friends were prepared to make to obtain his pictures.

Pierre too felt that powerful sense of possession, a sentiment that was inseparable from the enjoyment of his art. He must have been avid to know what his friends might have paid for his paintings. But more than that, he wanted his unique collection of drawings to stay in France, intact, for the benefit of amateurs and artists. He offered them to the king for a hundred thousand livres. The offer was refused. The first minister, Cardinal Fleury, responded that *"Le roi avait deja assez de fatras sans encore en augmenter le nombre"*—The king already has enough jumble without adding to it further.

It was a major blow to Pierre, made worse by his instinct that these drawings and the rest of his fabulous collections, including the Raphael *St. George*, were soon to fly out of the hands of the Crozat family. He had collected art all his life, driven to it as if by a sickness. Now it was to be dispersed. Who would he be without the Crozat collection intact? His name, his legacy to history depended on it.

On the night of May 24, 1740, Pierre Crozat died at his home in Paris, ensconced in the palatial chambers of his great gilded shell. He was seventy-seven years old. The Raphael *St. George*, owned by kings, earls, and dukes, was hanging in the room next door to his bedroom, a symbol of the heights to which he had advanced in his trajectory from commoner to intimate of the king. He was buried in the cemetery of St.-Joseph, close to his brother and to Molière, author and mocker of social climbers. His keenly observed comedy *Le Bourgeois Gentilhomme* might have been written about the Crozat family.

Pierre Crozat's paintings and his myriad other treasures went to his nephew, Antoine's eldest son, Louis-François Crozat, marquis du Châtel, who died less than a decade later. Most of the paintings were then passed on again to the marquis's younger brother, Louis-Antoine, Baron de Thiers.

In 1750, wrapped in silk and rags and a protective wooden case, the Raphael *St. George* made a short journey across Paris to the house in Place Vendôme which was now the home of baron de Thiers. Crozat's huge collection of drawings had been sold and dispersed, enriching art collections all over Europe. His unique collection of engraved gems had been bought by the regent's son, Louis Duc d'Orléans. But the heart of his obsessions, the five hundred superb masterpieces that had brought him such tangible status, remained together in this exclusive residence, gathering admirers and envy. From time to time the collection swelled with the baron's own acquisitions. And by the time Louis XV made a visit to view them a few years later, the Crozat collection was acknowledged as the most famous and important private art collection in France.

And there the Raphael *St. George* stayed, hanging in an ornate room of what was to become the Ritz Hotel, until a new and even more greedily power-obsessed collector managed to wrangle it out of French hands and transport it to another faraway land.

6.

MOST ORDINARY PARISIANS RUMBLING in creaking carts over the cobbles of Place Vendôme on their way to the fishing quays of the Seine had no idea what lay inside that palatial house owned by the baron de Thiers. Looking up at the grand façade, lit at night with a blaze of candles, they might have glimpsed elaborate gold cornices and twinkling chandeliers. But they could never have imagined the treasures that lay within. Only members of Paris's exclusive art world knew how fabulously well stocked this house was.

Paris in the mid-eighteenth century was a world of intense playground pleasures for the aristocratic elite. Balls and masquerades at night gave way to decorous flirtation in parks during the day, when elegant lovers, dressed impeccably in contemporary silks or historical costumes, found diversions in plays, concerts, carnivals, and other amusements. The lives of these Parisians were unrepentantly attentive to fashion, in art, clothes, interior decoration, even in forms of eating and drinking. With their courtships, costumes, and dramas, they whiled away their time enjoying the nostalgic pleasures of an aristocracy in retirement.

The Crozat collection of paintings was naturally the subject of intense interest to these people. It had by now become so celebrated that collectors and connoisseurs, artists and amateurs were constantly asking to view it. Permission was granted on request, and a catalogue of the paintings, containing a room-by-room description, was prepared in 1755. Louis XV honored the baron with a visit, keen perhaps to see what exactly his closest art-collecting rival owned. Over the years, the Raphael *St. George* became the most famous star of the collection. It was written up at adoring length in Crozat's *Recueil Crozat*, which ranked it with works owned by kings and emperors all over Europe. Now in its gilded chamber in Place Vendôme, the knowledgeable and the merely curious flocked to admire it. Connoisseurs adjusted their pince-nez to study the gilded garter around St. George's leg and Raphael's superb treatment of the horse's muscular white flanks. Clusters of beautifully dressed ladies, the cream of Parisian society, twittered and fluttered their fans in front of it. It was inevitable that in time the painting came to be viewed as an important part of France's national heritage.

So when the baron de Thiers died in 1770, and his three daughters made it known that they were interested in selling the *St. George* and the rest of their famous collection, this was sensational news. As soon as the rumor was let off the lead, it raced around the salons of Paris, darting in and out of these social and intellectual gatherings. One of the first to pick up the news was Madame Geoffrin's salon. Mme. Geoffrin was a wealthy socialite who hosted a dazzling assembly of French gentlemen, all of them distinguished by birth or brains, in her rooms in Rue St.-Honoré on Monday and Wednesday evenings. Nothing flattered Mme. Geoffrin so much as her association with the intellectual and social elite. She was a skillful hostess. She cultivated the art of conversation at her weekly meetings, drawing in the philosophers and encyclopedists, steering conversations and guiding arguments so that the sinuous streams of sparkling talk would lure them back again the following week. Apart from herself, no ladies were admitted to these events, the wives, mistresses, and other hangers-on being mollified with their own *petits soupers* on Thursday evenings. But of course Mme. Geoffrin much preferred Mondays and Wednesdays, when, her decorative bust puffed out with self-importance, she welcomed dozens of bewigged gentlemen to sit around eating and drinking in her paneled rooms, admiring her paintings and sculptures, quoting poetry, and batting intellectual witticisms back and forth.

In addition to the highbrow philosophical debates, there was always talk of art. At times the place must have resembled a dealers' den. Mme. Geoffrin was always on the lookout for prospective art purchases for her grandest and most heavily titled friends, and her salon members were always eager to exchange the latest gossip about who was selling or buying what, and for how much.

One of the members of Mme. Geoffrin's elite salon was Denis Diderot, the author of the encyclopedia and also an experienced art critic. Diderot was an unquenchable talker when he became fired up, spewing out ideas and arguments and engaging in ardent tirades as he slurped his liquor and gobbled his dinner. Diderot was present at the Rue St.-Honoré when early rumors of the Crozat sale reached Mme. Geoffrin's salon. One can imagine the smoky gathering of gentlemen, their fingers fluttering at their throats as the news danced around the room. Diderot was aghast. On hearing the news, as he later put it in a letter, he "exploded like a volcano." Diderot had good reason to explode, but it was not with fury. He exploded into action, because as well as being an encyclopedist and art critic, he had another, rather grand job on the side. He was an art scout for Catherine the Great, empress of Russia.

Diderot was a member of a huge and handsomely paid network of eyes and ears spread out across Europe whose job it was to notify her first of potential sales of fine art. No important art collector died without Catherine's being immediately informed. Naturally, Diderot rushed from the Rue St.-Honoré to send word to his patron. To his great satisfaction, she was shaping up into one of the greediest buyers of art in all of Europe.

∽

Eight years earlier, just before dawn on June 28, 1762, Catherine had been summoned by Aleksei Orlov, the scar-faced brother of her current lover and one of the principal backers in her bid for the throne. She was already estranged from her husband, Emperor Peter III, and was staying in the small palace of Mon Plaisir, some thirty kilometers outside St. Petersburg. Catherine had dressed quickly to be told that everything was prepared for her to be proclaimed empress. As her carriage hurtled toward the imperial capital, the preparations were finalized. By the time she had reached the Kazan Cathedral, several regiments of Russian troops had assembled there, and she was received as sovereign by the archbishop of Novogrod. Some soldiers kissed her hand. Others wept with joy. The first phase of the coup had proceeded without a hitch. One week later, a crumpled note was delivered to Empress Catherine stating that the emperor had perished abruptly. She swiftly issued an announcement that he had died of hemorrhoidal colic. The Orlov brothers had judged that she wished her husband eliminated.

Catherine the Great was the supreme potentate of the East, the eighteenth century's most omnivorous ruler, with sexual, territorial, and cultural appetites that were nothing short of gluttonous. She was larger than life, in physical stature, animal energy, and determination, and has few equals in the annals of grasping ambition. Having seized the Russian throne through a palace putsch and incited the imperial guards to murder her husband, she governed with the cooperation of a long list of official lovers, from Grigory Orlov and Grigory Potemkin to Platon Zubov, who was thirty-eight years her junior. Her sexual lusts were famous throughout Russia, and for years after her death, people were willing to believe the rumor that she had died after the failure of a machine called "Catherine's Winch" while trying to make love to a horse.

Catherine was the daughter of a titled major general in the Prussian army, but it was through her mother's connections, as aunt to Peter, heir to the Russian throne, that Catherine gained her access to power. When she was a child, a palm reader had claimed he saw three crowns in her palm, which she immediately interpreted as a sign that she was to marry her cousin, Peter. "Child that I was," she wrote in her memoirs, "the title of queen delighted me. From then on my companions teased me about him and little by little I became used to thinking of myself as destined for him."

She first met Peter when she was ten. She quickly established a friendship and within four years had extracted from him a promise of marriage. A year later, in 1744, the fifteen-year-old Catherine married the heir to the Russian throne.

Married life in the Russian imperial family was far from straightforward. She spent the next seventeen years at the court of the domineering Empress Elizabeth, her mother-in-law. She maintained careful relations with her but largely avoided her husband, Grand Duke Peter, who had turned out to be both sickly and mentally retarded. In some ways his incapacity suited Catherine perfectly. She simply got on with the business of grooming herself to rule. She learned Russian, studied Russian history, and demonstrated a great devotion to the Russian Orthodox Church.

Her moment came in 1762, a year after the Empress Elizabeth's death, when she carried out the coup d'état and ascended the throne. As she grew into her role of absolute ruler, the Empress Catherine found it increasingly difficult to curb her gargantuan cravings. She already governed the world's largest country. But under her rule, Russia's remorseless territorial expansion continued. She took over a large part of Sweden and Finland as well as chunks of Poland and Lithuania. She invaded the Ottomans' Black Sea provinces and Crimea and moved against Persia and Central Asia. She extended her boundaries right across Siberia to the Pacific, where she began to size up Alaska, establishing a permanent settlement there in 1784.

In cultural terms, Catherine's appetites were equally rapacious. At her accession to the throne, she had inherited the beautiful baroque Winter Palace, built by the Empress Elizabeth, as grand and elegant as any royal palace in Europe but bigger than them all. It had over a thousand rooms, nearly two thousand windows, hundreds of stairs and many miles of corridors. But it had scant furnishings and very few paintings. The place was a desert for the visual arts. Peter the Great had left a handful of works depicting himself winning battles; Elizabeth had acquired a clutch of rather dull German, Dutch, and Flemish pictures. The imperial art collection ranked below even that of a minor Italian duke.

Catherine was fully aware that the most powerful nations were now judged not only by the size of their armies and navies and the grandeur of their palaces, but by the value, glamour, and fame of their art collections. Naturally she decided to improve on her collection. At first she began buying artworks to furnish her bare palace, but addiction quickly took hold, and she began to buy on an imperial scale.

In 1770, when rumors emerged of the possible sale of the Raphael *St. George* and the rest of the Crozat collection, Catherine had already dabbled her toe in the world of international art buying. She had achieved gratifying results. Her first acquisition had been in 1764 when she bought a collection of old master paintings put together by the Berlin dealer Johann Gotzkowski. The collection included three Rembrandts, a Frans Hals, and some fine Dutch works. It had been intended for Frederick the Great of Prussia, the most cultured monarch of his age. Frederick had commissioned Gotzkowski to gather the treasures together in the first place, but distracted by the Seven Years War with Austria, he had been forced to turn it down. This was an early triumph for Catherine. She had beaten the emperor to a fine collection of paintings. Her appetite was whetted for more.

Through her ambassador in France, Prince Dmitry Golitsyn, Catherine next turned her attentions to Paris, the center of the world art market. She was fortunate in Golitsyn, for he put her in touch with the man who was to become her most productive art scout, Denis Diderot. In 1766, Golitsyn alerted Catherine to the fact that Diderot's financial affairs were in such a state that he was being forced to offer his library for sale. He was asking fifteen thousand livres. This was a huge sum of money. A Paris working man earned no more than five hundred livres a year, a provincial lawyer something between two and three thousand. Catherine immediately offered Diderot sixteen thousand livres, and on the condition that the books remain in Diderot's home in Paris. She also wished him to act as her librarian during his lifetime, with a salary of a thousand livres a year, to be paid for fifty years in advance. In other words, she was offering him a lump sum of sixty-six thousand livres in return for the promise of his library after his death. Diderot was overcome with gratitude. "Great Princess," he wrote, "I bow down at your feet; I stretch my arms towards you but my mind has contracted, my brain is confused, my ideas jumbled, I am as emotional as a child, and the true expression of the feeling with which I am filled dies on my lips.... Oh, Catherine! Remain sure that you rule as powerfully in Paris as you do in St. Petersburg."

Diderot was an excellent choice of counselor and friend for Catherine. He was a respected member of the intellectual elite, which had long fascinated the empress. He was well connected in the art world, and he had impeccable taste. Diderot was so bowled over with the generosity of his grand Russian patron that he readily agreed to comb France for the finest paintings money could buy.

One of Diderot's first successes on Catherine's behalf was the purchase of the Gaignat collection. When Louis Jean Gaignat, who had been Louis XV's secretary, died in 1768, Diderot immediately sent word to Catherine, informing her that Gaignat "had collected some wonderful works of literature almost without knowing how to read, and some wonderful works of art without being able to see any more in them than a blind man." Others had clearly made the same observation: there was unexpectedly fierce competition at the sale. In the event, Diderot only managed to acquire three canvases by Gerard Dou and one each by Murillo and van Loo.

A year later, having just won a war against the Turks, Catherine won an equally important victory in Dresden by acquiring for one hundred eighty thousand Dutch guilders the hotly contested collection of the recently deceased Count Heinrich von Bruhl. A nobleman and minister of foreign affairs to Augustus III of Saxony, von Bruhl had managed to build his own private art collection in parallel with that of the king. Thanks to the numerous etchings of works in the collection, von Bruhl's hoard was well-known throughout Europe, and Catherine was delighted when it arrived, by boat, from Hamburg. There were over six hundred paintings—four Rembrandts, five Rubenses, some Dutch masters, and a range of contemporary works by Watteau and Bellotto. There were also more than a thousand drawings carefully mounted in fourteen leather-bound volumes. Catherine was not particularly interested in drawings, but if they had to be part of the package, she was content to buy them along with the rest.

As her taste for artistic plunder and prestige grew, she began openly to wage her art-buying campaigns as a form of diplomatic warfare against the other monarchs of Europe and their richest subjects. Competition to acquire great works of art in Catherine's day was ferocious. Many of the finest treasures had already been bought with the assumption of permanence. But Catherine, with her often spiteful motivations, her immense determination, and her apparently unlimited resources, hovered over Europe like a great eagle, ready to swoop down and snatch up any prize that became available.

Catherine's most sensational coup, which was to be her most important art purchase of all, was her acquisition of the Crozat collection in 1772. She was well aware that within it lay the treasured Raphael *St. George*, a prize whose fame far exceeded its gemlike size.

As soon as Diderot had obtained the empress's permission to go ahead with the purchase, he summoned his elderly friend François Tronchin, a banker, collector, and art connoisseur, who cut short a holiday to rush back to Paris and examine the collection. Working at great speed, Tronchin drew up a catalogue, rejecting one hundred fifty-eight paintings that he considered to be of questionable merit and unworthy of the empress. That left roughly five hundred great works of art. But the purchase was by no means straightforward. As soon as Diderot's intentions began to leak out, the disposal of this incomparable collection became a public issue and a question of national policy.

Would the French government allow such a collection, so famous throughout Europe and an adornment to French culture and prestige, to leave France? Of course, the thought that the French government wanted to keep the collection only fueled Catherine's desires to have it for herself. Some exquisitely delicate diplomacy would be required, and the Russian empress recruited the most silver-tongued sophisticates to her side.

Within a few months, half the leading writers, artists, and intellectuals of the French Enlightenment, moved by respect for Diderot and admiration for his magnificent benefactress, became involved in what amounted to a conspiracy of the intellectual elite on behalf of Catherine. As one observer noted, M. de Marigny, the director of fine arts, had to stand by and see these treasures go abroad, for want of the funds necessary to buy them on the king's behalf.

After prolonged negotiations, the coup was finally completed in January 1772, when Catherine paid four hundred sixty thousand livres for some five hundred superb paintings. As well as the star Raphael *St. George*, there was Giorgione's superb painting *Judith* (thought at the time to be by Raphael), as well as eight Rembrandts, six Van Dycks, and works by Rubens and Veronese. It was a distillation of the best from an astonishingly good collection.

Diderot was delighted and described the French outcry in a letter to Catherine's French art adviser in St. Petersburg, Etienne-Maurice Falconet: "I arouse the most genuine public hatred, and do you know why? Because I am sending you paintings. Art lovers cry out, artists cry out, the rich cry out ... the empress plans to acquire the Thiers [Crozat] collection in the midst of a ruinous war. That is what humiliates and embarrasses them."

Russia was not only in the midst of a war but also deeply involved in precarious diplomatic negotiations when Catherine signed the contract of sale. She was bartering a deal with Austria and Prussia over the partition of Poland in the west, while still fighting the Turks in the south. "The collectors, the artists and the rich are all up in arms," Diderot wrote. "I am taking absolutely no notice ... so much the worse for France, if we must sell our pictures in time of peace, whereas Catherine can buy them in the middle of a war. Science, art, taste and wisdom are traveling northward and barbarism and all it brings in its train, is coming south." It was a victory for Catherine's broadest aims for Russia. It was also a major triumph for her personal glory.

Just one highly desirable picture had escaped her clutches. It was Van Dyck's portrait of Charles I. This superb canvas had been procured separately by Madame du Barry, who maintained that the du Barry family was descended from the Stuarts. To mollify his patron, Diderot pointed out that Catherine had acquired the collection for less than half its value—a view born out by the fact that in the same year, Catherine paid thirty thousand livres for two van Loos and a few months after that acquired the considerably less impressive collection of the duc de Choiseul—a hundred and fifty pictures—for four hundred forty thousand livres.

As the scandal of the Crozat sale raged around the streets of Paris, Raphael's *St. George* was packed, along with the other paintings, into one of seventeen enormous wooden crates, under the expert supervision of Tronchin. Then came what seemed to Catherine interminable delays. First the paintings sat in a warehouse on the edge of the Seine for three months, "suspended between the sky and the water," according to Tronchin, waiting for the ship's owner to complete his customs details. Then the boat that was to have taken them from Rouen set off without them. Further delays ensued while the insurance paid on the first ship was transferred to a new vessel, the *Hirondelle*.

Diderot remained in a state of nervous tension through these long months. Only a year earlier, a collection of paintings purchased from the Braankamp collection in Amsterdam, traveling by sea to St. Petersburg, had been lost during a storm when the captain joined his crew at prayers and the ship ran aground. Works by Rembrandt and many other old masters had sunk to the bottom of the Baltic, along with some members of the crew. The loss was serious—to art history, to Catherine's growing collection, to everyone.

Catherine's recorded comment was stoical: "Well, I only lost sixty thousand écus!" Perhaps her stoicism rested upon the anticipated arrival of the greatest art prize that was ever to enter the hands of the Russian imperial family: the Crozat paintings. Then, finally, on November 6, the best part of a year after the deal had been signed, the paintings arrived in St. Petersburg. Tronchin was rewarded with a sack full of sable furs with which to make himself a coat.

One can imagine the scene on the quay of the Neva outside the Winter Palace (the residence of the tsars that is part of the complex of buildings known collectively today as the Hermitage). The *Hirondelle* bounced and jumped in the waves as workmen struggled to unload the precious cargo in bitter winds. Catherine waited in her apartment relishing this moment, longing to see the treasures, which had evaded the clutches of the French and had finally come into her hands. At last the crates began to be opened, and hundreds of masterpieces were brought before her for approval. Catherine's eyes glistened at the glamour and the power embodied in these sensational works of art. In a stroke, Catherine's collection of paintings had been raised to match the world's leading collections of art.

She knew the most celebrated works from engravings, but seeing the real paintings before her for the first time, after a year's tantalizing wait, must have given her a burst of triumphant energy and refueled her passions for more. You can get a sense of that thrill still today walking around the Hermitage, where most of the finest paintings carry the Crozat label.

One freezing, black October night in 2004, Giles and I arrived in St. Petersburg in a flurry of early snow. As we drove through the outskirts, weaving between the interminable lines of Soviet-era apartment blocks, the place seemed shrouded in gloom. But we were lucky enough to be staying, through the kind introduction of Geraldine Norman, the art historian and the Hermitage's London representative, in a small apartment just five minutes from the museum. Geraldine's magnificent history of the Hermitage, published in 1997, was to become my constant companion in St.

Petersburg, providing me with much of the material for my Russian chapters. The next morning we awoke to glorious sunshine and hurried to the Hermitage. The façade was dazzling. Painted a sea green, with its white columns and gold capitals and rococo flourishes, it seemed to go on forever, doubling round and back in wings and additions that have been added to the building over its two-hundred-year history.

We were not of course alone as we stood and stared. Foreign tourists, the wealthy Americans, British, French, and Germans, were pouring out in steady streams from the back streets of the city and winding in little ant trails toward the museum. They seemed generally well-informed, with their guidebooks and headsets and earnest strategies for study. And there were Japanese, Koreans, and Chinese too, occasionally wandering in newly married coupledom, but more often in big tour groups, being simultaneously dragooned and educated by professional guides. And then there were the Russians, who turn up in magnificent numbers. Mothers with children, young naval cadets in their uniforms, schoolchildren, families, and elderly couples, they too poured in droves into the Hermitage that day to wander and stare, as dazzled as anyone else by the splendor and excess of their country's heritage.

We went first to the galleries of Italian art. No fewer than thirty-two rooms are required to display the Hermitage collections of Italian art from the thirteenth to the eighteenth centuries. The Italian collection was begun with, and is still based on, works collected by Pierre Crozat.

As we walked around the vast, gilded galleries, we found our eyes were torn between the superb paintings hanging on the walls and the architecture and decoration of the rooms. This is how it would have been in Catherine's day. Gilded cornices held aloft by seminaked caryatids demand your attention. Marble columns with golden capitals compete with extraordinary doors, finished with elaborate patterns of gilded bronze and inlaid tortoiseshell. There are huge malachite vases and candelabra studded with semi-precious stones. The atmosphere is potent and almost oriental, flowering with so much money and power that one quickly feels exhausted trying to absorb it all. And at every turn there are busts and portraits, sculptures and cameos of Catherine the Great and her descendants. But if you can keep your eye on the paintings, the search for Crozat labels is quite straightforward. Just look for the best, not just in the Italian galleries but all over the place. The Giorgione *Judith*, the finest Titians and Veroneses, fabulous paintings by Van Dyck, Rubens, Tintoretto, and Rembrandt all once hung in Crozat's house in Rue de Richelieu. The caliber is astonishing. Titian's *Danae*, painted in 1536, was his, as was Rembrandt's painting of the same subject, made exactly a hundred years later. To me, it was a revelation to see them all gathered there in one place, to appreciate the extent of his collecting passions.

Crozat's collection, centered on Raphael's famous painting of St. George, clearly lay at the heart of Catherine's lust for glory. It was the first big collection to come into her hands, and it remained the most important group of paintings in the Hermitage.

You can see how effectively Catherine satisfied her unbounded desire for fame with stupendous collections of art. She fully understood the importance of using the arts to further her political ascendancy. Most of her ambition was about expanding her fame abroad. But she also harbored a vain desire to bring enlightenment to the Russian people. She wished to import culture, knowledge, and civilization, to push her vast and unruly country out of its barbarism and ignorance and into a new era of progress. Even in St. Petersburg, Russia's international window to Europe, the rude manners of Asia still threatened to sully the recently imported polish of Europe.

On the one side were splendid fashions, elegant diamond-studded ball gowns, sumptuous feasts, theaters, and concerts. Catherine lured French professors, artists, writers, and philosophers to her court to add further luster to her reign. She set the tone for all members of the nobility by sending to Paris for her clothes and furniture. And she had a French theater built, where nobles were forced to attend performances under pain of a fine.

It was only fifty years since Peter the Great had visited Paris, London, and Vienna and brought back to the Russian court a new vision of behavior. Drunken brawls still occasionally occurred at her grand soirées, so Catherine drew up a set of rules to ensure that everyone behaved properly in the polished sanctum of her palace:

1. All ranks shall be left behind at the doors, as well as swords and hats.
2. Parochialism and ambitions shall also be left behind at the doors.
3. One shall be joyful but shall not try to damage, break, or gnaw at anything.
4. One shall sit or stand as one pleases.
5. One shall speak with moderation and quietly so that others do not get a headache.
6. One shall not argue angrily or passionately.
7. One shall not sigh or yawn.
8. One shall not interfere with any entertainment suggested by others.
9. One shall eat with pleasure but drink with moderation so that each can leave the room unassisted.
10. One shall not wash dirty linen in public and shall mind one's own business until one leaves.

It is not surprising that such rules were needed, for the vast mass of the Russian population, and many thousands in St. Petersburg, were still sunk in servitude, poverty, and drunkenness. Shopkeepers, coachmen, servants, and peasants wore Asiatic dress, thick and pungent sheepskins with long woolen bands wound round their legs and feet. They had long beards, fur caps, and long fingerless gloves of skin and short axes hanging from their crude leather belts. While the tiny minority of proud aristocrats danced and displayed themselves in their glittering splendor, the vast majority of the people under Catherine's rule trudged around hopelessly in the snow looking like primitive barbarians.

Catherine made efforts to improve her country. She built academies, schools, and hospitals, but she was not popular and never won the affection of her subjects. In truth, she probably cared less for the opinion and sentiment of Russia than she did for the admiration and applause of her counterparts in Europe. As the English ambassador Robert Gunning noted shrewdly, the motive of all her patriotic labors was not benevolence but an insatiable thirst for fame.

In spite of all her efforts, Catherine was considered mildly ridiculous by the ruling classes of Europe. None of her counterparts was under any illusions about how she had seized power, and they were regularly entertained by the variety and energy of her many amorous affairs. Gunning's reports were generally damning: "The Empress, whatever may have been reported, is by no means popular here, it is not indeed in this country that she aims at becoming so. She neither bears any affection to the People of it, nor has she acquired theirs."

In practice, her lack of success in domestic affairs impinged little on Catherine's view of herself and of her position of ascendancy in Europe. Now, with the Crozat treasures in her possession, she could bask in the fame of having whisked three Raphaels out from under the noses of the French: the *St. George and the Dragon*, the *Holy Family with a Beardless Peter*, and the *Judith*, only much later revealed as a Giorgione. Of the three, the *St. George* must have touched her most profoundly, for St. George was the patron saint of Moscow and accepted by the people as the protector of all Russia. Catherine herself had always made a point of displaying her interest in St. George. In 1767, in imitation of the English whom she most admired, she had instituted an Order of St. George, making it the most illustrious of all the Russian military distinctions. On feast days, she wore a Russian dress of brocade or velvet with the sash of St. George, and a high coiffure topped by a small crown. She observed St. George's Day every year with great and pointed ceremony.

St. George became one of her tools of leadership, and she used it, as had the English kings Henry VII and Charles I, as a means of uniting her people behind her. She must have been delighted when at last she finally held Raphael's depiction of the saint in her hands. Here was a rare and exquisite painting, by her favorite artist, of a figure of heroism, chivalry, and enlightenment. At least, that is how she would have seen it. Catherine had already had herself flatteringly painted on a handsome white charger. No doubt she now imagined herself as a latter-day St. George, triumphing over the enemies of Europe, and bringing prosperity, stability, and enlightenment to the fair maiden Russia.

In claiming a particular passion for Raphael, Catherine was not showing any great individuality in her taste. The most highly prized painters in the late eighteenth century were not Titian, Rubens, Van Dyck, or Rembrandt, but Raphael, Leonardo da Vinci, and Correggio. In particular, the name of Raphael was awesome and powerful. For more than a hundred years, the highest prices had consistently been fetched by Raphaels. High prices and high demand signaled to Catherine that Raphaels were worth having.

So, inspired by her first purchases and hungry for more, she sent her scouts out to comb Europe for further additions to her Raphael collection. Of course, there was virtually nothing available.

Drooling over the books on architecture and the collections of engravings and prints sent to her by her art scouts in Italy, she still dreamed of a collection of Raphaels to surpass any other in the world. And then in the autumn of 1778, Catherine saw the beautiful colored engravings by Volpato of the Raphael frescoes in the Vatican. She conceived the idea of having Raphael's loggia copied in St. Petersburg. No time was lost, and by November scaffolding was up in the Vatican Palace. Christopher Unterberger, who had done paintings for the Villa Borghese and had worked on the decoration of the Vatican library, was commissioned to execute exact copies of the frescoes and a scale model of the building. Unterberger painted cartoons of the original size in tempera and even reconstructed the damaged portions. From these, and from various engravings, oil copies were made on canvas, which were rolled up and shipped to St. Petersburg in sections. Meanwhile, the great Italian architect Giacomo Quarenghi was commissioned to build a new extension to the Hermitage incorporating a loggia to match the original in the Vatican. When the fresco copies arrived, they almost fitted the new building. With a few subtle nips and tucks, they were fitted into the spaces allotted and the work was finally completed in 1782.

Catherine's enthusiasm for Raphael did not stop at having his Roman frescoes copied. When she reported on progress of the rebuilding of her palace in Tsarskoye Selo, in a letter to Friedrich Melchior, Baron von Grimm, in 1781, she told him that eleven of the rooms were to be dedicated to "Raphaelism." But her passion was patchy. When suggestions were made that she should acquire copies of the Raphael cartoons for tapestries, with themes from the Acts of the Apostles (now in London's Victoria and Albert

Museum), she declined, noting on the report, "I cannot imagine what they are like, but if their subject matter is sad or too solemn, I am not interested in them."

The empress had become used to investing in art blindfolded. She could never attend auctions, and she could only ever buy what her agents proposed, choosing on the strength of their recommendations and the descriptions published in the sale catalogues. But her unsurpassed networks of informers snooped and listened for every twitch of the market, and as a result, Catherine was, at the height of her buying spree, the most successful collector in Europe, probably in the world. She had money at her disposal, she had information, and she had a ruthless determination to win.

Spurred by her diplomatic triumph over the French with the Crozat collection, Catherine then went on, in 1779, to buy the superb collection built up by Sir Robert Walpole, Britain's first prime minister, when it came up for sale at Houghton Hall, shipping it to St. Petersburg for her own enjoyment.

Walpole's collection was filled with masterpieces by every painter whose work was admired by the cognoscenti in the reign of George II. There were twenty Van Dycks, nineteen Rubenses, eight Titians, five Murillos, three works by Veronese and three by Guido Reni, two by Velázquez, a Frans Hals, a Raphael, and a Poussin. When the question of its sale came up, the radical politician John Wilkes had advised the British parliament to turn it into a national gallery: "A noble gallery ought to be built in the garden of the British Museum for the reception of this invaluable collection."

Catherine's motive for her swoop on the Walpole collection seems to have been purely political. Britain was at the peak of its international powers, with an empire stretching from India to North America. Catherine had long admired Britain, ever since her early married days when she had been a friend of Britain's ambassador. By buying the splendid collection of the nation's first prime minister, Catherine was playing a little game of one-upmanship. To Catherine's delight and to the fury of the British, this magnificent collection of pictures was scooped from under their noses, and in exchange for a sum somewhere between thirty-five and forty-five thousand pounds, left British shores for Russia.

At her peak, Catherine was buying fifty paintings a year, most of them good ones. She was well aware that the splendor of her court would enhance her own reputation abroad and have a direct impact on diplomatic relations. It would also guarantee her own posthumous glory. By now her spending was driven almost entirely by political calculation. Her appetite for art precisely matched her appetite for power; and both were rapacious. She knew it too. "It is not love," she confided to von Grimm, "it is voracity. I am not a lover—I am a glutton."

Her gluttony showed itself particularly in the field of antique gems, carved with portraits and other images, which she accumulated with absolute abandon. She loved the massive extravagance, the excess of her gem collection, the fact that no other could match hers in size. In the spring of 1782, she wrote to her old friend and agent, von Grimm: "My little collection of engraved gems is such that yesterday four people could only just carry two baskets filled with drawers containing roughly half the collection; and, so that you don't get the wrong impression, you should know that they were using the baskets that carry wood for fires in winter and that the drawers were sticking out a long way; from that you can judge the gluttonous greed that we suffer from under this heading."

Five years later, she bought fifteen hundred more engraved gems from the duc d'Orléans, the most famous gem collection in Europe, which had come from Pierre Crozat. With this hoard now in her possession, she confided eagerly to von Grimm, "all the cabinets of Europe are only childish accumulations compared to ours."

Catherine continued this muscular strategy of acquisition and artistic patronage for all thirty-four years of her reign, turning St. Petersburg into a thriving cultural center, buzzing with artists, dealers, and craftsmen from all over Europe. Nowhere else was so much money being lavished on the arts. In 1790, six years before her death, Catherine wrote a letter to von Grimm, in which she ran through the inventory of her artistic triumphs. "Besides the paintings and the Raphael loggia," she wrote, referring to her four thousand old masters and the Raphael fresco copies, "my museum in the Hermitage contains thirty-eight thousand books; there are four rooms filled with books and prints, ten thousand engraved gems, roughly ten thousand drawings and a natural history collection that fills two large galleries." In all this, her collection of some sixteen thousand medals and coins seems to have slipped her mind.

It was an accumulation that outclassed those of all the other monarchs of her day. She had already admitted to von Grimm that her passion for building was addictive: "It devours money, and the more you build, the more you want to build. It's an illness like alcoholism." Her passion for art was much the same.

Occasionally, privileged foreign visitors were invited to visit the Hermitage. They found the place utterly astonishing. Baroness Dimsdale, the wife of the English doctor who successfully inoculated Catherine and her family against smallpox, visited Russia in 1781 with her husband, as the guests of the empress. Elizabeth Dimsdale kept a diary in which she wrote about the magnificent collections of pictures and jewels, the amazing porcelain and glass, and the massive luxury of the palace itself. She spent days being escorted around the various palace galleries and apartments, through room after room filled with pictures from floor to ceiling, dazzled by the profusions of portraits, landscapes, and unrivaled masterpieces by all the great painters. She was also shown the glass-covered apartment on the top floor that was used by the empress in winter. It was warmed with stoves and filled with the scents of exotic flowers and shrubs, the air palpitating under the beating wings of birds. In another apartment she saw "all kinds of Animals stuffed, a Skeleton of an Elephant, and one stuffed with the figure of a Turk riding as they do in Turkey, there were a great many bones of Elephants found in Siberia." Alongside these curios, there were two gruesome stuffed animals: Peter the Great's horse and his favorite spaniel.

In 1773, Diderot finally made a visit to St. Petersburg to meet his great benefactress. He spent several weeks there, spending long hours chatting with the empress. He was aged sixty by this time, and the journey from Paris had been a hard one. He was disappointed by her lack of interest in his advice. "Monsieur Diderot," she told him, "I have listened with great pleasure to the outpourings of your brilliant mind; your great principles, which I understand perfectly well, make fine theory but hopeless practice." She sent him back to Paris laden with gifts: a ring, a fur, his own carriage, and three bags each of a thousand rubles. "If I deduct from that," he wrote to his wife, "the price of an enamel plaque and two paintings which I am giving to the Empress, the expenses of the journey and the presents I must give . . . we will only be left with five or six thousand francs, perhaps even less." They were the thoughts of an elderly and irritable genius, whose bones ached from the Russian winter just as much as his hurt pride. One cannot help thinking that the sentiment was somewhat ungrateful given the empress's massive earlier generosity over his library.

Catherine's relations with Diderot had changed, but so had the Hermitage. Now it was beginning to take on the character of a museum. No account from a well-heeled traveler to St. Petersburg omitted a reference to a tour of the galleries, although of course no one from the lower classes was allowed in. In 1792, four years before Catherine died, an English visitor named John Parkinson was given a tour that revealed the feel of the place. "The Empress having graciously permitted all the foreigners in Petersburg to see the Hermitage—this morning we repaired thither between the hours of ten and eleven.... We were not permitted to enter with swords or sticks; but they were required to be delivered up before we went in. Quarenghi joined us there and was of great service to us in pointing out what particularly deserved our attention. In so short a time, however, and in such a crowd, it was impossible to see such a profusion to any good purpose or with any satisfaction. We first saw the Royal apartments, which occupy that side of the building which fronts towards the river, we then passed through the picture Galleries which form the three other sides of a square. Afterwards we went by Raphael's Gallery to the Cabinet of Medals, Mineralogy and what I must call for want of a better word 'bijouteric.' ... The Apartments as well as the Galleries are crowded with paintings, good and bad placed promiscuously together."

Catherine had created a vast and celebrated art collection, unmatched anywhere else in the world. And she had housed it in buildings which she had planned and commissioned herself. The art was just one of the many triumphant achievements of a woman determined to leave her mark on the world. But while many of us have forgotten the foreign policy triumphs, the domestic advances, and the diplomatic points that she won during her reign, millions of visitors from all over Russia and the world still pour into the Hermitage every year, to wander the miles of corridors admiring the collection that has become synonymous with Catherine the Great. She must have known that future ages would forget the soldiers and the statesmen. Somehow she knew that only the art would make her fame endure.

∞

More than two hundred years after her death in 1796, Catherine remains the presiding power at the Hermitage. Everywhere you can see her image, smiling out of flattering portraits, dressed in ermine and diamonds, or sitting elegantly on horseback. Her face is also preserved in dozens of tapestries, statues, and cameos dotted about this gilded and cupid-encrusted rococo wedding cake of a place as if she is still watching and enjoying the reactions of the millions of visitors flocking to get a taste of her passions.

After Catherine's death, her son Paul I inherited the collection and reigned briefly until his death in 1801, at the hands of assassins. His twenty-three-year-old son, Alexander, had collaborated in the plot to oust Paul from the throne but had probably been unaware of the plan to kill him. Alexander was devoted to the memory of his grandmother but had little feeling for art. His main contributions to the museum were his restructuring of its administration and the acquisition of art from the collection of Napoleon's estranged wife, Josephine. His interests lay largely in the military, but he did appoint a well-known art collector and bibliophile, Count Dmitry Buturlin, as administrator to the museum. Buturlin pointed out that an art collection is judged by the quality of paintings it hangs, rather than its number. Catherine had tended to overlook this basic truth in her headlong pursuit of fame. He advised an enlargement of the Italian school of paintings and that the museum should be open to the public "at a fixed season of the year, on condition that certain inviolable rules be observed and under the supervision of specially appointed staff."

But art and the running of the Hermitage were never uppermost in Alexander's mind. He was much more interested in being a soldier. Alexander is perhaps best remembered for his victory over Napoleon in 1812, aided by a particularly brutal Russian winter against unprepared French soldiers. He personally led the

Russian army into Paris and was hailed as the liberator of Europe. He played a leading role among the crowned heads of Europe in the Vienna Congress in 1814 to resolve the shape of Europe in the wake of Napoleon's defeat.

Alone among the tens of thousands of paintings in the imperial collection, Raphael's *St. George* was to play a part in the glorification of the Emperor Alexander. When portraits were commissioned for the Waterloo Gallery at Windsor Castle of the leaders of the campaign against Napoleon, Alexander decided to create a similar gallery of his own in the Winter Palace. A British portraitist was commissioned to paint three hundred thirty-two head-and-shoulders portraits of the Russian generals who had fought in the wars against Napoleon. The paintings were not finished when Alexander died in 1825, but his brother, Nicholas I, who inherited the throne, completed the undertaking and hung them in the specially designed 1812 Gallery.

At one end he hung a vast portrait of Alexander as heroic military leader riding to inspect his troops on a white horse. It was large, no bigger than an average terraced house. Next to this magnificent painting was the Raphael *St. George*, picked out from the collection by the two soldier brothers and hung like an icon with a small candle burning day and night below it. Two members of the Russian Guard stood sentinel at the entrance to this long gallery, motionless as if sculpted from stone.

Nicholas, like his older brother Alexander, was enamored of St. George. This saint and mythical hero was considered the protector of the Russian army and patron saint of all the Russians. To them it was the perfect choice of painting to hang in the hall dedicated to celebrating Russia's great victory over the French tyrant.

Fantastic ceremonies and processions took place several times a year in the 1812 Gallery, the candle in front of the Raphael painting flickering and jumping as the soldiers stamped and marched up and down the inlaid wooden floor. The imperial family, decked out in their finery, had to stand for hours on end, receiving seemingly endless lines of visitors and exchanging kisses with them. By the close of these ceremonies, wax from the hundreds of mustaches covered Nicholas's face.

The displays of costume were magnificent. Lord Londonderry described a name-day celebration of 1836 as a marvel of luxury and pin-tight organization, a demonstration of the absolute devotion and obedience of Nicholas's subjects. Stretched out in a line that passed through the 1812 Gallery and several vast halls were the various hierarchical groupings of officials, the ladies in long veils and Russian caps covered in jewels, the senators in scarlet with gold embroidery, high-ranking civil servants in light blue dress coats, and the chief marshall swinging his diamond-studded mace. Then around the emperor were the generals, aides-de-camp, and officers of the armed forces. The uniforms of the cuirassiers, hussars, dragoons, and infantry of every denomination dazzled the visitor. "The admirable arrangement and order that reigned gave each his proper place, and without the least semblance of confusion. All appeared like clockwork, and I was never before so struck with the magical effect of order." The Empress Alexandra was arrayed in a blaze of jewels, wearing a full Russian gown and dragging a red velvet and gold train, hardly able to support her own weight. And her crown, which particularly impressed the marquis, was surmounted by rows of jewels, "some of which were nearly as large as pigeon eggs."

Some evenings finished with a dinner in the empress's "fairyland," a fantasy winter garden where guests dined on elegant porcelain before vessels of gold and silver. The air was filled with the aroma of immense orange trees whose stems had grown up through the tables. African boys in Moorish costume served "every delicacy in the world." An American visitor, John Maxwell, wrote that the setting "rivals the enchantment of an eastern story."

The Winter Palace, by this time, was enormous, a colossal edifice, painted in sea green, or at times in other bright colors, to give it a face-lift during the long months of whiteout snow. The suites of apartments were like enormous labyrinths, and even the chief of the imperial household in Nicholas I's day, who had held his post for twelve years, was not entirely acquainted with every nook and cranny of the place. Just as in the vast tracts of land owned by wealthy aristocrats, there were areas inhabited by colonies of which the owner took no notice, there were in the imperial palace such additional bodies living off the building, unknown or ignored. There were watchmen on the roof, for example, kept there to maintain the fabric of the building and in winter to keep the water in the tanks from freezing by throwing red-hot balls into the tanks. They lived in little makeshift huts between the chimneys, took their wives and children up there, and even kept chickens and goats, which fed on the grass growing on the roof. It is even said that some cows were introduced but that they were removed before the great fire of 1837.

The fire was generally blamed on the ineptitude of a French architect named Auguste Montferrand, who had wheedled his way into favor with Nicholas I by presenting him with a book of exquisite architectural views. He had rebuilt various halls and state rooms in the palace and had constructed a throne room as a memorial to Peter the Great. The fire is thought to have started in some defect in the heating flues for this room, and it quickly began to spread. Nicholas and his wife were at the Bolshoi Theater when news came of the fire. Without telling his wife what was happening, the emperor hurried back, arranged to move his young sons to the Anichkov Palace, and took command of a massive evacuation of paintings and furniture.

First in the line of danger were the Raphael *St. George* and the portraits hanging in the 1812 Gallery. With impressive speed, staff and firemen removed every one of these paintings and rushed them out into the palace square, dumping them in the snow before hurrying back in to save the thousands of other treasures. Sailors pitched in, peasants, palace guards, everyone threw themselves into retrieving Russia's imperial heritage, and everything was dumped in the snow. One of the empress's favorite gold ornaments was only found in the spring after the snow had melted. Helpers were working with such enthusiasm that Nicholas was eventually forced to restrain them. The story goes that a group was wrestling so hard trying to get a gilt-framed mirror off the wall, ignoring his commands to leave, that he was forced to throw his opera glasses at it to break it and persuade them to leave before they became caught in the fire themselves. "You see, lads," he said, "your lives are dearer to me than the mirror and I now ask you to leave the building." A poet described the fire as a vast bonfire with flames reaching the sky. It burned for several days and the Winter Palace was completely gutted.

The Raphael *St. George* had been saved. Amazingly, it was undamaged by its brief sojourn in the snow. It still occupied a central position in the collection on account of both Raphael's unrivaled fame and its subject. Nicholas was no less obsessed with the order of St. George than his grandmother had been. In his eyes, it was probably the most important work of art in the entire imperial collection.

He had had a disastrous start to his reign, and had clung thereafter with all the more fervor to St. George as his guide. The Decembrists' uprising, which took place on his accession in December 1825, had been planned as a demonstration in favor of the succession's passing from Alexander to his brother Konstantin, whom they believed would be a reformist tsar and give Russia a constitution, exerting a restraint on autocratic power. They did not know that Konstantin had renounced his claim to the throne on marrying a Polish woman who was not of royal birth. Nor did they know that Alexander had prepared a secret manifesto recognizing his younger brother Nicholas as his heir. In St. Petersburg on December 26, some three thousand demonstrators gathered around the statue of Peter the Great in the Senate Square. One of the first decisions of Nicholas's reign was to have his guards fire on them, killing about eighty and dispersing the rest in chaos. A few hours later Nicholas wrote to Konstantin: "Dear, dear Konstantin, your will has been done. I am Emperor, but, my God, at what price! At the price of my subjects' blood!"

After this appalling start, Nicholas had had to begin the process of ceremonial validation of his rule. He turned to St. George and the Russian army, still bathed in the aura of glory following its defeat of Napoleon. Using the drill field, the immaculate rows of marching soldiers, to confirm his power, Nicholas presented his rule as a triumph of good and morality embodied in the imperial family and St. George, over the subversive forces of evil. The emperor was demonstrating his role as the hero, the protector of the people, and his model was St. George.

The first performance of this identification took place in the palace square when he brought his eight-year-old son, Alexander, to be presented before the Sapper Battalion, which had "saved" the imperial family from the insurgents. Nicholas made it clear that he and his heir were one and asked the troops to love his son as they loved him. Then he placed Alexander in the arms of several cavaliers of the Order of St. George, and at his command, the first officers in each line rushed to the boy and kissed his hands and feet.

This must have been unnerving for the boy, who had been brought up, like all imperial children, as if he were a precious doll. All his life, his world had been protected and his every need attended to by an army of personal servants that included a nanny, two night maids, four chambermaids, a nurse, two valets, two footmen, eight domestic servants, and eight drivers.

When that eight-year-old boy, Alexander, became Emperor Alexander II in 1855, he instituted, despite his conservative upbringing, what were later to be known as the Great Reforms. He emancipated the serfs, introduced a new elective system of local government, and made the judiciary independent of government. His people did not express their thanks. Political opposition, which had been suppressed for so long, broke out in a flood of revolutionary activity, and in 1866 a disgruntled student took a shot at the emperor. He missed, but the incident put Alexander under the close protection of the army and St. George for the rest of his life.

Alexander had grown up with the expectation that St. George would protect him, an expectation he had inherited from his father. He valued the Raphael painting as an icon, an object of devotion, but his wife, the Empress Maria Alexandrovna, had a completely different view of this exquisite painting. She had an art lover's appreciation of it, and in time she managed to procure it for her own private enjoyment.

Maria Alexandrovna had arrived in St. Petersburg, a shy sixteen-year-old, from her home in Darmstadt. Her future husband, the heir to the Russian throne, the Grand Duke Alexander Nikolaievich, had undertaken a tour of Europe in 1839, the purpose of which was, in part, to choose a bride from a list of candidates that had been drawn up on his behalf. During an unscheduled stop in Darmstadt, the young man fell in love with Princess Maximiliana Wilhelmina Augusta Sophia Maria of Hesse-Darmstadt, who was not on his list of aspiring fiancées. When he eventually succeeded in persuading his parents to agree to the match, the young princess converted to the Orthodox religion and received the rather more manageable name of Maria Alexandrovna. They were married in 1841, in a wedding of unsurpassed splendor. The celebrations, which lasted a full fortnight, were designed to play to Europe. Forty-two thousand invitations were reputedly sent out for the main ball hosted by the newlyweds.

The poor girl did not find it easy adjusting to her new position in the world. Her mother-in-law enforced strict Prussian etiquette and remained intolerant of the more relaxed manners of her own family. The young woman often sat in her room and wept, and soon after her arrival in St. Petersburg, her face broke out in a rash, an affliction that affected her at tense moments throughout her life. She had to wear a veil and remain indoors for several weeks.

Maria Alexandrovna consoled herself with the marvelous art treasures to be found in the Hermitage collection. It was bigger than ever, for important works were still being bought in large quantities. Whenever a major art collection came up for auction as the result of the misfortunes of some once great French, German, or English family, Romanov agents were quickly in attendance, cash in hand. Vast amounts of European art flowed into the Hermitage to enrich the royal collections, much of it the debris of lost wars and squandered fortunes.

Not long before Maria Alexandrovna married, her father-in-law, Nicholas I, had acquired Raphael's famous *Alba Madonna*, from the London banker William G. Coesvelt. Nicholas had adored the collections of the Hermitage and knew them intimately. A few days before his death in 1855, as he wandered through the galleries for the last time, he was heard to murmur, "Yes. Here is perfection!"

When Maria Alexandrovna became empress herself, she boldly selected a few treasures from the imperial collection to decorate her rooms. The *Alba Madonna* was the first of these, and then a few years later, in 1867, she asked for the Raphael *St. George* to be removed from the Hermitage Italian room and brought to her own private apartments.

These rooms, at the southwest corner of the Winter Palace, were vast galleries with high-vaulted ceilings and elaborate cornices picked out in gold leaf. Raspberry brocade wallpaper covered the walls, and the ormolu cabinets, gold candlesticks, gilt chairs, and chandeliers all contributed to a scene of twinklingly opulent splendor.

In her favorite room right on the corner, she had an arrangement of large potted plants, which allowed her to peek down into the square by the river and watch the goings-on there without being seen herself from the window. It was in this room that she gathered all her favorite art treasures. What a position to be in! She had the pick of the finest art collection in the world, a cache of treasures that numbered something like one million objects. Her choice was possibly influenced by the roaring approval for Raphael that hovered over the art world. But she was not such a naive girl anymore. Here, in her private apartments, where she sat daily, reading, embroidering, and entertaining her most intimate visitors, she hung her favorite paintings: the *St. George*, the *Alba Madonna*, and the Murillo *Immaculate Conception*, which had come to the Hermitage from the Walpole Collection. She also chose, as an accompanying piece to the *St. George*, da Vinci's delicately beautiful *Litta Madonna*. It was an impressive choice.

The *St. George* hung in that gilded raspberry room until the empress died in 1880 and the Raphaels were returned to the Italian room in the new Hermitage. There they remained until a certain Karl Baedeker made a visit and wrote his 1914 guidebook. It was to trigger all kinds of upheavals at the Hermitage. In this book, he awarded the Raphael *St. George* two stars. The accolade was a rarity in the world, and even in the Hermitage a very great rarity among so many top-class treasures. Ironically, it may be that the Baedeker two-star rating was seen and noted in 1914 by the collector who was to come swooping in, within a few years, to acquire and remove the great painting and send it on the next leg of its journey. But not before it survived other dangers.

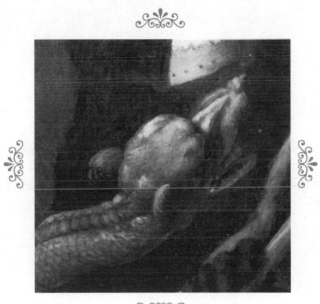

7.

"I OPENED MY WINDOW wide and realized that it was the chatter of a machine gun; then I saw an incredible sight—all the well-dressed Nevsky crowd running for their lives down the Mikhailov-skaya Street, and a stampede of motor cars and sledges—to escape from the machine guns which never stopped firing." Bertie Stop-ford, a British diplomat, was changing for dinner in the center of St. Petersburg in March 1917. "I saw a well-dressed lady run over by an automobile, a sledge turn over and the driver thrown in the air and killed. The poorer-looking people crouched against the walls; many others, principally men, lay flat in the snow. Lots of children were trampled on, and people knocked down by the sledges or the rush of the crowd."

Just three years after Baedeker awarded Raphael's *St. George* the highest possible accolade in his art guide to the Hermitage, events began to unfold in St. Petersburg that placed the beautiful little painting in grave danger. The Russian Revolution of 1917 unleashed political, social, and cultural turmoil on the country. Thousands of people were killed, institutions were toppled, beliefs smashed, and cultural artifacts burnt, broken, and ruined. Rapha-el's painting, having been cherished, appreciated, and adored for four hundred years, was suddenly facing an entirely unexpected threat.

In March 1917, the first Russian revolution took place. Al-though it later took on the colors of a political revolution, it began as an undirected popular movement, an expression of common, accumulated rage by thousands of ordinary, cold, and hungry people in St. Petersburg. There were plenty of things for them to protest about, but one of their greatest grievances was the mass slaughter of young Russian boys being sent by the emperor to the front lines to fight the Germans. Huge demonstrations against the war had been building up daily in the center of the city, and before long bakeries and other food stores were broken into and emptied by hungry crowds. When the soldiers of the city garrison were ordered to clear the streets, many abandoned their posts to join the protestors. Within days, virtually every barracks in the city had mutinied, and vast crowds of demonstrators began to surge through the streets. The police mounted guns on strategic buildings and began to fire indiscriminately at the masses below.

Similar dramas were occurring all over the city, and the following day the crowds of workers and soldiers and their families fought back, setting fire to prisons and police stations. The Winter Palace was invaded and the Fortress of St. Peter and St. Paul, the Russian Bastille, where so many political prisoners had died, fell to the rebellious crowds. The Duma, inaugurated in 1906 and the chief critic of imperial policy, rejected the emperor's decree of abolition, and around midnight on March 12, a new political order was installed. A provisional government was to rule Russia until democratic elections could be organized. Three days later, the emperor abdicated.

The Hermitage Museum had been closed since the beginning of the month because of the uprisings in the streets, but it was far from safe. The night before the emperor abdicated, a company of soldiers, whose barracks faced the Raphael loggia, had threatened to fire on the Hermitage and flatten it if machine guns were not immediately taken off the roof. No such guns existed, but two dozen drunk and excited young soldiers had broken into the Hermitage waving their rifles and spoiling for an argument with the curators. Fortunately they were placated and drifted off, nursing almighty hangovers. The incident blew over, but it was indicative of the threats that were to hang over the museum during the rule of the provisional government.

Within a few months, the dangers had mounted again. Following an attempted Bolshevik coup in July led by Lenin and Trotsky, which almost succeeded, Alexander Kerensky, a brilliant young former justice minister, was elected prime minister and moved the seat of the provisional government into the Winter Palace. Kerensky took over Alexander III's study and library for himself. Hordes of attendant office workers occupied the palatial rooms where the rest of the imperial family had lived. Soon secretaries and other support staff were crawling all over the place like ants.

The political situation was so volatile and dangerous that the provisional government required a military guard. Large numbers of soldiers moved in, and the state rooms on the first floor were turned into their barracks. As the situation worsened and support for the Bolsheviks grew, more young soldiers, the so-called *junkers*, were recruited from the military academy to guard the palace. These soldiers swarmed all over the grand ballrooms and state apartments, and soon their dirty mattresses and blankets filled the Gold Drawing Room, the White Hall, and the Raspberry Drawing Room, where Raphael's *St. George* had hung in more peaceful times. Wet towels were left hanging on marble statues. Straw and cigarette butts littered the parquet floors. The place stank of stale tobacco and unwashed humanity, and there were crusts of bread and empty wine bottles discarded in corners. Machine guns were mounted on windowsills and rifles stacked in rows between the mattresses.

The palace treasures were clearly in grave danger of abuse by ignorant young soldiers, so work began hurriedly on an inventory of the art treasures in all the imperial palaces. Meanwhile Count Dmitry Tolstoy, the director of the Hermitage, was far more worried about the advance of the Germans. They had occupied Riga, just two hundred miles to the south, on September 2, and were heading for St. Petersburg. The Germans posed a much more specific threat to the Hermitage treasures. Tolstoy's particular concern was for a group of paintings, including a Rembrandt, four Claude Lorrains, an Andrea del Sarto, as well as many other major masterpieces, which Alexander I had bought from the heirs of the Empress Josephine in 1814. She had received them as war booty from an important German collection, and Tolstoy was convinced that the approaching Germans would claim them back again. They might try to carry off other priceless paintings too.

Tolstoy called a meeting with his team of curators. Late into the night they debated what to do until finally, and with considerable trepidation, they agreed to recommend the evacuation of the entire contents of the museum to Moscow. It was a solution of a sort, but it was by no means a guarantee of safety. Before they could change their minds, the provisional government accepted the recommendation and carpenters were called in to knock up enough crates to accommodate every movable object in the Hermitage. There were more than a million pieces, and the carpenters ended up making eight hundred thirty-three crates to carry them.

Tolstoy was beside himself with worry. "With terror I asked myself—when and in what state will these precious things again see the light of day? The Hermitage was living in a feverish, difficult time; it seemed as though we were caught in a nightmare, or burying someone very near and dear. The whole of the curatorial staff were working very intensely, our scholars themselves wrapping up and packing the objects they were responsible for ..."

∞

Backroom dramas still seem to be intrinsic to life at the Hermitage. During my visit to the city, I encountered more emotional mercury in my four days among the Hermitage staff than I had for months. One of the first people I met was a librarian named Anna, a plump, middle-aged woman dressed in the standard Russian winter ensemble of thick, gray woolen turtleneck sweater and brown skirt. Her long blond hair was curled and pinned behind her ears. She was pretty, with delicate pale skin and pink cheeks, but this afternoon she was not prepared to smile. She looked frazzled. It was almost the end of the day, and she was evidently unhappy about many things. For a start, I could see she was angry about the glass top of one of the reading desks, which had been smashed by an anonymous visitor the previous morning. She was concerned about her burdens of work and her lack of support staff. She was worried about the state's dwindling support for the Hermitage, her lifelong workplace and that of her parents. And now she was additionally irritated by being asked to dig out old books, documents, and photographs for a visiting foreigner. My appearance signaled a lousy end to a lousy day.

Before I could apologize, she had shrugged her shoulders and with a practiced scowl bustled off into the deeper recesses of the book stacks, the rapid tap-tap of her court shoes making a point to me about how little time she had for such niceties. A minute later she reappeared clutching the Benois catalogue, the inventory made in 1913 by Alexandre Benois, one of Russia's leading art historians and curators. She put it down on the desk in front of me. I opened the front cover carefully, hoping to find a familiar image as its color frontispiece. And there it was, tiny but powerful: Raphael's *St. George and the Dragon*. I was deliriously pleased to see it.

Benois had singled it out as the finest painting in the entire collection. "It was small in size," Anna said, coming closer to look at the picture and suddenly warming up in spite of herself. "But it had a far greater impact than you could ever expect." Anna sat down and we talked about the extraordinary allure of this painting, of how it had seduced so many powerful people over so many years. And how, even during its stay in Russia, it had been snatched this way and that by men and women desiring its calming, protective presence. She ran through the movements of the painting, how it had hung as an icon in the 1812 Gallery and then moved back to the Italian room before being summoned by Empress Maria Alexandrovna, wife of Alexander II. "Yes, they all loved that painting. There's a kind of vague folk memory among the guards here of it as an icon, hanging in the 1812 Gallery as a state emblem, a symbol of protection."

I told her about photographs I'd seen of Nicholas II on horseback holding up small icons with which to bless the Russian soldiers before their departure for war in 1914. Might he have brought out the *St. George* to bless the soldiers? After all, St. George was the symbol of protection for the Russian army. Anna and Lena, my translator, thought about this. "It's possible," ventured Anna, nodding slowly and smiling now. "The painting was small enough. It had been treasured as an icon. And it carried a very powerful message. I've never seen any photographs, but the emperor might well have carried it out and blessed the troops with it."

Later, Anna brought out a few old photographs taken in 1917 of curators and scholars wrapping and packing objects ready for evacuation. Eminent academics can be seen at work, slowly enclosing the pieces for which they are responsible in nests of shredded paper, laying them gently like tiny babies in the large wooden crates. Their faces betray their emotions at handing over these precious objects to an unknown fate. In sending away the cream of Russia's artistic heritage, they were also sending away the reason for their employment. The photographs offer a poignant record of the heightened emotions and uncertainties that hung over this treasure house. And watching Anna and Lena studying them, I could see that they too had a feeling that their fate in 2004 hung, to a far lesser degree, but still hung, in the balance.

The fears of the Hermitage staff back in 1917, however, looked a great deal more serious and more urgent. Within a few weeks of agreeing on the evacuation of their treasures, these men and women, whose agonized features I could still make out so clearly, were caught up in a new drama.

On October 24, the Bolshevik uprising was launched. Its command center, ironically, was the Smolny Palace, home of the famous Young Ladies' Institute, where the daughters of the Russian aristocracy had been schooled in manners, decorum, and elegant dancing. Machine guns and cannons stood at the palace doors, and inside there were scenes of feverish activity: councils of war, mass meetings of mutineers, seething crowds of soldiers, workers, and sailors everywhere. Other groups of Bolsheviks were massed in several other command posts, in the Fortress of St. Peter and St. Paul, in the Pavlovsk Regiment's barracks, and on the cruiser *Aurora*, anchored in the Neva, only a few meters from the Winter Palace.

Gradually during the course of the day, Bolsheviks and their supporters moved through the city, and by noon they had surrounded the Winter Palace. Demanding the unconditional surrender of the provisional government and receiving no answer, they signaled for attack at 9 p.m. with the firing of a few blank rounds from the *Aurora* and the fortress. The bombardment was kept up for most of the night. Some live shells were fired and parts of the pediment were damaged. Most of the *junkers*, having no stomach for fighting, departed and returned to their school. Then the Cossacks left, declaring themselves opposed to bloodshed. By midnight few defenders remained apart from a company of women and a few cadets. The assault on the palace, the climax of the Bolshevik victory that night, was essentially a victory over a handful of women. By 2 a.m. the palace was taken.

In the adjoining Hermitage, Tolstoy and his loyal scholars had barricaded the entrances to the museum from the Winter Palace and had gathered in the Italian Room, where they had spent the night dozing fitfully in a semicircle of velvet-covered chairs. A few hours before dawn, one of the guards woke them to announce that the Winter Palace had fallen to the Bolsheviks.

As they swarmed into the Winter Palace that night, the Bolsheviks fell upon an amazing array of treasures and precious objects. An American journalist named John Reed, who was with them, later recounted the events in his book, *Ten Days That Shook the World.*

"Carried along by the eager wave of men we were swept into the right-hand entrance, opening into a great bare vaulted room, the cellar of the east wing, from which issued a maze of corridors and staircases. A number of huge packing cases stood about, and upon these the Red Guards and soldiers fell furiously, battering them open with the butts of their rifles, and pulling out carpets, curtains, linen, porcelain, plates, glassware.... One man went strutting around with a bronze clock perched on his shoulder; another found a plume of ostrich feathers, which he stuck in his hat."

Books in luxurious bindings were snatched from the emperor's former quarters. Statuettes, sheets embroidered with the imperial monogram, gold-handled swords, even blankets and bars of soap were looted. Tables and cupboards were smashed, paintings defaced, and bayonets used to tear apart portraits of the imperial family. In the rooms of the ladies-in-waiting, dozens of court dresses and ball gowns had been pulled out of cupboards and thrown all over the floor in shimmering mounds of colored silk.

Those searching the courtyard soon found the palace cellars

and flung themselves upon the stocks of food and drink, dragging cases of wine and hams out into the square and off to their barracks, like wolves with their prey.

The imperial cellars contained one of the largest and finest collections of liquor ever put together. In it were tens of thousands of bottles of superb wine collected over the centuries for the pleasure of the imperial family and their guests. During the following days, hundreds of crates of wine were stolen from the vaults, and a strange kind of public bacchanalia reigned. Bolshevik workers and soldiers helped themselves to bottles of Château d'Yquem 1847, the last emperor's favorite vintage, and sold off hundreds of bottles of vodka to the crowds outside. Soon the drunken mobs went on the rampage, vandalizing the palace and looting shops in the city. Sailors and soldiers raged around the wealthier districts, robbing and killing for sport.

In vain the Bolsheviks tried to stem the violence by sealing off the liquor supply. They appointed guards who repeatedly became drunk on the job. They posted more guards, who began selling off more bottles to the crowds. They walled up the cellar with bricks, but holes were bored, and people gathered to lick and to suck out anything they could get. Hundreds of bottles were broken until a sea of wine two feet deep was sloshing about in the cellar. They started pumping the wine out onto the street, but the crowds only came and drank it from the gutters. Hundreds of drunken men and women were arrested and thrown into jail. Machine guns were set up to deter more drinkers, but still they came. The anarchy continued for days until, at last, the alcohol ran out.

Had our precious little Raphael painting been caught up in all this madness? Could it have been slashed or crushed by vodka-maddened revolutionaries? The chaos taking over the city was such that nobody could really be sure of anything anymore. A trainload of Hermitage treasures had left the city on the night of

September 29. Over six hundred crates of valuables, many of them containing fabulous and famous canvases, had taken all day to be loaded. Careful lists had been checked and double-checked at the station to ensure nothing had gone missing. Yakov Smirnov, one of the curators, had accompanied the train to Moscow and reported back that three hundred twenty crates had been duly stored in the imperial apartments of the Great Kremlin Palace, two hundred twenty-seven in the armory, and sixty-seven in the History Museum. Tolstoy fervently believed that our Raphael was among those stored at the Kremlin.

On the second train, which left St. Petersburg on October 19, the Hermitage was only allowed five carriages. The rest had been reserved for important objects from the Winter Palace, including the cream of the imperial wine store, disguised as archives. Bottles of hundred-year-old cognac and the finest Madeira and Hungarian wines had been included in this consignment. For months after it arrived at the Kremlin, the tantalizing smell wafting out from broken bottles triggered repeated break-ins and put the Hermitage treasures at risk. But there were other dangers to come.

As soon as the Bolsheviks seized power, a multitude of revolts broke out all over Russia, setting off the most terrible and ruthless of rebellions within the country, a civil war.

Among the first to rebel against the Bolsheviks were the Cossacks, a privileged military group that had always supported the tsar. Quickly, other volunteer armies were recruited to fight with the Cossacks under the White flag. Gathered behind the Bolsheviks' Red flag, meanwhile, was an armed rabble of ex-soldiers, intoxicated with their new freedom and brutalized by drink, as well as an anarchic mass of rebellious peasants and industrial workers and their families.

They were a hopelessly undisciplined force. They lost huge tracts of territory to the White armies and found themselves trapped in a small area around Moscow and St. Petersburg. These two cities were the strategic and symbolic centers of Russia, and the Bolsheviks refused to relinquish them. From Moscow, they continued to declare themselves the legitimate government, fighting against mutineers. They also had foreign invaders to consider, for all the great powers, still fighting each other in the First World War, had begun helping themselves to pieces of the dying Romanov empire.

Although foreign troops never approached Moscow or St. Petersburg, these two cities did see the fiercest battles of the civil war. In the weeks following the revolution, the fighting between Bolsheviks and moderates was most brutal of all in Moscow and focused in a small area around the Kremlin Palace.

On November 15, word reached St. Petersburg that all the Hermitage treasures had been destroyed in artillery bombardments of the Kremlin Palace. Lenin's appointed minister of culture, the Commissar for Enlightenment Anatoly Lunacharsky, instantly handed in his resignation, issuing an emotional public statement: "I have just been informed, by people arriving from Moscow, what has happened there. The Cathedral of St. Basil the Blessed, the Cathedral of the Assumption, are being bombarded. The Kremlin, where are now gathered the most important art treasures of Petrograd and Moscow, is under artillery fire. There are thousands of victims. The fearful struggle has reached a pitch of bestial ferocity. What is left? What more can happen? I cannot bear this. My cup is full. I am unable to endure these horrors. It is impossible to work under the pressure of thoughts which drive me mad! That is why I am leaving the Council of People's Commissars."

Count Tolstoy, the aging and embattled Hermitage director, instructed a French journalist in rather more measured tones to "tell the civilized world that Russia no longer has the Hermitage."

Had all those hundreds of thousands of priceless treasures been instantaneously destroyed in the fury of mindless civil war? Had the Raphaels, the Titians, and the Rembrandts, not to mention the porcelain, statues, and other classical antiquities, so carefully collected and preserved over hundreds of years by generations of tsars, been blown up? After centuries of slavery and brutal treatment by their masters, the pent-up force of the Russian people was finding its outlet in hideous atrocities. Armed robbery and looting was rife; the rabble of soldiers, intoxicated by revolution and drink, raped and robbed as they went, blowing up buildings and killing peaceful citizens at will. Given the lack of military discipline on either side of the conflict, it was quite possible that the reports were correct.

Wisely, Tolstoy decided to send a member of his staff to confirm the truth. Yakov Smirnov, the elderly expert on Oriental silver, who had accompanied the first train to Moscow, volunteered to go. Braving a train packed with drunken revolutionaries, so full that hundreds made the journey singing and shouting on the roof, Smirnov reached Moscow and made his way to the Kremlin. He went to the History Museum first, where he found crates of paintings, drawings, and engravings still intact in spite of bullet holes in the windows. The bullets had ricocheted off the ceiling without doing any damage. When he got to the imperial apartments, he was horrified to find no crates. After some frantic searching, he discovered that they had been dragged down to the ground floor as the bombardment began and had become mixed up there in a chaos of other palace treasures. Smirnov was barred from entering the armory—the new revolutionary bureaucracy required a pass which he did not possess—but men who had been inside assured him that the hundreds of crates were still inside and still intact.

Smirnov dispatched a two-word telegram to St. Petersburg, "All safe," but the telegraph office assigned it such low priority that it was never sent. Smirnov eventually arrived back in person to reassure Tolstoy and his colleagues that their treasures were relatively safe for the moment.

Meanwhile, the prospects for the conservation of art and culture in St. Petersburg were deteriorating fast. Tolstoy and his teams of curators continued to show up for work every day, but all the best of their collections were in Moscow, four hundred miles away, and the Hermitage Museum was closed to the public. They busied themselves rescuing private collections and drawing up inventories of works that Tolstoy had taken into the museum store for safekeeping in the early days of the Revolution.

Naturally this scholarly group was determined to save Russia's cultural heritage, which they had been educated to study and preserve. Lenin however was impatient with such "trivial matters." Instead he gave his encouragement to the avant-garde art groups who rejected the old bourgeois art and believed that art should have a social agenda and a mission to communicate with the masses. Tolstoy's staff was by nature a conservative lot, highly educated, many of them elderly. Large numbers of them were of noble lineage. They were not destined to get on well with the new guard.

In August 1918, Tolstoy and his team were horrified to discover that the futurist art historian and critic Nikolai Punin had been appointed commissar of the Hermitage. The futurists were part of the nihilistic wing of the avant-garde and were on record as favoring the destruction of all "old art." Punin and the futurist poet Vladimir Mayakovsky set to work fast. The Hermitage was renamed the Palace of the Arts, and a conference was organized there for the working masses under the title "A Sanctuary or a Factory?" Mayakovsky, a swaggering and egotistical cultural vandal, suggested turning the Hermitage into a macaroni factory.

"We do not need a dead mausoleum of art where dead works

are worshipped," he wrote, "but a living factory of the human spirit—in the streets, in the tramways, in the factories, workshops and workers' homes.... It's time for bullets to pepper museums ... to dynamite the old world." Vladimir Kirillov, another poet, followed suit, equally anxious to shock. "In the name of our tomorrow we shall burn Raphael, destroy the Museums, crush the flowers of Art."

The futurists believed themselves to be as vigorously revolutionary as their political comrades. Their world was art, and they were determined to radicalize it. While most of their fellow citizens were entirely absorbed in the bitter, day-to-day struggle for survival, these artists paraded around, reveling in their destruction of the old and embracing the new in all cultural forms.

At every turn they threw out the methods and the tools of outdated expression. Paintbrushes were passé, canvas was outmoded. Realism was obsolete. Now these revolutionary painters embraced abstraction. As Mayakovsky declared to anyone who would listen, "The streets shall be our brushes, the squares our palettes." Museums of new art were set up all over the country and art schools reorganized according to abstract painting programs. Trains decorated with revolutionary themes were dispatched all over the country, carrying news of the Revolution, both political and artistic, to the masses.

For a few spectacular months, the avant-garde art movement pursued some wildly experimental forms. Poets rejected punctuation and grammar. Orchestras played without conductors, both in rehearsal and performance, claiming to be forging the way toward true collective work. Concerts were performed in factories using sirens, turbines, and hooters as instruments. In one "factory concert" there was such a cacophonous din from the hooters and sirens that even the workers failed to recognize the tune of the "Internationale."

There were similar attempts to bring theater closer to the masses by setting it in the streets, factories, and barracks and performing it there too. The most spectacular example was *The Storming of the Winter Palace*, staged in 1920 to celebrate the third anniversary of the October Revolution. For this enormous production, the streets of Petrograd were turned into a vast theater. With a cast of ten thousand actors, probably more than had taken part in the actual insurrection, key scenes were reenacted on three huge stages set up in Palace Square. The Winter Palace was part of the set with various windows lit up at different times to reveal scenes inside. And an appreciative audience of some hundred thousand spectators cheered wildly during the assault on the Winter Palace.

With all this exuberant revolutionary energy, it was not long before the visual arts too were taken out onto the streets. Clothes, furniture, offices, and factories were redesigned in a new "industrial style" with primary colors, geometric shapes, and straight lines, all believed to be conducive to liberated rational thinking. Buildings and trams were decorated and avant-garde posters put up around cities to mark the numerous revolutionary anniversaries and festivals. The artists of the avant-garde were attempting to turn the streets into a Museum of the Revolution, hoping that these expressions of the power of the new regime would impress even the illiterate. But the illiterate were not easily moved. The artistic tastes of the workers and peasants of Russia were profoundly traditional. While left-wing artists, such as Chagall and Rodchenko, believed they were creating a new aesthetic for the masses, in fact they were merely creating a modernist aesthetic for themselves.

In 1918, when Chagall had decorated the streets of Vitebsk for the first anniversary of the October revolution, he was asked by Communist officials: "Why is the cow green and why is the house flying through the sky. Why?" And when the Bolshoi Ballet toured the provinces during 1920, the peasants were said to have been so profoundly shocked by the display of bare arms and legs that they walked out of the performances in disgust. The Russian masses were ultraconservative when it came to artistic matters.

When several thousand peasant delegates came to St. Petersburg in November 1918 to attend a Congress of Rural Poverty, organized in the newly named Palace of Art, it was discovered after they left that they had filled the palace bathtubs and many rare Sèvres, Meissen, and Oriental vases with excrement. Maxim Gorky, the most famous writer in Russia, who was an active supporter of the Revolution, was particularly shocked by what he saw as an insult to Russia's cultural heritage. "This was not done out of need," he wrote. "The lavatories in the palace were fine and the plumbing worked. No, this hooliganism was an expression of the desire to break, destroy, mock and spoil beauty."

During these first few years under the Soviets, the values attached to historic works of art fluctuated wildly. At times art was viewed as a source of prestige, a fantastic and unsurpassable cultural showcase. At other, more pressing times, Russia's treasuries of world-class art were regarded as hugely valuable bargaining chips to be used, as we shall see later, in dealings with the outside world.

But first the Hermitage treasures had to survive a bitter battle of ownership within Russia. Natalya Trotsky, the wife of Leon Trotsky, had her eye on them. She knew all about Raphael's *St. George and the Dragon.* She knew about the *Alba Madonna,* and the Titians, the Rembrandts, and all the other thousands of fabulous works sitting locked up in crates somewhere inside the echoing chambers of the Kremlin Palace. She lived with her husband in an apartment a few floors up from those very treasure chests. Perhaps she went to look at them. Perhaps she even tried to open them up. But her chance came in July 1918 when she was appointed head of the Museums

Department at the Commissariat of Enlightenment. This was a ministry of education and culture rolled into one. Within a few days of her appointment, she had fired off a telegram to the Hermitage, informing the staff that she intended to hand over the Hermitage collections to the Moscow Museum of Fine Arts.

The elderly staff of the Hermitage had been through dramas enough in the last twelve months over their treasures. But this news set them quaking in their boots once again. By now Tolstoy, sickened by the news of the murder of the imperial family, had resigned and emigrated. Sergei Troinitsky, a former Hermitage keeper, had been elected director in his place. In this first battle with Natalya, Troinitsky managed to win the backing of Anatoly Lunacharsky, head of the Commissariat of Enlightenment. Lunacharsky was Natalya's boss, so Troinitsky was able to squash Mrs. Trotsky's idea. But she was not to give up so easily.

When the Hermitage staff sent word to Moscow in December 1918 calling for the return of the collections to St. Petersburg, they found themselves facing another stiff challenge. In the newspaper they read that the Council of People's Commissars (Lenin's inner cabinet) had decided to open the crates of treasures from the Hermitage and other St. Petersburg museums and put on an exhibition in Moscow. Natalya Trotsky was behind the move.

Horrified, the eleven senior Hermitage keepers rushed round to Gorky's flat and, with his help, put together a telegram to Lenin: "Extremely concerned," it read, "at the danger threatening the treasures of the Hermitage, Russian Museum and Academy of Arts in the Kremlin palace, as a result of the exhibition idea which will mean the unpacking of the boxes without the observation of proper guarantees of safety. The council of the Hermitage has gathered in the home of Maxim Gorky and unanimously sends a plea that you prevent the organization of the exhibition and do everything you can to achieve the return of the collections to Petrograd which is the sole means of saving the treasures."

The telegram worked. The crates again remained unopened. But the keepers' request to have the treasures sent back to St. Petersburg was denied because there was no transport available to move them, and no food available anyway for transport workers. The delay suited Mrs. Trotsky very well.

She had been born Natalya Sedova in 1879, the daughter of rich parents. In her late teens she had been expelled from her ladies' college for reading seditious literature and had moved to Paris to study history of art at the Sorbonne. There she was swept by idealism into the blossoming revolutionary movement. When Trotsky arrived in Paris in 1902, sent by Lenin to give a series of talks to émigré Russians, Natalya was twenty-three and possessed of a coolly exotic beauty. Trotsky was also twenty-three and had just spent three years in exile in Eastern Siberia. Both were married. They became lovers.

By 1918, when she began her tug of war with the Hermitage staff, Natalya and Leon were living in an apartment in the Kremlin, across the corridor from Lenin, and not far from Stalin's flat. Leon was now war commissar, and Natalya effectively cultural commissar. They generally dined with Lenin, from plates decorated with the double-headed eagle, correctly positioned by an old servant who had waited on more than one tsar in his time. Natalya, the former Sorbonne history of art student, was wielding increasing power and was fully aware of the value of what lay inside those crates stored downstairs in the Kremlin Palace.

In May 1919, the Hermitage staff discovered that Natalya was at it again, this time planning a new ruse to open a Museum of Western Art in Moscow. She intended to use the fabulous collections from the Hermitage as its core. Troinitsky wrote a deftly conciliatory letter, conceding that some of the Hermitage collection might be shared with other museums but arguing that all the art works must first be returned to St. Petersburg for assessment. Troinitsky was summoned to Moscow to discuss the issue. Realizing that in this new Soviet world, his class origins would work against him, he sent a member of the engravings department who had been a humble clerk before the Revolution. When he arrived in Moscow, he discovered that Natalya's department had already decided to open the crates and hold an exhibition in Moscow before dividing the spoils between the two cities. Demanding to see the exhibition spaces, he was horrified to see that the skylights were broken, which meant that rain could easily get in and damage the pictures. He also pointed out that it would not be easy to hang the pictures on marble walls.

Natalya Trotsky was formidably ambitious, but eventually she grasped the fact that this kind of exhibition was not going to be possible without the cooperation of the Hermitage staff. She also saw that this was not going to be forthcoming. Once again the danger had been lifted.

While the civil war raged, there was no possibility of moving the artworks from Moscow to St. Petersburg. But as soon as it ended, in November 1920, the reevacuation was finally arranged. A special train had been organized with a battalion of guards to accompany it, to prevent looting during the regular stops for fuel. A team of keepers was sent from St. Petersburg to supervise the packing. But the tug of war was not over. Natalya Trotsky made one last-ditch attempt to prevent the departure of the treasures. She refused to supply trucks to transport the crates from the Kremlin to the station. In the end, after a long delay, a fleet of trucks had to be sent from St. Petersburg on another train. As Natalya Trotsky fumed in defeat in her office in the Kremlin, the vehicles were filled and then driven in convoy to the station in the dead of night to avoid robbery. Raphael's *St. George* and the other paintings had evaded her clutches.

The first crates arrived back in St. Petersburg on November 19, and that night a modest banquet was held in the Malachite Room to celebrate. Gradually more and more crates were unloaded and opened, and over the course of several weeks, the paintings were rehung on the walls and the objects replaced in their allocated positions. Remarkably, given the circumstances of the last three years, virtually no damage had been sustained. The Rembrandt room was opened on November 27, the other Dutch paintings restored to view on December 12, and the Italian paintings on December 19. Raphael's *St. George and the Dragon* had survived three years of being carted back and forth on trains and trucks across the wintry wastes of the Soviet Union, surrounded by drunken revolutionaries, and bombarded with artillery fire as well as the repeated threats from Natalya Trotsky. It had come through all this unscathed.

Exactly one week after the *St. George* was returned to its wall in the Italian room, reunited with the *Alba Madonna*, the pipes burst. The palace had remained unheated through the food and fuel shortages of the last three years. In winter, temperatures had hovered between minus two and minus eight degrees centigrade, and the staff had worn fur coats and gloves to work. Then, to mark the return of the treasures, the Hermitage had been granted a special supply of fuel to heat the museum so that the temperature of the galleries would not damage the art. The ancient pipes were not accustomed to the heat. They disgorged their contents, drenching the paintings with hot water. The varnish turned milky. Once again the poor curators quaked in their boots. But happily the damage turned out to be temporary and the paintings were soon restored to clarity.

Raphael's *St. George* had spent three years locked away in a dark packing case. When it came out into the light again, Russia was a different country. The painting was to enjoy just ten years of relative peace before being removed from the wall in the dead of night, wrapped once again, and smuggled out to another faraway home.

8.

ONE MORNING IN THE early spring of 1930, one of the curators at the Hermitage, a young woman named Tatiana Tcher-
navin, received unusual orders from her director. She was to stay
on late after closing time, take one of the museum's most famous
paintings from the wall, and hand it to an unnamed representative of the People's Commissariat for Foreign Affairs. Then she was
to rearrange the remaining pictures so that the public would not
notice the gap. She was to ask no questions.

Over the next few months, twenty-one of the museum's finest
masterpieces of European art, including Raphael's *St. George*, were
secretly removed from the walls of the Hermitage. Each time, the
gaps left behind were disguised with a hasty rehang. The paintings were packed at night by candlelight under tight security.
Then they were dispatched in small batches from starving Leningrad and taken to Berlin, where they were exchanged, all told, for
nearly seven million dollars.

The final buyer was waiting in Washington, a solitary and elderly
patrician gentleman with high cheekbones and a silver mustache.
He might have come straight out of a Henry James novel as he sat
in his fifteen-room apartment on Pennsylvania Avenue, dressed
in pinstripes and attended by his butler. Spread out around him
were the trappings of wealth and success. Fine pictures hung on
the walls, polished mahogany furniture glowed, and as he read his

newspaper, all he could hear was the gentle and regular ticking of clocks. Wild elation was not his style, but on hearing the news of his successful purchase, he permitted himself a quiet but heartfelt smile.

The buyer was Andrew Mellon, treasury secretary of the United States, one of the richest Americans of his time and arguably the most powerful man in Washington. The deal he had done amounted to the most significant sale of artworks ever agreed. It was also a deal that was exceptionally complicated and so bizarre that no writer of fiction could possibly have imagined it. For Mellon's part, it was technically illegal, and for five years he denied he had done it.

But no wonder, because here was business done between the representatives of two systems of government so deeply and determinedly opposed to one another that it seems extraordinary that any such transaction could ever have taken place. The bare facts are almost unbelievable. During the course of that year, Andrew Mellon, senior representative of U.S. capitalism, did a secret deal, via a string of middlemen, with Joseph Stalin, leader of a Communist regime which the United States did not recognize.

At the center of this historic deal was the Hermitage, at the time perhaps the greatest museum in the world. Its collections had been augmented over the centuries by generations of tsars, and now it was being forced, by its own government, to part with its finest treasures. For the Hermitage this was a massive tragedy, a blow from which it has still not fully recovered. But for Mellon, already known as a notoriously hard-nosed collector, the deal was a spectacular triumph. There he was spending unprecedented sums of money on pictures that he had never seen and of whose existence, let alone authenticity, he could never be fully sure. But at the end of the yearlong negotiations, he found he had acquired the absolute cream of the Hermitage, twenty-one of the greatest paintings in the world. All of them were authentic. And all of them he had bought at bargain prices.

The story of how this exchange came about is the story of a string of strange coincidences. Throughout the 1920s, rumors had swirled around the European art world that the Soviet government was about to start selling off either the Romanov crown jewels or the paintings of the Hermitage. European and American collectors were aware of a hoard of fabulous artworks in Leningrad, as St. Petersburg had been renamed, but it was not until 1924 that they were given a direct report on the extent and condition of these treasures.

That year, Martin Conway, a British collector and MP, visited Leningrad and was invited by the government to make a privately escorted inspection of Russia's art collections. Over the course of several weeks, he visited palaces, monasteries, and vaults to view paintings, jewelry, icons, and fabulous jeweled Fabergé treasures. Everywhere he went, government representatives broke seals and opened boxes to show him the extent of their holdings. Even the family possessions of the murdered Romanovs were opened up for his delectation. The accounts of his tour, which first appeared in the *Daily Telegraph* and later in book form, were ostensibly designed to dampen the rumors of possible sales. But they were, of course, just the first part of an extraordinary Russian sales campaign to titillate potential buyers in the West.

Although the Soviets still denied it, they had been planning to sell for some time. In the early months of the Revolution, Lenin had realized that Russia's unmatchable collections of artworks could become a valuable export commodity that would earn credits—both economic and political—in the United States. Huge quantities of wealth and valuables had been expropriated from wealthy Russians at the time. Lenin reasoned that the conversion of those valuables into useful capital was a logical next step.

In 1920, Lenin had set up a store to house precious art objects that might some day be traded abroad to obtain foreign currency. Thousands of tons of valuables had been confiscated from churches, museums, palaces, and private homes all over Russia and placed in this storehouse.

By 1924, when Conway made his visit, some art objects were already being sold abroad. These were small-scale sales of rugs, tapestries, coins, clocks, and porcelain, organized through Russian trade delegations. It was nothing compared to the torrent of big sales that would follow. Returns were not good. The sales were badly organized and often unsuccessful either because the goods were not valuable or because they arrived in the West damaged. But still the demand in Russia for foreign capital was racing ahead.

Behind this demand lay Stalin's intoxicated vision of Russia transformed into an advanced industrial nation. In December 1929 Stalin celebrated his fiftieth birthday. Lenin was dead. All Stalin's rivals had been eliminated, and he had completed the process of taking over Lenin's memory. He was consolidating his power in new and ominous ways. On December 21, every Soviet newspaper was filled with eulogies to Stalin. *Pravda* spent five days listing the thousands of organizations that had sent him greetings. Even former opposition members joined the chorus of frenetic adulation for their leader. Enormous portraits covered the walls of the Kremlin. Statues and busts dominated the squares and public buildings of every town. Stalin, the Man of Steel, was commemorated in new names for cities and towns, and the highest mountain in the Pamirs was renamed Mount Stalin. The name and the portrait became a part of everyone's daily life. It was the beginning of the Stalin cult, which was to be developed on a phenomenal scale.

His grip on the Russian people was tightening, but Stalin ruled a nation in tatters. After years of world war followed by more years of civil war, the Russian economy was badly damaged. Its agriculture was the most primitive in Europe. Its factories had been all but destroyed. If Soviet Russia was to survive in what seemed to be an increasingly hostile world of fascism and capitalism, it needed above all else to have a strong economy. Stalin realized that he needed to introduce new systems of agriculture and technologically advanced industry.

In 1929 he officially launched his first five-year plan, setting out hugely ambitious goals for industry and plans for a massive collectivization of agriculture. With ruthless use of force and terror, he coerced the peasants onto collective farms and at the same time insisted on deporting en masse the more efficient farmers, pejoratively labeled kulaks. One result was the famine of 1932–33, in which some six million died.

The industrial campaign was pushed through at an equally brutal pace. In 1927 Stalin had proposed a fifteen percent rate of increase in output, but two years later the fever of industrialization had taken hold and he was demanding a fifty percent annual increase.

To achieve these immoderate targets, Stalin desperately needed new technology. He needed the most sophisticated farming equipment and the most modern factory machinery available, as well as engineering know-how. Obviously this was not something that Russia could produce for itself. Such things could only be bought from the enemy it most feared: the West. And this was Stalin's big problem. Russia could only buy from the West if it had foreign currency, and it could only obtain foreign currency by selling goods to the West. The trouble was, Russia was so backward economically that it produced virtually nothing the West wanted to buy. The brutal truth was that Russia needed American tractors and industrial machinery much more than America needed Russian furs and badger bristles.

The only things Russia had to sell (apart from grain and other essential foods) that the West might want to buy were works of art, especially those Western European works of art that had been acquired by Catherine the Great. These European masterpieces were ideologically unsavory to Stalin. Painted by foreigners, owned by the Russian nobility, they were saturated with the smell of everything Stalin loathed. They seemed all too expendable during a time of need. As one Soviet museum curator was quoted as saying, such sales were a perfectly good Socialist method to "turn diamonds into tractors."

Following the small-scale sales abroad of minor antiques, Stalin implemented an urgent and more carefully organized policy of art sales. By 1929, Russia was exporting more than a hundred tons of antiques and jewelry every month to the West. But the really big business came with the famous paintings, which the Russians began to sell off secretly.

The first buyer to get wind of an opening in the market was Armand Hammer, later chairman of Occidental Petroleum, who had links through his father with the Soviets. Hammer made an absurdly low bid, together with Joseph Duveen, the most famous art dealer of his day. They specified forty masterpieces including works by Raphael, da Vinci, van Eyck, and Rubens. For this they offered a flat five million dollars. Fortunately the Russians realized that the sale of paintings of this importance required long and careful negotiations. They dismissed the offer out of hand.

Next up to test the market was Calouste Gulbenkian, an immensely rich Armenian businessman with British citizenship. He was known to the Russians as the head of the Iraq Petroleum Company. Some years earlier, he had helped them with sales of Baku oil on the Western market. As a known art collector himself, Gulbenkian was an obvious prospect for potential sales of art.

Gulbenkian bought four separate groups of artworks from the Hermitage between 1928 and 1930. On his first trip he came home with twenty-four pieces of fine French silver and gold tableware from the late eighteenth century. He also got a painting by the Flemish master Dieric Bouts and a Louis XVI writing table. His second buying spree netted him fifteen more pieces of silver and a Rubens, the portrait of Helene Fourment. On his third trip he got Houdon's marble statue of Diana, two Rembrandts, a Watteau, a ter Borch, and a Lancret, all for £140,000.

Gulbenkian was a compulsive art collector who described his passion as a disease. Now that he had his toe in the Hermitage door, he was reluctant to pull out. But the Russians had begun to suspect, probably rightly, that Gulbenkian was stealing them blind. He managed to extract one more bargain old master out of them in 1930, Rembrandt's *Portrait of an Old Man*, which he got for £30,000. But then negotiations stalled: on Gulbenkian's side because he thought he was paying too much, on the Russians' side because they thought he was paying too little.

The Russians had lost interest in Gulbenkian because by then a new, and more profitable, sales channel had opened up. Antiquariat, the state organization formed expressly to sell art abroad, had begun negotiating in early 1930 with the Matthiesen Gallery in Berlin, which was in turn negotiating with Colnaghi's in London and the Knoedler Gallery in New York. At the end of the line sat the United States treasury secretary, Andrew Mellon.

At the age of seventy-five, Mellon was enormously rich and enormously powerful. He was divorced with two grown children and by nature a bit of a recluse. But the one thing he was passionate about was art, and his private life revolved around his own collection of paintings. The contrast could hardly have been greater between Stalin's regime with its starved, beaten, and oppressed peasantry, and Mellon, the rich, sophisticated, and powerful banker, government official, and art collector. Although poles apart in every way, they were linked irrevocably in this most unlikely embrace.

My journey following the Raphael *St. George* was nearing its end, and I was getting restless to reach the finale. When I started out, I had known only vague snatches of the story of this painting, its adventurous life and the people it had encountered. Now I had a fair idea about the collectors who had coveted it and the thoughts that had run through their minds on getting it. Mellon was the final mystery, and with that in mind, I flew in February last year to New York and traveled by train down to Princeton, New Jersey, to meet Professor David Cannadine, the eminent historian and the Queen Elizabeth the Queen Mother Professor of British History at London University. David was just completing his biography of Andrew Mellon, and he had offered to talk to me about him and to share relevant parts of his research. It was an immensely generous offer. Professor Cannadine had been commissioned some years earlier by Paul Mellon, Andrew's son, to write a full-scale biography of his father. Not long after the commission was finalized, Paul died.

We met in the Firestone Library, where he has an office, and he set me up with a desk and a selection of tottering piles of research. Later, we picked our way across the icy footpaths of Princeton University, past incongruously copied elements of Oxbridge colleges, to a busy Italian restaurant for lunch. There, over pasta drenched with tomatoes and aubergines, he fleshed out the story of this mysterious millionaire.

Andrew Mellon was born in 1855 in Pittsburgh, one of six sons of Judge Thomas Mellon. The Mellons were Scots-Irish Presbyterians, and Andrew Mellon inherited many of their characteristics. He was shrewd and strong-willed and a hard bargainer. He was also deeply reserved and, in spite of his ultimate wealth and fame, both austere and unostentatious.

During the course of his life, Mellon made several fortunes. When Mellon was still a boy, his father had spotted his potential, so when he came of age, although he was not the eldest of his sons, the judge gave him the family bank to run. This was a nickel-and-dime organization that had concentrated mainly on advancing small-scale loans to the working classes of Pittsburgh. During the last quarter of the nineteenth century and in the years leading up to the First World War, Mellon managed to convert this bank into a major vehicle for promoting the economic transformation of western Pennsylvania.

His method was simple. He put his money behind his shrewd judgment of businessmen. While most of his great plutocratic contemporaries, men such as Frick, Carnegie, Ford, and Rockefeller, were entrepreneurs, Mellon remained a banker all his life. In a sense he was the first great American venture capitalist.

When people had an idea for a new business but needed capital to get it started, they went to see Mellon. If the idea had sufficient potential, Mellon would lend money, taking shares in the company in return and often a seat on the board. As the company prospered, Mellon got richer, and with the income he backed more ventures. He was incessantly acquisitive, and by the early twentieth century, Mellon had interests not only in coal, steel, and railroads but also in the new industries of aluminum (he owned Alcoa), chemicals (he owned Koppers and Carborundum), and petroleum (he owned Gulf Oil). As a result, the Mellon fortune straddled both the great industries of the nineteenth century and the new industries of the twentieth century. By 1914, Andrew Mellon was, along with Rockefeller and Ford, and his own younger brother, one of the four richest men in the United States.

One of the first men to tap into Mellon's capital resources was Henry Clay Frick. His idea was to develop the coking business to supply the country's burgeoning steel industry. With Mellon's help, Frick's coking business prospered, and by the time Frick was thirty, he was a millionaire. His life, like that of other newly enriched American industrialists, was one of rich and methodic formality pursued within a rigid code of propriety. He worked hard during the day and in the evenings he would dress for dinners and dance parties, or sometimes for a game of poker. His ladies whiled away the days in decorative silk dresses, perfecting their large, generously staffed houses, arranging flowers, reading poetry, attending tea parties, and playing occasional gentle games of lawn tennis.

Naturally the millionaires of Pittsburgh spent time together, socially, and Frick had become good friends with Mellon. Although Mellon was not disposed to attend parties, during the 1880s, the two men started making trips to Europe together, and it was during one of these voyages that Mellon met Nora McMullen on board ship. Nineteen years old, educated, beautiful, and a member of the family that held the Guinness stout franchise in the United States, she was enchanting. Frick introduced Mellon. He was older than Nora, but he was handsome and gracious, and very, very rich. After a brief courtship, the two became engaged.

A delegation of important Pittsburghers made the journey to Hertfordshire in England in September 1900 for the wedding and a week of parties. The couple looked blissfully happy, but it was not to last. Back in the United States, Nora found herself living in a gloomy house in dark, sooty Pittsburgh, her life constrained by the dry rituals of long, dull teas with Mellon aunts and uncles. Her husband was not there much, and when he did come home, he closeted himself in his study to work. Two children were born, Ailsa in 1901 and Paul in 1907, but still Nora was unhappy. Her painfully honest memoir reveals how they drifted apart: "Nights that I spent in my baby boy's bedroom, nursing these thoughts for his future, my husband, locked in his study, nursed his dollars, millions of dollars, maddening dollars, nursed larger and bigger at the cost of priceless sleep, irretrievable health and happiness. Always new plans, always bigger plans for new dollars, bigger dollars, robbed him and his family of the time he could have devoted far more profitably to a mere 'Thank God we are living.'"

Perhaps in an attempt to brighten up the bleak family home, Mellon began buying pictures. He had bought his first painting in 1880 on a trip to London with Frick, spending a thousand dollars on it. Judge Mellon considered this wildly exorbitant, and Pittsburgh businessmen, who had previously admired Mellon's wisdom, began to question their own judgment.

Frick, who was five years older than Mellon, had been buying paintings seriously for some time, and he introduced Mellon to a partner in Knoedler and Company, the great New York art dealers. Knoedler's had recently opened a Pittsburgh branch to tap into the resources of the newly enriched Pittsburgh bourgeoisie. Like most of the Pittsburghers buying art to cover the walls of their large homes, Mellon generally preferred the rather undistinguished landscape and anecdotal paintings of the Barbizon school. At first sight he did not seem to be a natural collector. He was tightfisted and not particularly knowledgeable or discriminating. And he was almost inarticulate on the subject of his art. Knoedler began offering him the kind of placid works that would suit his taste. Mellon bought a Millet in 1896 and then started buying regularly, four or five canvases a year, typically mediocre pictures of cows in meadows, moonlight on ponds, and children with kittens.

Mellon and his fellow Pittsburgh art buyers were unknowingly contributing to a trend that was sweeping the United States. A new era was opening up in the matter of American artistic taste and collecting. The fortunes being made as the country transformed itself from an agricultural to an industrial economy were often spent on acquiring art. Works by Millet and Corot were particularly popular, appealing to a sentimentality in the viewer still left over from the nineteenth century.

Even the earliest big collectors of Mellon's generation—J. P. Morgan, Isabella Stewart Gardner, and Frick—first indulged in the vogue for buying this kind of mawkish work before turning their attentions to what we now consider to be the more distinguished old masters. But the American approach to art collecting was different from that of Europe. In the Europe of earlier centuries, groups of connoisseur collectors had grown up with an expert knowledge of the works in their collections, but in America these buyers were men of commerce, not of art. Inevitably, their business activities shaped their collecting attitudes and habits.

Mellon was a businessman to his fingertips. He was a member of the boards of over fifty companies, charged with sound management of business. In the boardroom he was an archconservative, and in the acquisition of art, his instincts were just the same. For years he continued buying four or five paintings a year, occasionally more, all of them through Knoedler. Yet with all those acquisitions, almost sixty during the years up to 1908, he did not manage to get his hands on anything particularly distinguished. The really serious buying was still to come.

At this stage, the pattern of his buying still reflected the pattern of his steady, predictable, wealth-accumulating life. But then in 1909, all that changed. His marriage to Nora collapsed. For several years, she had been seeing one of her old English friends, and the two of them had spent months together abroad, trailed by Andrew's detectives. The marriage breakdown dragged on for three years and eventually ended with an acrimonious and heavily contested divorce. Each parent was given custody of the two children, Paul and Ailsa, for six months of the year.

When his marriage fell apart, Mellon stopped buying paintings. He had found the breakdown of his marriage extremely traumatic, and also, some of his buying had been an attempt to appease Nora's unhappiness in Pittsburgh. For ten years he coasted along, immune to Knoedler's attempts to interest him afresh in buying more paintings.

Then, equally suddenly, his appetite changed again, this time triggered by another dramatic change of circumstances. In 1921, Mellon was appointed secretary of the treasury by President Warren Harding, a position he would also hold under presidents Coolidge and Hoover. It was to be a record-breaking term of office that continued until 1932.

When Mellon was offered the job, he was the third richest man in the country, yet he was utterly unknown outside Pittsburgh except to the banking community and some powerful political conservatives. Even Harding, as president-elect, on hearing the suggestion of Mellon as a possible treasury secretary, had responded, "Who?" Mellon was probably the least visible influential man in America.

Mellon was keen to make the move. He had piled up many millions and was losing interest in business. Frick had died two years earlier, and simple retirement was out of the question. To retire as treasury secretary would be a perfect way to cap a brilliant career in finance. And the glamour of Washington compared favorably with that of drab Pittsburgh. Even if he was not naturally a social person, he could extract some pleasure by osmosis from being in the more exciting atmosphere.

In early 1921, he resigned from the boards of fifty-one companies and moved to Washington. The city he arrived in was small but growing. It was also still southern but becoming increasingly cosmopolitan. The grand residential streets of Connecticut, Wisconsin, and Massachusetts Avenues boasted rows of handsome mansions and town houses. Mellon chose an 11,000-square-foot apartment on Massachusetts Avenue. It was in the McCormick, a Beaux-Arts building known as the finest apartment block in the city, with the biggest rooms and highest ceilings. Mellon took the fifth floor in its entirety, the only apartment with a balcony running along the twenty-two windows facing the street.

Mellon's apartment had six bedrooms, six bathrooms, and a huge servants' wing containing five maids' rooms, two more bathrooms, and a servants' dining room. The formal entrance, reached by elevator, was a kind of public hall flanked by cloakrooms. This opened onto an oval reception hall and then again to a large salon and two huge reception rooms.

Here, still spry at the age of sixty-five, Mellon settled into a life of great style, sometimes kept company by his daughter, but otherwise rattling around alone with only an army of servants. It was to decorate this vast apartment that Mellon began buying paintings again. He wanted to do some entertaining, in his own unostentatious way, with his daughter acting as his hostess. But he was also perhaps prompted by the sudden growth in the transatlantic market in art.

Rich Americans like Mellon were beginning to buy old masters from British aristocrats who were selling their estates, their houses and furnishings in the aftermath of the First World War. The man who did much to bring together the rich aspiring buyers and the poor reluctant sellers was Joseph Duveen, whom some credit with single-handedly creating the transatlantic art market of the twenties. It is a measure of Duveen's success that from the 1920s onward, Mellon bought as often from Duveen as from Knoedler. Duveen was ruthlessly efficient in his courting of potential buyers. Some said he had both Mellon's butler and his valet in his pay. Others claim that Duveen watched Mellon's movements to the extent that the contents of his wastepaper bin had been analyzed within an hour of Mellon's setting off to walk home from his office.

Either way, the two dealers now both regarded him as a "worthwhile" client and vied for his business. Mellon was now spending well over half a million dollars a year on increasingly good-quality paintings. He bought works by Van Dyck, Gainsborough, Reynolds, as well as Goya, Rembrandt, El Greco, and Vermeer. And the interesting thing was that Mellon found that the paintings boosted his social life. To his surprise, he found that he rather liked the change. He had rigorously avoided any social events in Pittsburgh. But in Washington, free from the demands of his complex business empire, he opened up.

The snobbishness of the narrow Washington social scene was overwhelming. The formidable grandes dames who dominated it had devoted their lives to demonstrating their own elevated position, and they spent their days examining and appraising every twitch in the party calendar. Naturally, they longed to have the U.S. treasury secretary at their elaborate parties and events. Never mind that their champagne was just transmuted shoe polish or steel girders. Mellon brought with him not only unbeatable cachet but also the possibility of a return invitation to his apartment, where there hung what was increasingly being recognized as one of the finest collections of art in the country.

His brother commented that Andrew "delighted in the sensation that his pictures made. He was as happy when the pictures were being admired as he was unhappy when the attention was focussed on himself." Of course thick embossed invitations poured in a steady stream through his letterbox. Mellon sorted them carefully with the assistance of his social secretary, a key staff member in the world's most social-climbing city. Only a very select few were accepted.

Meanwhile, as treasury secretary, Mellon was presiding over the longest boom in American economic history to date. As befitted a rich man, he believed in tax cuts, debt reduction, and trickle-down economics. His policies were not only making him and his million-aire friends very much richer, they were also helping to promote the great bull market. By the mid–1920s, Wall Street inspired visions of boundless wealth. Confidence blossomed. Buying stocks on credit became at first a fashion, then a frenzy. Brokers' loans increased from one billion dollars in 1920 to seven billion in 1929. A boom psychology developed. Real wages were advancing modestly. Trade union membership was declining. Interest rates remained low. And the prospects for international peace looked bright.

Mellon was also responsible for the enforcement of Prohibition (even though he owned a brewery and continued to send whisky to all his friends). He oversaw the redesign of the dollar bill and the planning of the Federal Triangle in Washington. And in an era when so much of his business concerned foreign loans and international debts and war reparations, Mellon was also running a large proportion of American foreign policy. More than anyone else he became identified with the good-time government of the 1920s. He was hailed by his admirers as the best treasury secretary since Alexander Hamilton. And it was said, only half in jest, that three U.S. presidents had served under him.

It was at this time, at the height of his powers, during the mid–1920s, that Mellon conceived an ambition to found an American National Gallery in Washington. It would house a great collection of art, held in perpetuity, for the benefit and education of the American people. This gallery, although funded and filled by Mellon, would not however be named after him: Mellon's dislike of publicity and ostentation was sometimes carried to almost self-indulgent lengths.

It was a kind of inverted arrogance, a subtle but potent vanity that seemed to be pushing him to do this. Art had never been a truly elemental passion of his. Money had filled that role in his life. But there was still a peculiar logic to this idea. In a national gallery, he saw a way of establishing his name in the history books, a way all the more effective for its blaring modesty.

This new gallery would be modeled on London's National Gallery, a place he visited regularly, sometimes with his adolescent son, Paul, who was by this time an undergraduate at Cambridge. Mellon's national gallery, like London's, would have no entrance charge.

On paper it looked like an appropriately grand ambition for one of the richest and most powerful men on the planet. There was only one problem. It was not the funding or the building of the gallery: Mellon could afford the money many times over, and as treasury secretary he would have no difficulty in allocating a large site to the gallery on the Mall near the Capitol. The problem was what to put in the gallery. He needed a large number of very high-quality paintings. The big question was where would they come from?

Most of the great galleries of Europe had already been in existence for centuries, gathering in superb paintings all that time. And even in the United States, it would not be easy to trump the extensive collections in the Metropolitan Museum in New York and the Museum of Fine Arts in Boston.

It is true that Mellon himself was now buying with unprecedented extravagance, through both Knoedler and Duveen. In October 1928, with the help of Duveen, he bought his first Raphael, the *Niccolini-Cowper Madonna*, for the then enormous sum of $836,000. This event signaled a serious gearing up for Mellon. Raphael represented the greatest prize for any collector, in particular for the American plutocrats who were investing huge sums in their art. These men, all self-made millionaires in banking, heavy industry, and other fields of business, had never been speculative buyers of art. They had no plans to resell for profit. They were making their choices as long-term investments. So the question of exceptional quality or importance in the history of art came well below that of authorship. What they wanted were works by great artists.

While the reputations of even the greatest artists rise and fall with time, it is not easy to appreciate how truly exceptional was Raphael's fame. His prestige had endured all changes of taste and fashion up to the end of the nineteenth century. Bernard Berenson, the art historian, referred to him without exaggeration as the "most famous and most beloved name in modern art." Raphael's name was almost synonymous with Art. His works were also very costly and very scarce.

As a result, all the major American collectors shared one ambition: to crown their collections with a painting by Raphael. Twenty years earlier there had been no Raphaels in America. Then, with the economic boom in the United States coinciding with the post-war recession in Europe, these rare trophies began to move in a slow trickle across the Atlantic. In 1909 Isabella Stewart Gardner bought the first two. More followed.

Mellon's purchase of the *Niccolini-Cowper Madonna* was sensational. The press coverage was widespread and perhaps shocked Mellon into a desire for greater secrecy in the future. Now buying some fifteen paintings a year, and spending three or four million dollars on them, he had reached levels of expenditure and accumulation far beyond anything that could possibly be required to decorate a Washington apartment.

With a national gallery in mind, Mellon's rapidly expanding and now superb-quality collection would certainly provide the core to which other private donors in turn might contribute. But even at this rate, it would not be enough to establish a significant national gallery. What he needed, to jump-start a national collection on a sufficient scale, was to buy in bulk. He needed to buy an entire preexisting, top-class collection, just as Catherine the Great had established her Hermitage collection with the purchase of the Crozat paintings.

In retrospect, and with the information we now have, it is clear that by 1929, Andrew Mellon and Joseph Stalin were set on a convergence course. Ironically, neither party knew it at the time. The Russians were not aware that Mellon was planning a major expansion of his collection. Mellon had always been secretive about his dealings and his ambitions, mainly because, as a hard-nosed businessman, he knew that secrecy would give him the advantage in obtaining a good price. Equally, Mellon was not aware that the Russians, by now desperate for foreign currency to force through the first five-year plan, were about to make a new and determined effort to sell artworks that were absolutely unrivaled in the world. The Russians too were attempting to push for the best possible prices by negotiating in secret. And they were determined to conceal from the West a domestic economic situation so desperate that they had to sell off their own national treasures.

Then in October 1929, one final development added to the inevitability of the handshake between Stalin and Mellon. The New York stock market crashed, and an economic hurricane struck the American economy. On Black Tuesday, October 29, the worst day of panic selling, paper losses amounted to ten billion dollars. It was more than the entire national debt, almost as much as America had spent on the Great War, and twice the amount of all money in circulation throughout the United States at the time. Even the wealthy were subjected to a leveling process. Cornelius Vanderbilt III, for example, lost eight million dollars in an hour that day.

Few Americans were left unscathed. As the crash gave way to the Great Depression, America tightened its belt. Consumer confidence shrank to virtually nothing. Industrial output fell and unemployment rose. Banks failed, prices fell. Even capitalism itself was called into question.

Mellon's fortune had taken a hit too. But the Mellon millions had been piled so high and were so prudently spread that for him the crash was like a scratch on a Rolls-Royce. Indeed, Mellon's continuing wealth gave him the luxury of a perspective that allowed him, later, to describe the Depression as "a bad quarter of an hour."

Mellon's determination to acquire a great deal more top-quality art was in no way dimmed. In fact, his chances had improved: the economic slowdown with its accompanying drop in prices meant that his remaining wealth could buy all the more. But still there seemed to be insurmountable difficulties in reaching a deal between Andrew Mellon and the Soviet government. To begin with, the United States had still not recognized the Soviet Union and would not do so until 1933. It was illegal to trade directly with the Soviets and, even in this age of relatively relaxed regulations, the secretary of the treasury could hardly be seen to break the rules in such an extravagant fashion. On top of that, could Mellon, the archconservative capitalist, trust these unpredictable Communists to give him what they were promising?

The Soviets faced equal constraints. They had not yet succeeded in making even one great sale. There was mounting opposition from within the Hermitage and elsewhere to such transactions. And in addition, how could they be sure that these rapacious capitalists would honor the bargain and hand over their dollars in secret?

So the chances of a deal's coming off were very slim when, early in 1930, Knoedler and Company in New York learned of the Gulbenkian negotiations. Immediately the firm concluded, rightly as it turned out, that the Russians were ready to sell art of a very high quality and in unprecedented quantity. If Knoedler was to be involved in such sales, it had to find a buyer. There was no question as to who this ideally should be: its best and richest client, Andrew Mellon.

Knoedler's had been tipped off by the London dealers Colnaghi's of Bond Street, which employed the nephew of Knoedler's president, Charles Henschel. Colnaghi's in turn had heard from an art dealer in Berlin named, at different times in his life, Francis Catzenstein, Zatzenstein, and eventually Matthiesen. He was an experienced dealer who had made his name with some outstanding sales from German princes and nobles in the aftermath of the First World War. Matthiesen had his own representative in Moscow who negotiated directly with Antiquariat, the Russian organization set up for the purpose of the art sales.

This was the European-American syndicate that was in place when rumors of the Gulbenkian purchases, and of the possibility of more, began to circulate. By April 1930, Knoedler's had reached an agreement with Mellon, who had authorized the company to purchase on his behalf what were described as "certain paintings from the Hermitage collection."

From then on Knoedler's was responsible for most of the negotiations, although the firm tried to avoid involving Matthiesen, whom it increasingly, but not always wisely, regarded as a costly and unnecessary middleman. With Mellon and the Soviets now primed for a deal, negotiations proceeded very rapidly, and by late April 1930, two Rembrandts and a Frans Hals were on their way from Leningrad to New York. Mellon had paid $560,000 for them. That was only the beginning. In early May, Charles Henschel of Knoedler's sailed for Europe hoping to negotiate more sales directly. While still on board ship, he received a telegram from Matthiesen's agent in Moscow, saying that the Russians were prepared to sell van Eyck's *Annunciation* for half a million dollars. Mellon agreed immediately, and within days, the Russians had handed over the painting to Henschel in Berlin.

Henschel went on to Leningrad, where he had an uncomfortable but highly profitable stay. Most of his time was spent in his hotel room waiting endlessly for Antiquariat representatives to call. He found it difficult to communicate without any Russian and subsisted almost entirely on caviar and vodka. On one occasion Henschel offered a cigarette to a Hermitage official, only to find it wistfully refused. The official explained that unless Henschel gave a cigarette to everyone in the Hermitage, including laborers and guards, the acceptance of this gift might very well cost him his job.

In the end Henschel's efforts were rewarded. During the remainder of 1930, he negotiated the sale of two more Rembrandts and three Van Dycks, which Mellon acquired for just over a million dollars.

Meanwhile in New York, Knoedler's was busy sending Mellon bulky packages of notes and art books containing information on the works he was expecting to buy. On May 6, 1930, a large package from Knoedler's arrived on the overnight train in Washington. It was picked up by Mellon's chauffeur and brought to the treasury secretary's apartment. Inside Mellon found a copy of the Hermitage collection catalogue, with a marker on page nine. Opening the book at the page, he saw a reproduction of Raphael's *St. George and the Dragon*. "This picture is beautiful and in a perfect state, in a word irreproachable," read the notes from Knoedler's. More pages of details gave the provenance of the painting: Duke Guidobaldo, Henry VII, Henry VIII, earl of Pembroke, Charles I, marquis of Sourdis, Pierre Crozat, Catherine the Great, Hermitage Gallery. And then Mellon read through over a dozen references in published books, reproduced for him by Knoedler and Company, and all confirming the full extent of its provenance.

Telegrams were now whizzing back and forth across the Atlantic from Matthiesen and his partner in Moscow, and from Colnaghi's as the pace of sales picked up. In early 1931, Matthiesen wrote that while he had succeeded in securing some more old masters, he was still unable to lay his hands on the Raphael *St. George*. Were the Russians balking at selling this extraordinary painting? Did its symbolism, its significance as an icon, and its unique provenance make it just too precious to part with? Were the scholars at the Hermitage trying to block its sale?

Ever since January 1930, a "shock work brigade" had been assigned to the Hermitage to select valuable works suitable for sale. The decisions as to which paintings should be sold were therefore out of the hands of the Hermitage staff. The sales were undertaken in relative secrecy, but of course the staff could see what was disappearing. Some brave scholars and curators protested by trying to block or delay the removal of the paintings. Sometimes they claimed that the order notes had not arrived. Occasionally they deliberately failed to understand the illiterate telegrams demanding urgent delivery of the paintings. Van Eyck for example had been written as "Van Dyck," Houdon's *Diana* as "Vandondiana." But such sabotage resulted in inquiries and demands for speedier transfers. And the staff involved risked very serious punishments: the gulag or death.

Requests continued apace during 1930 and 1931, and in late February 1931, Mellon finally heard that he had successfully acquired Raphael's *St. George and the Dragon* for $745,500. The Hermitage curators had failed. There was more to come: another million dollars for a Botticelli and a Rembrandt, half a million dollars for a Veronese, a Van Dyck, a Frans Hals, and a Chardin. And then finally in 1931, the last three paintings were hand-delivered directly to Knoedler and Company in New York by Antiquariat: a Perugino, a Titian, and Raphael's *Alba Madonna*, all for just under two million dollars.

Mellon had paid less than seven million dollars for twenty-one of the finest paintings in the world. For the Matthiesen-Colnaghi-Knoedler syndicate, it was an absolute triumph, the greatest deal they had ever clinched, and probably the greatest art coup of the century. They had acquired superb, authentic pictures at very good prices after exceptionally complex negotiations with the still-unrecognized Communist regime. For Andrew Mellon it was the greatest triumph of his career as an art collector.

This was not how it seemed in Russia, least of all in the Hermitage. Other paintings and objects had also been sold to museums around the world, although none on the scale of the Mellon purchases. All told, fifty masterpieces had vanished from the walls of the Hermitage. To the scholars there, assessing their heavily depleted collection, the sales seemed like a total disaster. After decades of dreadful, tormenting, dispiriting problems, the Hermitage had now finally reached its absolute nadir. The humiliation was total.

The museum had suffered the worst of both worlds, Communist and capitalist, as the government in Moscow had allied itself with a rich American, with the shared aim of plundering a great Russian museum of some of its finest treasures. What made it worse was the fact that there could be no public acknowledgment that any such sales had taken place.

That is no longer the case. When I visited the Hermitage Museum in 2004, I found Mikhail Piotrovsky, the fifty-nine-year-old director, still vividly emotional about the whole affair. "I still feel terrible about the sales. It was a crime that they were ever sold, and

Russia was cheated by the Americans. There's no doubt about that. Andrew Mellon was the biggest shark among them. He chose well. He got the best things. But it was still a crime."

Piotrovsky sat in his office beneath a portrait of Catherine the Great. He is cosmopolitan and highly sophisticated: the face of the new, twenty-first-century Hermitage, with fluent English and ten other languages comfortably in his grasp. But no amount of international polish could prevent his composure's dissolving on this subject. He talked in a great gush of fury, allowing me little to do but put slalom posts in his headlong conversational path.

"These paintings had become part of Russia's heritage. Nobody had any right to sell them. The Russians were not complete idiots, they got what they wanted. They got the possibility of trade with the United States. They got dollars, but actually an amount in total that was equal only to three or four days' worth of the national budget. They used the money to build a tractor factory in Stalingrad. It was later turned into a tank factory. So what did we gain in the long run? Nothing. There were always other ways of getting foreign currency, and other ways of bribing U.S. officials."

Unfortunately for Russia, Stalin obviously preferred tractors to a Raphael, and he believed that the Raphael must be sold to pay for the tractors.

Piotrovsky was still angry and humiliated over an event that took place fifteen years before he was born. But clearly he fears it could happen again. "Catherine the Great understood that the creation of a good art collection was as important as having a good army. She made Russia the great state and power that Peter the Great never did. She knew about how to demonstrate greatness. She knew that a fine art collection would win far greater status for Russia than any number of wars. My government needs to remember this as it carries on fighting in Chechnya."

There is one small compensation, however, for what he calls the

"Mellon robbery." A program of loans has been organized, bringing back the lost works to the Hermitage for temporary exhibitions. "It's a very small compensation. It's for the education of our people. The *Alba Madonna* has been back, and the *St. George* is next on my list. This beautiful little painting was considered the best picture in the Hermitage. It was the frontispiece for the Benois catalogue. It was the finest work ever to come to this museum. I feel dreadfully saddened and angry that we no longer have it. And for what?" He tailed off into rueful silence, as if the loss had finally deprived him of any more words.

Very few words at all came out of the mouth of Tatyana Kustodieva, when I tracked her down later that day to discuss the same subject. The curator of Italian paintings met me with a frown. *"Niet, niet, niet!"* she hissed. "I will not talk about it!" Kustodieva is in her late sixties, with brutally cropped gray hair and a censorious outlook on life. Sitting tight-lipped in her voluminous black dress and black crocheted shawl, she was clearly irritated at having to talk to me on Piotrovsky's orders, and furious that the subject was Raphael's *St. George.* No amount of charm would melt this icy refusal. Perhaps the subject was simply too painful. Our brief meeting over, she returned to one of the huge ash buckets around which the Hermitage curators gather for warmth and cigarettes, sharing sandwiches, gossip, lines of poetry, and occasional tots of vodka. Every time I passed her in the Hermitage corridors over the next few days, she glared angrily at me.

The following day I went to the Hermitage archives, where I met Elena Solomakha, the chief archivist. She is a young and enthusiastic woman and seemed much more willing to help. As she searched for documents related to the *St. George,* I looked around the archive, the former apartment of Franz Labienski, a nineteenth-century keeper of paintings. Its rooms overlook the Neva at its broadest point. From the strangely low windows you can gaze right out over the expanse of icy blue water, an outlook which gives you a sensation of flying. A bronze bust of Labienski serves as a hat stand for Elena's woolly bobble hat.

"I've got it," called Elena suddenly, with a gratifyingly excited little shriek. She rushed in brandishing a clear plastic file. Inside was a faded piece of incredibly thin paper, typed over and rubber-stamped to within an inch of its life. Extracting it with great reverence and faintly shaking fingers she put it on the blotter in front of me. URGENT and TOP SECRET glared the bold red stamps at the top. Underneath, the order from Moscow demanded that the deputy director of the State Hermitage remove two paintings from the walls of the gallery: Raphael's *St. George and the Dragon* and Rembrandt's *Woman Holding a Pink*. It then ordered him to surrender them to a Mr. Prussakov, the representative of Antiquariat. Clearly Prussakov was to arrange for them to be spirited out of the country. The Hermitage staff was left with the task of rehanging the two rooms and disguising the gaps.

My heart was racing as I scrutinized this flimsy little piece of paper. This Russian memo, typed out more than seventy years ago by some indifferent party stenographer locked inside the Moscow bureaucratic machine, symbolized the final leg of the painting's journey. It was the final leg of mine too. I was nearing the end of my quest.

"This order had to be carried out immediately," explained Elena. "Nobody had any time to think about it or try to come up with delaying tactics. It was far too dangerous by this time. Staff at the Hermitage had already tried to delay sales and save some of the paintings, but they had received terrible punishments. None of their efforts had worked in the end."

So that night, after closing time, on February 27, the little Raphael was taken down from the wall of the Italian room, wrapped by candlelight and, with great reluctance, handed over to Prussakov. The Hermitage staff had been neither involved nor consulted in the negotiations. They had been given no explanations. This priceless little Raphael had survived many threats since its arrival in Russia in 1772. It had been treasured and protected through fire, war, and ignorant greed. On several occasions it had been removed for safekeeping, and each time the Hermitage had ensured its return unblemished. This time, though, the staff knew they would never see it again.

There were very good reasons, both in the museum in Leningrad and in the government in Moscow, to deny that these sales had ever taken place. Across the Atlantic too, Andrew Mellon also had good cause to deny that his extremely risky and controversial purchases had ever happened. Here was a man who was bearing the full brunt of criticism for the crash and for the resulting worldwide slump that was to last the best part of a decade. Mellon had not foreseen the crash, nor had he prepared any policy for dealing with it.

In an effort to stimulate growth, he cut taxes, but this was immediately dubbed "rich relief," since it affected only high earners. Mellon made plain his belief that for the less well-off, the slump was not altogether a bad thing: it would "purge the rottenness out of the system" and encourage moral virtues like thrift and hard work as well as ensuring the survival of the fittest. It was not a popular stance.

Ten million Americans were unemployed, but only a quarter of them were receiving relief. Two million vagrants roamed the country looking for work. In some states, ninety percent of the nation's schoolchildren were underweight. Desperate people resorted to eating wild greens, violets, and forget-me-nots, as well as what leftovers they could scavenge from restaurants.

In Mellon's home town of Pittsburgh, a charity drive in the autumn of 1931 had fallen far short of its six-million-dollar goal, with only a $300,000 contribution from the Mellon brothers.

If Mellon had admitted that he had just lavished almost seven million dollars on paintings, illegally buying them from a government his own administration did not recognize, he might have been lynched.

He had other reasons for his denials. During the very period when Knoedler and Company was negotiating to buy paintings from the Soviets on his behalf, Mellon found himself as treasury secretary making decisions on larger issues of Soviet-American trade in which his private art purchases were intertwined. Privately, Mellon welcomed Soviet dumping of art on the Western market. Publicly, Mellon was under fierce and relentless pressure from American businessmen to bring a stop to Soviet dumping of any kind. The problem became exacerbated in 1930 when the Soviets started selling goods in huge quantities at bargain prices, in order to corner the market. In the West, the common response was to throw up protective tariff barriers. In the United States, a long debate in Congress finally produced the Smoot-Hawley Tariff Act in an attempt to protect the domestic market from foreign imports.

Mellon delayed the legislation as long as he possibly could so that his private purchases would avoid customs duty and other scrutiny. It was signed by President Hoover in June 1930, and then Mellon fudged the dates to indicate that he had purchased most of his paintings in April and May that year. Many of them, including Raphael's *St. George*, were actually delivered much later.

During the early 1930s, he was already in the process of setting up the A. W. Mellon Educational and Charitable Trust. His plan was to donate all the Hermitage paintings to the trust, along with many more from his private collection and a large sum of money. It would be the job of the trust to hold these pictures and the funds until his imagined National Gallery of Art could be created. In the meantime, Raphael's *St. George and the Dragon*, reframed and cleaned by Knoedler's, sat, along with the other Hermitage paintings, in the darkened basement of the Corcoran Gallery in Washington. There it remained for some time, evidence of a dirty little secret, hidden just under the skin of one of America's richest and most prominent public figures.

The irony of the whole affair was overwhelming. Here was a painting of transparent beauty and simplicity that had been traded with the darkest greed and duplicity by two of the most powerful men on earth.

Almost immediately after the paintings arrived in Washington, rumors of the Hermitage sales began inevitably to trickle slowly around the press. Mellon was asked at least five times whether he had bought any paintings from the Hermitage. Repeatedly he denied that he personally owned any paintings that had hung in the Hermitage. It was a denial that was technically correct (his trust was the owner, not Mellon himself), but only just.

Mellon's long career as treasury secretary was unraveling before his eyes. By this time he was coming under increasing criticism for what was seen as his mishandling of the slump. Attacks were mounting on his inappropriately close relations with business. His public world was becoming increasingly uncomfortable.

Then in January 1932, a Texas Democrat stood up in the House of Representatives and demanded the impeachment of Andrew Mellon for "high crimes and misdemeanors." The charges related to conflict of interest: the fact that as treasury secretary, Mellon maintained a substantial interest in three hundred corporations capitalized at more than three billion dollars. A month later, Mellon resigned.

President Hoover immediately offered him the post of ambassador to Britain. Mellon spent a brief few months there, wandering the halls of the National Gallery and using his position to further the interests of Gulf Oil, one of the Mellon companies. Then in

November that same year, his public career ended with Roosevelt's landslide victory in the polls.

Mellon returned to Washington. He was seventy-six years old and ready to rest. But his problems were only just beginning. Not only was he a marked man among Republicans for what was deemed to have been his hopeless mismanagement of the crash. He was also a prime target of Roosevelt's New Deal. Mellon was precisely the kind of rich businessman whom FDR inveighed against on account of his unacceptable wealth. He was the perfect scapegoat for America's woes.

Having forced him out of office, the Democrats now sought to convict Mellon of tax fraud. After extensive investigations, the Internal Revenue Service charged Mellon with failing to pay just over three million dollars in taxes in 1931. Mellon immediately declared the charges to be "impertinent, scandalous and improper" and hired a top lawyer. At issue was the taxable status of the Hermitage paintings, which he had claimed as a deduction on his 1931 income tax return.

For the first time in his life, Mellon found himself in the full glare of publicity. It was inevitable that during the course of the sensational and much-publicized court hearings, the details of Mellon's often-denied Russian purchases finally came out into the open.

Art experts and dealers, including the flamboyant Joe Duveen, were summoned to give evidence on Mellon's behalf, testifying to the value of his collection and his intentions to donate it to the nation. Duveen told the court that he even had a site picked out in Washington.

After several years of investigation, testimony, and appeal, Mellon was acquitted in February 1937 of the charge of tax evasion. Immediately the government began new prosecutions against him.

Mellon was deeply hurt by these attacks, which darkened his declining years. But they did not distract him from his ambition to secure his place in history. Ironically, it was while he was still locked in battle with Roosevelt and the New Deal that he finally wrote to the president, late in 1936, with his offer. He planned to give his pictures and his money for the creation of a national gallery where great art would be freely available to the American people for ever. Roosevelt invited Mellon round to his office. As they sipped their tea, their respective lawyers were attempting to paint each other in the worst possible light in their Board of Tax Appeals presentations. Then in March 1937, just five months before Mellon died, Congress accepted his gift on behalf of the American people. Mellon had got himself into deep trouble on account of his art, but he had characteristically turned the situation around to work in his favor. Mellon had bought his immortality.

So confident was he that his national gallery would be built that he had already hired an architect for the job. John Russell Pope had considerable experience in designing art museums and had converted the New York mansion of Mellon's old friend Frick into a museum. Mellon, who had in mind the kind of palatial, Palladian building that Pope favored, became involved in every detail of the building. He didn't care how expensive the decoration was, but with typical inverted snobbery, he just didn't want it to look expensive. For the building's exterior, for example, he personally specified expensive pink Tennessee marble because it was, like himself, unostentatious and austere. According to one of his aides, "he chose it because it didn't look like marble. Here, too, perhaps, his choice indicated an expression of his desire for silence; he didn't want the marble to admit that it was marble."

The Washington National Gallery of Art that they designed was a conventional but nevertheless impressive piece of monumental architecture. It was an appropriate symbol of a triumphalist urban

America that was beginning to sense the approach of superpower status in an emerging new world order.

Less than ten years earlier, in 1928, Mellon had been appointed to oversee the fifty-million-dollar development of a series of new government office buildings. These were to be built in the Federal Triangle, an area of slum land between the White House and the Capitol, south of Pennsylvania Avenue. It was a task of heavy symbolism, for these new buildings were to be designed for the aggrandizement and embellishment of both the city and the nation. Mellon ensured that they rose up as monumental edifices to rival those of any other world capital. The buildings that emerged on this patch of land were vast classical monoliths, bristling with pediments and columns, and with a grandeur and richness of detail that reflected the economic, political, and human aspirations of America. They were all about the appearance of strength, power, and majesty. And within the plans for this impressive new world, Mellon had quietly, but with the approval of then president Hoover, reserved a site for his future national gallery.

On the edge of a huge continent, on the coast closest to the lodestone of European history, Mellon was creating an audacious new capital city that would be the window onto America's new power. His bold vision paralleled the creation, two hundred years earlier, of St. Petersburg, built on the edge of another huge continent, again on the coast closest to Europe. That city had been a symbol of Russia's modernization, developed by Catherine the Great as the grandstanding center of Russian imperialist power, culture, and superiority.

And just as Catherine the Great, with her limitless wealth, built and filled her Hermitage with the finest art treasures Europe could offer, Mellon too, a hundred and fifty years later, followed in her footsteps. He too spied and gathered into his possession every gem of European art history he could lay his hands on. And he created a grand gallery in which to display it. Like Catherine, his motives were not those of a truly passionate art lover. He was driven, as she had been, by the value and the spectacle that this amazing collection of art would make.

In August 1937, Mellon died at the age of eighty-two. Ever since his scandal had erupted, he had been frail and tired. But he had not been defeated. Shortly before his death, he had seen the plans for the building and had learned that construction work had begun. Pope himself died the day after, but the gallery's completion was overseen by Paul Mellon, by David Bruce, who had married Ailsa Mellon, and by Donald Shepherd, Andrew Mellon's lawyer.

The building cost some sixteen million dollars, and Mellon's nucleus collection was valued at fifty million. It was probably the largest single gift to the American people in the nation's history. The Washington National Gallery of Art was completed in 1941 and opened by President Roosevelt in March that year. Almost immediately it began attracting other bequests and donations of art.

In the Founders' Room you can see a painting of Andrew Mellon, whose monument he never intended that gallery to be, but whose monument it nevertheless is.

As an art collector, Mellon was not easy to evaluate. He was not a connoisseur. Despite his enormous wealth, the homes he lived in and the art he initially bought were all mediocre. They were pleasant, placid pictures. He did not like nudes or contemporary paintings or paintings of unpleasant scenes, gaudy colors, or excessively dark paintings with black backgrounds. He was not enthusiastic about religious paintings either. All his paintings had to be pleasant to live with.

No one would dispute that the paintings he bought later were superb artistic treasures, all proven paintings, which the centuries had already deemed to be great. And once he had conceived his idea for a national gallery, he relaxed some of his earlier restrictions. He bought crucifixions, dark paintings, unpleasant scenes, even seminudes. But he never bought a painting by a living artist, and he certainly made no discoveries nor patronized creative people in the art world. His Raphaels, Rembrandts, Titians, and van Eycks were blue chips. He was not interested in the speculative new issues, the wild Picassos and Cézannes that had yet to stand the test of time. By buying through Knoedler's and Duveen, the two most establishment dealers in the world, he avoided exposure to the explosive new art world of his day. As for his choice of paintings, John Walker, who later became director of the gallery, wrote that Andrew Mellon was "inarticulate on the subject of art. Even the names of the artists whose works he owned occasionally escaped him." He just liked the look of them. He was a lonely man who, as one acquaintance remembered him, was content to sit among his luxuries, nursing his loneliness and conversing with his soul.

His ambitions were grander and more self-serving than mere love and appreciation. When once asked why he collected art, Mellon stared long and hard into the distance and eventually replied slowly,: "Every man wants to connect his life with something he thinks eternal." His beautiful little Raphael *St. George*, which had been loved and lusted after by so many powerful men and women, was the ultimate gem, linking his name back in time to those of English kings and earls and Russian empresses.

As soon as the gallery opened, the public came pouring in, some fourteen thousand on the Easter weekend and three hundred thousand during the month of April. Again Raphael's *St. George* was under threat, although this time it was not too serious. A restorer's report written in May 1941, just two months after opening, reveals that the painting had been scribbled on in pencil: "A fingerprint appears on the dragon, and someone has drawn pencil lines across the dragon." The pencil lines, the report continues, are similar to those drawn on the Canaletto a week ago. Other paintings had been damaged more seriously: a Van Dyck, a Rembrandt, and a Pintoricchio had all been permanently marred and needed repainting. The report recommended increasing the number of gallery guards to one per room.

Today the Raphael *St. George* hangs in Room 20 on the first floor of the National Gallery. It's in good company. There are four other Raphaels in there too, but the *St. George* stands out, like a polished diamond. It is something more treasured than a Madonna or an altarpiece, something more hopeful, a more exquisite *thing*, to have and to keep. The light, the detail, the incredible clarity in such a small painting draws you in as if on a string. William Thorne was the guard on duty when I went there most recently. "Oh yes, man! That one's real famous. That's Raphael's *St. George*. Most people come into this room and go straight over to that painting first. They stand there for a long time. It has a kind of magic in it, that one."

He smiled at his neatly prophetic words as another group came in and walked straight over to the painting. It was a man and two women, perhaps a husband and wife with their daughter. They stood there for a long time, in worshipful silence, seduced by the mystique of this extraordinary painting. If only they knew its full story.

Epilogue

THE GAME OF TRACING the life of a much-traveled object is fascinating. But it is seldom easy to do. Unfortunately museums still have a habit of labeling their treasures in the simplest possible way. They give us the name of the creator, the date of creation, and possibly a mention of the previous owner. It's as if no object has ever had a life to speak of prior to arriving in this grand and important repository. And the assumption of course is that it will stay there forever. We should know better.

Great and memorable art has always been traded and appreciated as much for the power it symbolizes as for its aesthetic qualities. It has always been a kind of currency. The various owners of Raphael's *St. George and the Dragon* wanted that painting because of the status it would confer on them. It spoke of wealth, sophistication, and power. They acquired it as a commodity because it would be useful to them.

These days, when we look at great, historic paintings, we should be entitled to a little more background about them, some clues about the power plays that have gone on in their lifetimes, the stories of the kings and collectors and institutions that have fought to have them. We need a bit more of the lowdown on the *life* of these things.

Most of these works, it is true, were never painted to be viewed by ordinary people like us. Being able to see them now in public museums is one of the great privileges of the modern democratic world. And although they seem to be nailed down permanently, many of these works of art are still moving around. Country-house owners, faced with rising maintenance bills, occasionally find themselves forced to "deaccession" the odd old master. Sometimes, such as in the case in Britain of Raphael's *Madonna of the Pinks*, put up for sale by the duke of Northumberland, they are "saved for the nation" with the help of corporate, government, and charitable funding, and bolted firmly to the walls of the National Gallery in London or another such institution. Occasionally corporations themselves invest in art, much as they would in equities or property. In 1987, for example, the Yasuda Fire and Marine Insurance Company paid just under forty million dollars for van Gogh's *Sunflowers* to hang in the art gallery of its Tokyo headquarters. The company believed it would bring publicity and fresh business. It did.

But the circular movements of these treasures are not always smooth. The Hermitage Museum faces constant demands from the descendants of those whose artworks were seized by the Soviets and nationalized in the aftermath of the Russian Revolution. The grandson of the great collector Sergey Shchukin recently filed a lawsuit for the return of a Matisse painting when it was on exhibition in Italy, prompting the Hermitage to order its immediate return to Russia. The Hermitage director, Mikhail Piotrovsky, has now said that he will not lend any Hermitage objects for exhibition in any European countries without a government indemnity to protect them from seizure.

In the end, unless stolen to order, perhaps during wartime, as was the case with ancient treasures in Iraq, it is the man or woman or organization with the deepest pockets that tends to get the art. And this explains the steady but ineluctable flow of artworks into institutions such as the Getty Museum.

The fact that these places are open to ordinary people for

pleasure, study, and debate is to be celebrated. If we go to the Getty Museum in Los Angeles today, we see ordinary people looking at great works, chatting about art, and generally enjoying the atmosphere of that remarkable treasure house. So we end, in a way, where we began, with the Florentines of Raphael's day, the babble of people, ordinary men and women, the tradesmen, tailors, bakers, merchants, and their children, gathering in the piazzas of their city to discuss the artworks of the moment, the tides of opinion rising into the air like the chatter of finches.

Index